W9-BIG-752

Between Revolutions

Between Revolutions

An American Romance with Russia

Laurie Alberts

University of Missouri Press   Columbia and London

Library of Congress Cataloging-in-Publication Data

Alberts, Laurie.
   Between revolutions : an American romance with Russia /
Laurie Alberts.
      p.   cm.
   Summary: "Documents the author's experiences in the Soviet
Union in an American Field Service exchange program during
the last years of the Cold War. Looks at the lives of ordinary
Russians and the difficulties of American/Soviet relations"—
Provided by publisher.
   ISBN-13: 978-0-8262-1598-7 (alk. paper)
   ISBN-10: 0-8262-1598-X (alk. paper)
   1. Alberts, Laurie. 2. Novelists, American—20th century—
Biography. 3. Americans—Soviet Union—Biography. 4. Soviet
Union—History—1953-1985. I. Title.
PS3551.L264Z463 2005
813'.54—dc22   2005016243

♾ This paper meets the requirements of the
American National Standard for Permanence of Paper
for Printed Library Materials, Z39.48, 1984.

Designer: Jennifer Cropp
Typesetter: Crane Composition, Inc.
Printer and binder: The Maple-Vail Book Manufacturing Group
Typefaces: Bergell and Minion

Note: Although this is a work of nonfiction, some characters'
names have been changed.

Some material from the chapter "Russia Is a Fish" first appeared
in *NIMROD International Journal of Prose and Poetry.* All photos
are from the author's collection.

To Sergei and Lyuda

Contents

Between
Revolutions

A Kiss at Sheremetyevo—September 1982

On first glance, Russia was forest, spreading endlessly below the plane's wing; an ocean of firs and yellowing birch leaves. The turning leaves surprised me. I'd assumed, unreasonably, that seasons belonged to New England. This landscape could have been northern Vermont, but for the vastness—a forest stretching thousands, not hundreds, of miles.

The airfield rushed up, a grassy gash against the line of trees, and the plane bumped onto the runway. Seat belts clicked open; joking voices suddenly stilled. I thought I detected a subtle stiffening in the passengers—a planeload of Soviet officials back from foreign junkets, Africans returning to Patrice Lumumba University, several Western businessmen and exchange students, all reaching for their hand luggage. Perhaps it was only my own apprehension. We trailed down a staircase onto the tarmac, and then there were soldiers everywhere. *Okay,* I thought. *Russia. Now it begins.*

The soldiers, improbably young, with blandly handsome faces, blond hair, and pale blue eyes, shuttled us along the underlit passageways of Sheremetyevo, into the bottleneck of passport control. The airport interior was sepia-toned, dim, and metallic, with tubular soundproofing stalactites hanging from the ceiling and multilingual customs declaration forms littering the floor. Despite the soldiers, the lines were chaotic, and I was quickly cut off by a shoving group of thirty Soviet athletes in warm-up suits.

"So much for Western privilege," said my former seatmate, a shaggy,

1

bespectacled American Ph.D. candidate in linguistics headed for a semester at Moscow State.

Two men in synthetic suits abruptly pulled a couple of African students from our line and led them through a door. They reappeared behind a glass partition, where one of the Soviets began pawing through the Africans' hand luggage.

"If you're black, get back," the grad student said loudly.

"Shhh," I hissed, looking around wildly to see if he'd been heard. Behind the glass wall, the African students stared glumly at their feet as their belongings piled onto the floor.

"It's true, they hate it here. The Russians hate them—they spit on them in the street. They only come because the Sovs give them bucks so they'll go back and tell their poor little underdeveloped countries how wonderful communism is."

I veered away into another line. Now my stomach hurt, fear intensifying the jet-lagged biliousness of a night without sleep, too many cups of stopover coffee in Orly Airport, and an Aeroflot lunch of sausage, sturgeon, and mineral water at six a.m. eastern standard time. At the passport control booth another teenage soldier stared at my papers, my face, the mirror behind my head, back at my face. He put my documents down and picked up a phone, filling me with panic. They'd found me out. Somehow they knew that I had phone numbers and addresses of friends of friends jotted in faintest pencil in the middle of my Russian-English dictionary. And now they weren't going to let me into their country. Or worse, they wouldn't let me go home.

"Alloo?" the soldier said into the phone, all the while staring at me with the deepest intensity through the pane of glass. "Alloo?" He shrugged, replaced the receiver. It dawned on me that he had received the call; it had nothing to do with me. The boy stamped my papers, shoved them back under his window, offered a shockingly lascivious grin, and waved me through.

On the other side of passport control, a pretty but haggard woman in a leather coat and a yellow chiffon scarf over her bleached hair waved a cardboard placard printed with the name of my exchange sponsor, the American Field Service. I pointed emphatically at my chest, in Tarzan jungle language—Me Laurie!—nodding my head frantically with international goodwill.

"Lawoo-rie?"

"Yes."

"Welcome." She stuck out her hand. "I am Irina Alekseyevna, but you may call me Irenie like the heroine in Sir Walter Scott. You speak Russian?"

"A little." Very little would be more honest. I'd had three semesters of college Russian a number of years ago, enough to qualify for this apparently underapplied-for teaching exchange—my skills as a teacher of English had actually clinched the deal—but not enough to give me any clue as to what the people all around me were saying. I hoped that Irenie wouldn't be too disappointed.

"So. Russian for you is not important. We are eager to exploit you for your English!" Irenie laughed gleefully. She gripped me by the upper arm and propelled me toward the luggage carousels, chattering brightly in a bizarre, semi-British, Russian-inflected English.

"These lines are ghastly. You must be horribly tired. I also was horribly tired when I arrived in your country. I was exchange teacher seven years ago in Los Angeles. I met many very nice capitalists there. I especially loved the Disneyland. I visited the Disneyland four times! Excuse me Lora, may I call you Lora? Do you see your suitcases? Americans always have many, many suitcases. You see, I was also Intourist guide at one time. But when I arrived in your country I had only one little valise."

My two enormous duffels, heavy with textbooks and gifts for my as-yet-unknown school, packed with a semester's worth of toiletries that couldn't be found in Russia, shamed me. Moreover, I could barely drag them into the customs line. A second leather-coated woman joined us, a squat, middle-aged bulldog who lifted my bags with frightening ease.

I took her for some kind of peasant laborer, a female porter. Irenie introduced her as Elena Glebovna, her boss from the Ministry of Education, a high official in charge of the American Teacher Exchange. No matter that she spoke no English, some other logic was at work here. Lesson one in Soviet bureaucracy.

The customs agent did a three-second inspection, and Elena Glebovna hurried away with one of my duffels, as I dragged the other across the airport lobby in exhausted pursuit.

The first man I met in Russia—not counting the passport soldier and the bored customs agent—kissed my hand. He was a kindly porter with the strong-boned face of a peasant, summoned to cart my bags to the waiting Ministry of Education car. He gave me a Russian coin as a gift and couldn't stop exclaiming over the "pretty Amerikanka." I'd heard it was illegal to give foreign currency to a Russian, so I bestowed on him a New York City subway token in return. The ministry women looked on with impatience. They didn't realize that with eight hours' time change I'd been magically transformed from another invisible New York female to an exotic foreigner.

It was late September, and in accordance with all the tourist clichés, Russia did look bleak. Riding into Moscow on a flat highway punctuated by olive drab army trucks, and mud-colored delivery vans that appeared to be riveted at the seams, under a cloud ceiling that wouldn't lift for months, I had the sense that I was looking at a photograph developed without sufficient contrast. Everything, even the enormous billboards advertising Lenin, appeared oddly familiar, as though I'd visited this place in an ancient black-and-white dream.

"Elena Glebovna says you will have a tour of Moscow later," Irenie translated. "It is a shame that you cannot see more now, but we do so want to put you to use right away. We will only have you for six weeks before we must share you with a school in Leningrad. Do you see those big metal barricades? They are to mark the German lines during the Great Patriotic War for the Fatherland."

I peered out at the big steel X's in the waning light. So, six weeks in Moscow, then Leningrad. I had no idea who made these decisions. Everything—where I'd work, whom I'd work with, where I'd live—was out of my hands. We sped past bulky women in overcoats waiting at a bus stop in front of a pre-revolutionary estate turned chemical institute—its elaborate iron fence enclosing a forest of delicate birch—and into the monochromatic, low horizon of downtown Moscow. The swirled onion domes of St. Basil's Cathedral, dwarfed by the vast emptiness of Red Square and the concrete high-rise Rossiya Hotel, looked disappointingly small, even fake—like the plaster Matterhorn at Irenie's Disneyland.

To save the ministry money, I was lodged in a Russian—not a tourist—hotel called the Pekin—Peking, vestige of warmer relations with China. It was a fourteen-story yellow wedding cake with a spire and clock tower overlooking Mayakovsky Square. I was given a pile of rubles the size and shape of Monopoly money, and left alone in my out-of-scale hotel room with its grand high ceiling and sagging, cot-sized beds, its flimsy plastic radio that wouldn't turn off, massive color TV that wouldn't turn on, and a telephone that kept ringing with wrong numbers. On the other end of the telephone line, tinny voices kept asking for "Masha" or "Sasha." Either the phones were incredibly bad, or someone was checking on me.

If I wanted to leave the hotel I had to give my room key, weighted with an enormous cone of what felt like lead, to the *dezhurnaya,* the floor lady, who knit silently behind a desk like Madame Defarge. A mysterious crew of bored-looking, blue-jeaned Soviet youth flashing Marlboros hung around the elaborate, Chinese pagoda–style entrance to the restaurant at the Pekin. Children of the *apparatchiki,* high-level Soviet officials, I supposed.

I made my only foray into the Pekin's downstairs restaurant. It was rumored that the restaurant used to have a Chinese chef, but when I went in alone with my Russian dictionary and tried to order from the enormous menu, I was informed by the waiter that everything was "*nyetu*"—not available. Finally I let him bring me his choice, a *kutlyet,* a greasy patty of indeterminate origin. The privileged youth came and went, danced herky-jerky to the overly loud band, and blew smoke rings. I retreated to my room.

Looking down at the city from my room, I was swept by a premonition of terrible isolation, dreariness betokened by wet pavement, and the dim glitter of streetlights over a six-lane thoroughfare bereft of cars. Russia looked closed and out of reach. I was sure that I would spend months being shunted around by broad-shouldered women in leather coats. I would never meet anyone, never know this place. Yet, when I turned away from the hotel window, the wet kiss of the porter lingered on the back of my hand—a startling intimacy, almost a promise.

I woke to the radio and the first melodious bars of "Moscow Evenings," then beep, beep, beep. A smooth female voice announced the news about horrifying American *imperialisti* and glorious Soviet achievements, and a hearty-sounding physical health instructor led listeners through exercises, chanting "Opa. Opa. Opa." Beyond my window I could see the statue of Mayakovsky, revolutionary poet and square-jawed suicide.

The head English teacher at School Number 45 arrived at my hotel lobby to show me my metro and trolley route to school. Alexander

Zakharich was a fat, balding man with nervous little piggy eyes and an impressive set of stainless steel choppers. But for his teeth and the lack of a top hat and spats, he looked exactly like the Soviet propaganda cartoons of fat capitalists. He hurried me across the square, past the Tchaikovsky Concert Hall, to Mayakovsky Metro Station on the corner of Gorky Street. He showed me how to buy a monthly subway pass, impatient at my fumbling with the toy money, and we descended into the famous Moscow underground on steep escalators that carried the stale whoosh of air generated by trains far below. I wanted to ogle the passengers ascending across a slick expanse of polished stone but Zakharich demanded my attention. I praised the famous cleanliness and splendor of the Moscow metro and described the filth of the subway in New York, hoping to score trust with my honesty. Within seconds an olive green train rushed up and sucked us in.

We sat side by side in the subway car, making awkward conversation while the train whizzed in and out of elegant, chandeliered stations. Across from us the bundled passengers, clutching plastic bags and vinyl totes stuffed with produce, narrowed their eyes at the sound of spoken English. When Zakharich asked what my family did by way of profession, I unthinkingly answered that my father was a lawyer, my mother stayed at home, and my sister worked at Brandeis University. "Ohhhh?" said Alexander Zakharich thoughtfully. "And what did you say your surname was?"

"Alberts," I said, then panicked. I hadn't expected Alexander Zakharich, a man with steel teeth, to recognize the name Brandeis. How could I have been so careless? I feared that he could, through some mysterious Russian ability to ferret out secrets, read my heart and know the truth, despite my bland surname.

Before I left for Russia, the émigrés I knew told me not to mention the fact that I was Jewish. "You will be treated better that way," they said. But I was no troublemaker friend to refuseniks and dissidents, no freer of Soviet Jews. Back in Vermont, my mother attended the Unitarian Church, and my father kept asking how I could live in Manhattan in the midst of all those loudmouth New York Jews. "They don't have to behave," my father said with a mixture of disgust and envy. As a Cape Cod native, he considered himself a "white Jew" and was proud of the fact that in the navy everyone had thought he was Greek or Italian, he was so unlike the brash Brooklynites. Being Jewish meant nothing to me, I believed. I cursed myself—not even at school yet, and I'd already made a mistake.

The school, made of pale, gritty brick, looked like any of the apartment or office buildings on the street. Alexander Zakharich led me through a dim hallway into his office. Uniformed students gawked at me and giggled by the coatroom. Alexander Zakharich directed me to hang my coat in his private closet and proudly showed off his collection of American and British texts and phonograph records, his album devoted to the sacred visit of the last American, a smiling blonde named Sandy, whom he'd adored.

"Have you visited America or England?" I asked.

Alexander Zakharich's face tensed. "I believe one can know a foreign country perfectly without ever having seen it," he said, turning away. He selected an album and turned on the phonograph. I was surprised to hear the American satirist Tom Lehrer sing "National Brotherhood Week." When Lehrer got to the line "everybody hates the Jews," Alexander Zakharich chortled in delight and searched my eyes. I laughed politely and wondered what I had let myself in for. Still, on some level I had to admire the man's eclectic tastes.

He was a brilliant language teacher. I sat in the back of the room and watched a group of uniformed ten-year-olds play journalist to Alexander Zakharich's rescued Robinson Crusoe. The girls wore brown pinafores and fluffy white bows in their hair, the boys, dark blue pants and white shirts, all of them decorated with the red neckerchief of the Young Pioneers. They raised their hands in a stiff little elbow-on-the-desk salute, and rose when called on to ask Mr. Crusoe if he had a map, and was he eating fishes on his island?

"Fish," Alexander Zakharich corrected. "One fish. Two fish. Ten fish." In a frenzy to impress me, he sat down at a piano and made the kids sing "Good Morning to You" in their high, sweet, accented voices. When the bell rang, the hushed orderliness of the school was shattered, and the halls filled up with screaming, racing children—strenuous classroom discipline made up for by short-term corridor chaos.

That morning, at Zakharich's request, I gave my first lecture to an auditorium filled with high school students and their teachers, an informal account of my life in America—the places I'd lived and studied. New Hampshire, Massachusetts, Alaska, Vermont, Iowa, New York. I asked for questions. The students stared at the floor; none were willing to speak English in front of so large a group. Perhaps I'd spoken too quickly. Maybe they hadn't understood a word I said. They were being taught on a British model and were unused to American inflections. Finally, in the back of the room, a dark, young, bespectacled male teacher raised his hand. He introduced himself as Grigorii Vladimirich, with an unnervingly perfect British accent. "I would like to know what you think of the book I've just finished reading which states that the CIA was behind the James Jones massacre in Guyana as an experiment to see if people would willingly follow a leader to their deaths."

I was flabbergasted. My first day, and already I was being provoked. "I'm just a teacher," I said, "and I don't know anything about the CIA." *Sure,* I could hear them thinking, *sure you don't.* Russians sent on exchanges were party trustees, loyal team players, government reps. Of course they would think the same of me. "Unfortunately," I added, "I believe there are enough miserable people in the world looking for someone to tell them what to do that such a horrible event could happen anywhere." Alexander Zakharich ended the meeting, and I was shunted away to the cafeteria for lunch.

The cafeteria was a room of long tables, painted in cheerful folk murals—wheat stalks, bread loaves, and happy peasant girls in traditional dress cavorted on the walls. The same male teacher sat down across from me as I fought my way through a plate of kasha and gristly beef. His glasses had an odd greenish tint, and a Wimbledon insignia adorned the breast of his blue sweater.

"You lived in many different cities," he said. "Was it difficult to get permission?"

I looked up at him, wondering again if he was trying to provoke me in some way. "What permission? No permission is required. You just live where you want."

"Oh," he said. His eyes flickered, went out of focus. I was swept by a bizarre new sense of frustration—this man thought I was lying!

"Is Grigorii Vladimirich tiring you with his peculiar questions, Lora?" asked one of the women teachers with a tight smile. I looked down at my kasha. "Your lecture was very interesting," she continued. "Our children did so enjoy it. They did not ask questions, of course, because they are exceedingly shy."

Alexander Zakharich and I argued that afternoon. He brought me into his office to show me his favorite project, one he hoped that I could help him with. Through the generosity of Yevgeniya, an English teacher whose husband worked as a censor at Mosfilm, he'd managed to secure a copy of the old Audrey Hepburn/Peter O'Toole film *How to Steal a Million*. It was his life's work to make a transcript of the entire sound-track to use as a teaching tool. Unfortunately, there were still certain expressions that eluded him, and he needed my help. If I didn't mind, of course. "For example . . ." Alexander Zakharich switched on a reel-to-reel tape player and ran a few seconds of mumbled dialogue between Audrey Hepburn and Peter O'Toole back and forth. His face took on the intent, thoroughly obsessed expression of a bird-watcher, a music connoisseur, or perhaps a cat by a mouse hole. "There, that one. Did you understand?"

"Play it again." I hadn't the faintest idea what was being said. The soundtrack was muddy. After three more tries, I had to admit that I was stumped. Alexander Zakharich was very disappointed in me. Obviously, Sandy had done much better.

"I'd like to talk to you about my duties," I ventured.

"Oh?"

"I don't want to give lectures in the auditorium. The kids don't want to speak in that environment, and I don't blame them. I want to teach in a classroom. I'm here on an exchange, and part of an exchange is showing *how* we teach at home, right? Nobody in America teaches language by lectures."

Alexander Zakharich's face darkened. "You must forgive us if we wish to put you to the best use possible. We rarely have native speakers in our schools, and we consider ourselves very fortunate to have you here. It is of utmost importance that the largest number of students have the opportunity to hear you speak."

"I guess we disagree about what's the best use. I don't want to lecture. It's dull. And don't you want the kids to speak?"

Alexander Zakharich puffed his cheeks in annoyance. "Speaking isn't as important for them as comprehension, I'm afraid."

"Why not?"

"How often do you think they will be talking to foreigners? Certainly they won't have your opportunities for travel."

I could see his point, but I'd be damned if I'd stand in front of that sea of uniforms every day. I wanted contact. Then my nemesis in the Wimbledon sweater walked in. Perhaps he'd been listening to us from the doorway. Alexander Zakharich and he spoke rapidly in Russian. I crossed my arms and waited, irritated that they would be so rude in front of me, and nervous because I hadn't any idea what they were say-ing but I was sure that they were talking about me. Wimbledon looked very animated and intent, his dark eyes glinting behind his weirdly tinted glasses. I had to admit he was kind of good-looking with those black eyes, that mustache—something between Groucho Marx and Omar Sharif. I imagined the report: uncooperative foreigner.

Alexander Zakharich broke off suddenly and turned to me. "All right, you will have it your way if you must. Tomorrow you will begin teach-ing the eighth, ninth, and tenth formers. You will take over two classes from Grisha here, and a class each from Natasha and Emma. You know our Grisha? Grigorii Vladimirich?

"We've met," I said, offering my hand yet refusing to meet his eyes. So there was my punishment. I'd be stuck with this provocateur twice a day. "And won't I at least have a chance to watch a few classes, to get some idea of how your teachers work?"

Alexander Zakharich bit his lip in fury. "If you must."

I headed back to my hotel. My doubts about School 45 gave way to curiosity about the place through which I was passing, enveloped by the great, muffling cocoon of a language I didn't speak. In the metro, I won-dered at every person over fifty—survivors of war, what had they seen? Their faces looked hard, yet I envied the tenderness of the couples. On the escalators rising from the metro platforms, women rode a step above and turned to face their husbands or lovers, reaching out to fuss with collars or tuck already perfectly folded scarves back into their part-ners' coats. Inside the train I watched in fascination as a teenaged boy played with the zipper on his mother's brown parka. Up he zipped, over her mammoth breasts, then down again. The mother and son stared into each other's eyes with the contentment allowed only to those who have never read Freud.

A few seats down, a boy in glasses that made him look bug-eyed leaned sleepily against his father's shoulder. The father spoke animat-edly while the son snuggled close. Everywhere people were touching: roughly, pushing up against each other in the peak-hour metro throngs; gently, lovers leaning into one another as the trains came to a stop; companionably, as girlfriends, grandmothers, couples, and even sol-diers walked with locked arms down the street. Behind their blank, composed public faces, I could feel the mysterious warmth of flesh ra-diating like well-banked stoves. I wondered if I was the only lonely person in Russia.

Shorts in Central Park

I felt like Alice down the rabbit hole. Nothing was as it seemed. Although the Moscow streets were constantly swept by broom-wielding *babushki,* there was an air of fustiness, of grit and damp decay. School 45 was painted with cheery pastel colors and full of green growing plants, yet it seemed dark and somber. In Russia, the essence of things prevailed against appearances.

At school, I was treated with a solicitous attention that didn't seem quite personal. The teachers spoke English to me but Russian to each other in my presence. In the breaks between my classes, they crowded close to beg explanations of an elusive phrase from a trashy American novel they'd managed to get their hands on, or in the case of my nemesis Grisha, to judge the merits of a stilted translation of poetry from Russian into English. His moonlighting translation job depended on a shortage of native speakers, I supposed.

The kids lingered shyly to ask questions about current rock *musika.* My name was a big problem for them. Students ordinarily addressed a teacher by her first name and patronymic, but Laurie Murrayevna—Laurie, daughter of Murray—sounded ridiculous to me. "Miss Alberts," on the other hand, was ideologically unsound, too pre-revolutionary for Alexander Zakharich. I suggested simply "Laurie." Many of the students felt uncomfortable with such familiarity and adapted by calling me Miss Laurie.

"Excuse me Miss Laurie, do you like KISS? Do you like ABBA? Is The Pink Floyd very popular in America now? Do you like the great Dean Reed?"

Dean Reed? I was to hear about him often, an American Communist who'd married an East German and had found himself a sinecure playing anticapitalist folk songs in Russia and East Germany. No one believed he wasn't famous in the U.S.

After the students and I had agreed on the greatness of the Beatles, one of the senior teachers, Natasha, would grab me and say with a wink, "Oh, Lora, how we exploit you. Now you must drink tea and eat something tasty." Gripping me by the upper arm, she would propel me into the lunchroom, where the students, milling about with their glasses of tea and endless sugary pastries, would gawk at me, and a table full of teachers would jump up to make room.

Natasha reminded me of high school theater teachers at home, mildly bohemian and artsy. Although fiftyish, busty, and thick through the waist, she had a smooth, rounded forehead and wore her graying brown hair in a girlish braid, the tightly drawn strands of hair and her heavy black eyeliner emphasizing the shrewd Slavic tilt of her eyes. She tottered about, top-heavy, skinny legs rising from tiny, high-heeled ankle boots.

Natasha's classroom was decorated with photographs of student productions of Shakespeare and Dickens along with the requisite portraits of Pushkin and Lenin. She was no simple lover of literature and kids, however. Natasha had been to America on an American Friends Service exchange twelve years ago, a mark of her trustworthiness and political power. All she would say of her stay in America was that she'd missed her son terribly and met "many nice peace-loving Quakers who were different from most Americans."

The other English teachers I met were bony Nina and Emma, a former beauty gone to a soft middle, with a pinched, dissatisfied face. When there weren't any English teachers there to chaperone me in the lunchroom, I was left to the mercy of the history and gym and math teachers, who didn't speak English. My Russian was barely adequate to maintain a basic conversation. I smiled and nodded to express my idiotic pleasure at the fresh-baked pastries, the greasy soups. The fat, white-coated kitchen women behind the steam tables grinned at my bumbling attempts to give them the correct number of kopecks. For the first time I understood New York immigrants, their humiliated response to the assumption that a person who can't speak a language must be stupid. When I tried to speak Russian, I adopted an apologetic, fawning tone. I wanted them all to like me, to think that I liked them and whatever their school, their city, their system had to offer. But I didn't like the way they taught.

The teachers criticized their students mercilessly for a bad accent or a wrong answer, yet were as familiar as mothers, stroking the kids' hair in the halls, fussing with their clothes, reminding boys almost army age to say "thank you"—an odd mixture of maternal and despotic. The students rose when called on and stared at the ceiling in nervous concentration while performing amazing feats of memorization, reeling back whole chapters from last night's reading.

Only the best students were called on while the worst languished in the back of the room, in "Kamchatka." They considered my democratic attempt to call on every student either a perverse form of cruelty or an attempt to expose Soviet weakness. If a student didn't know an answer, the other kids whispered it to him shamelessly—a touching display of collectivity but futile pedagogically. Of a kid called on from "Kamchatka," a teacher told me, disgustedly, "That one wouldn't know how to answer even in his *own* language."

Sometimes I caught a glimpse of secret handholding in the coatroom, but whatever dramas were unfolding among the kids, I had no access. I was never allowed to be alone with them. In almost every class I taught, teachers sat in groups of two or three in the back of the room. They corrected my students' mistakes aloud, interrupted me to suggest which kids I should call on, giggled, and whispered loudly to one another in Russian. They were probably there as much to get exposure to my genuine American accent or for the novelty, the relief from the boredom of their own days, as to monitor me with the kids, but I found it disconcerting.

"Our children are like intelligent dogs," Natasha and Emma repeated often. "They understand everything but they cannot speak."

And do they obey their masters? I wanted to ask. I quickly grew irritated with the Russian love of axioms, the oft-repeated, unoriginal phrase. Their kids got graded and judged every time they opened their mouths; no wonder they wouldn't speak.

They were incapable of answering a direct question that wasn't in their reading or hadn't been drilled into them in another class—or they were afraid of giving an answer that would get them in trouble. If I asked "Why?" or "What do you think about . . . ?" some story from the reading materials I'd brought in, they fell into embarrassed panic.

"They are too young to know what to think on their own," the teachers assured me. "First they must learn the facts."

The "facts" were frightening.

"Why does your country want war?" a student finally rose to ask when I opened the class to questions. I tried to discuss the tragedy of mutual arms buildup, but they shook their heads. "Soviet tanks are for peace," the boy insisted. "American tanks are for war."

Words like *viewpoint* or *opposing theories* held no meaning for them.

"Why are there so many natural disasters in America?" another boy inquired.

I couldn't convince him that a country as large as the Soviet Union must have its share of earthquakes and floods also, but they weren't reported in the news. No, if they weren't in the news, they didn't exist. America was not only the land of massive unemployment and race riots, but also of natural disasters.

"America pulled the Soviet Union over the fortieth parallel in the war," a peach-fuzzy sixteen-year-old admonished. "You refused to open the second frontier."

I didn't know what he was talking about. All I knew of World War II was the TV show *Combat* and a few boring chapters in my high school history book. But this was a school with a shrine devoted to the Great Patriotic War for the Fatherland; a school with World War II helmets, rifles, and war slogans fastened in memoriam on the bricks in the stairwells.

I explained that I didn't know much about it; since that war my country had fought two more and my generation was involved with Vietnam. In fact, I told them, I'd joined millions in Central Park that summer protesting nuclear weapons. Actually, I'd attended that rally more out of curiosity than conviction, but my real point was a sneaky combination of self-justification and propaganda—I'm no Reaganite, and we can protest the actions of our government. I wanted them to think that the fact that Americans openly criticized their government meant something, and I felt peevish when they merely agreed with the criticism. Why protest Soviet nuclear weapons? They were for peace, not war.

When, in a frenzy to be honest and gain their trust, I described the homeless in New York, the exorbitant cost of a private education in America, they nodded their heads with recognition, but there was no turnabout. If what I said agreed with what they'd been taught, fine. If not, I was lying or misinformed. I was filled with frustration, the result of repeatedly biting my tongue.

What was I doing trying to propagandize them anyway? I was losing sight of the purpose of this exchange—was I supposed to be sharing information about American life or merely my American accent? They hadn't invited me here to criticize their system. And if I did, I'd get into trouble or make them so distrust me that I wouldn't learn anything. I wanted to share everything about us, just as I wanted to learn everything about them. But there was no chance of real exchange.

"Tell them about the American holidays," Alexander Zakharich counseled, making a nervous little steeple with his hands. I sighed in exasperation. Alexander Zakharich's private closet already held a cache of cardboard pumpkin and pilgrim cutouts, the beneficence of past American guests and their "holiday" lessons.

Although I damned myself for cultural chauvinism, I was sure that our way was better, that a school (supposedly one of the best in Moscow) that gave kids five glasses of sugary tea a day but no milk and had stinking primitive toilets couldn't possibly educate kids.

It's a poor country, I reminded myself. Toilets weren't what mattered. What was happening to the kids mattered. When I visited the youngest grades I saw seven-year-olds wriggling in their seats with excitement, children who could hardly contain their passion to be called on, to be beckoned to the board. By the time they reached the upper grades, their natural desire to learn had been annihilated, excitement replaced by deadly boredom and a protective public mask. They were being trained not to think, or if they did, to hide it.

To get more kids to ask questions, I had them write them out on pieces of paper that I read aloud. One day when I was, miraculously, left alone with the kids for a few minutes, I read aloud a small, dark girl's question, "Do you like your system of education?" I said a few words about the plusses and minuses, then turned the question around. "Do you like yours?" I asked.

"No," she said. "Not very much."

The class erupted into hisses and "oooohs." I didn't ask her why because it was clear she had broken some rule and would be reported. Not an hour later Natasha sidled up to me in the hall. "That girl in your ninth form class, the dark one, she is a very strange girl. Something is quite wrong with her mind, I think."

I wondered what would become of her.

Surprisingly, the only upper-form classes where the students showed any life were those of Grisha, my antagonist.

"What shall we do today? Shall we work or play?" Grisha asked his kids the day I observed his teaching.

"Play!" they screamed madly, like kids anywhere.

He kept them entertained with quizzes and games and drills. His teaching style was physical, almost frenzied—hopping about, scribbling on the board, swinging around to call on a sleeper. In Grisha's class, the kids spoke English, and it wasn't memorized. Although he seemed frantic to impress me, I admired his energy. When his back was turned, I couldn't help measuring the width of his shoulders or the roundness of his muscled butt— a nice body for a provocateur. The school was short on men.

Grisha piled me up with a selection of textbooks. They were badly printed on cheap paper, grammar lessons interspersed with essays on the achievements of the Soviet economy and the exploits of the heroes of the revolution. He added a dog-eared copy of *Catcher in the Rye*. I flipped it open and found a student's penciled commentary: "I think Holden loneliest person in world."

"And what do you think of our texts?" Grisha wanted to know when the bell rang and the kids rushed out of the room. He peered at me intently, his eyes burning behind his silly tinted glasses.

Was he waiting to trick me into a criticism that he could report? I wouldn't tell him what I thought—that language texts would be more interesting to kids if they taught the culture of English speakers instead of rehashing Soviet culture in English.

"I'm impressed that your kids are reading *Catcher in the Rye*," I hedged. "Our kids read it at the same age, but not in a foreign language."

Grisha smiled sardonically. "We are permitted to teach it because it provides a critique of your decadent capitalist society."

I gritted my teeth. Later, Grisha's use of the word *permitted* haunted me. Was he being ironic? Impossible, I decided. This was the man who'd asked about the CIA. I chided myself for being suckered into misunderstanding his intentions and determined not to let down my guard with him just because his class was lively and he spoke with that seductively perfect accent. I had to remember that he was Russian, not British. A hard-liner like Grisha probably thought being "permitted" to do anything was an honor.

After school, no one invited me home or even offered to walk me to the metro. To be fair, most of the teachers were harried, middle-aged women in a rush to meet the demands of their second job—standing in lines to buy food for their families. It was obvious, however, that no one was eager to be associated with me in an unofficial capacity. As foreigner, I was both superstar and suspect. Clearly, my involvement with the teachers would be carefully sanctioned and controlled.

Each day at four o'clock, after a stint of deciphering idioms from *How to Steal a Million* and fending off Alexander Zakharich's questions about my origins and hints about what teaching materials I might be planning to add to his hoard, I removed my overcoat from his private closet (protection against theft, I finally realized) and headed for the metro. At the city center, I wandered the streets alone, the only dawdler in the midst of Russians who walked with quick, determined strides. The streets were so wide and the motorists so disdainful of walkers that pedestrians had to use an underpass.

The city lacked any trace of Western street life: no charming outdoor cafés, few colors except the omnipresent red of banners and posters. Instead of street hawkers, there were *babushki* in white lab-style jackets over their padded coats selling ice cream. The occasional sale of bloody meat from an overturned box gathered a line down the block.

Walking home I glanced into shop windows filled with piles of political texts or synthetic fabrics that cost a teacher's monthly salary. How artfully the pyramids of mackerel cans were stacked, even if there was only one sort to choose from. The shoppers all around me seemed filled with utter seriousness, absorbed by the task at hand and by the weight of their laden string bags. No one but I glanced at the red placards, the huge propaganda posters everywhere exhorting us to FULFILL THE PLAN!

I rode the metro to the Arbat, Moscow's venerable artists' neighborhood, but in the bookstores the texts were limited to Jack London or Sholokhov's Soviet Realist opus *Quiet Flows the Don*. I watched the swimmers splashing in the enormous, steaming outdoor city pool. I wanted to join them, but I had no bathing suit, and I was afraid I wouldn't be able to make myself understood well enough to secure my document-filled purse.

At the Hotel Pekin, the floor ladies and old pensioners with armbands eyed me suspiciously as I passed. I sat alone over tea and cookies (my usual supper, because it was cheap and readily available) in a corner table of the "buffet," a small café on an upper hotel floor that sold wine and vodka and caviar, and sour cream that Russians ate straight from a glass for breakfast. Sometimes I communicated through hand signs to the chambermaids, who seemed to pity me for being so far from home. I gave them ballpoint pens and decals for their children and bribed them for toilet paper with sample tubes of hand lotion.

I sat for hours in my room, smoking cheap Bulgarian cigarettes, sitting on my narrow, sagging bed, or I opened the double windows and looked down on the pedestrians marching across Mayakovsky Square in their shapeless woolen coats. I couldn't follow the TV programs (a working television was eventually brought to me), and I found the whining, high-pitched folk choruses on the radio annoying.

I began to think of my old boyfriend Kim, a dangerous sign: thinking of Kim meant I wanted someone to bail me out of this misadventure the way the turtle in old King Leonardo cartoons used to cry, after some harebrained attempt to be a logger or a jet pilot had gone awry, "Take Me Back Mister Wizard, Take Me Back!"

An image of Kim began to haunt me at night at the Hotel Pekin: standing in his vegetable garden, leaning on a hoe and grinning—shirtless Kim, who knew how to fix his own car and who had read all the classics—glistening with sweat, smiling his benign smile, surrounded by green sprouts. Kim who thought living itself was pleasure enough—a good meal, a *Smithsonian* article on glaciers, seeds planted in the ground—and couldn't understand my restlessness. Why hadn't I been able to settle for that garden, that hoe? A life like a warm bath, a ride in a hammock? But it wasn't that simple. Kim had wanted to close out the world, experience it only through books. He'd wanted to keep me cloistered, away from everyone else. I wanted to be immersed in the world; I wanted adventure.

I'd moved to New York because I thought you had to live there to be a writer and because it was as unlike Iowa, where I'd spent two years in graduate school, as I could imagine. I'd taken, and, after only six months, quit a job in an Episcopal prep school where the headmaster had informed me that I'd have to attend chapel, but it shouldn't offend a "Hebress." I had a couple of short stories published in inconspicuous journals, a novel I couldn't finish, and a growing fear that I was never

going to be more than mediocre. Now I thought I needed a foreign ge-
ography to give me definition. I needed Russia.

I'd been obsessed with Russia for years. It was the land of my grandparents, though they'd been glad enough to escape the pogroms and
conscription into the czar's army. I loved the sound of the language, as
rich and musky as mushrooms and black soil. I loved the literature; its
mix of sentimentality and violence struck me as much closer to the
themes of American literature—and my home life—than that of our
accepted source, England, with its fixation on marrying well.

I wanted to know what it was like to exist under the largest of
thumbs. Half the globe woke up and went to sleep with totalitarian
rule; I thought if I were allowed to taste and smell it, I would understand something essential about the world—and though I didn't know
it yet, myself. I too had grown up under a minor form of totalitarian
rule. My siblings and I had quaked in the presence of our Stalinesque
father, who shared the madman's droopy mustache and prominent
nose. We'd done his bidding out of fear and were accustomed to his
paranoid, brutal outbursts, his extreme, arbitrary punishments (at six I
was locked in the attic for talking back; at eight I was permanently ban-
ished from the living room for spilling a glass of water). I used to think
that if my father were a country, he'd be Russia.

Such parallels, of course, were below the level of consciousness. Russia
held other attractions. I was fascinated by people who could never go
home again, fascinated by those who had been exiled. (My stalled
Alaska novel had a Russian defector as a character.) And I was drawn to
extremes. At eighteen I'd hitched around the West. At twenty-one I'd
worked as a deckhand on fishing boats in Alaska. I thought the only
way you could know a place was to work in it, alongside its denizens.
Now I feared that the only definition I'd find in Russia was that of outsider. I'd be consigned to an emptiness even more profound than the
one I'd left behind.

I wasn't motivated by a desire for a romance, had never been in any
of my travels. Romance, to me, was just part of the package. But New
York had proven impossible in that regard. Before I'd moved there, a
friend had told me that all her New York friends complained there were
no men. I'd pooh-poohed her warning, having never been short on
boyfriends. I had since read an article that said there were sixty-six men

for every hundred women in Manhattan. Perhaps it was sixty-six single men, or heterosexual men, I can't remember the details, but the message was clear. All over New York, on a Saturday night, beautiful, talented women were eating Häagen-Dazs and watching reruns on TV.

New York, it turned out, was full of men who never made a next date but said, "I'll call you," men who wanted me to convenience them by riding a subway sixty blocks, who then put me back on the subway at midnight to fend for myself, men who told me exhaustively of their therapists' opinions of their intimacy problems or their undying love for their last girlfriends, who'd left them for someone else. Sure, there were guys like that everywhere, but there seemed to be more of them in New York, where it was a seller's market. I wasn't going to settle for someone like my friend's boyfriend, who lived with his old girlfriend "to save rent" and went around asking, "Would you like champagne or would you prefer real pain? Would you like shampoo or would you prefer . . . ?" When I asked how she could stand it, she said, "Who else is there?"

A better question might have been, why did I stay in New York after the first flush of city excitement—gawking at the Madonna pinned with dollars in the San Genaro parade, or the dangling pimpled chickens in the storefronts of Chinatown—wore off? Why didn't I move back to Vermont where my mother lived? Why did I, and my friends, beat our heads against those concrete walls? It had to do with some vestigial dream, some persisting illusion of opportunity, a belief that by virtue of the sheer numbers of people there, by the presence of ambition and energy and variety all about, we were bound to receive whatever it was we wanted.

What was it that I wanted in Moscow? I wanted access, I wanted to understand, I wanted . . . contact.

At the end of the first week, I decided to call one of the phone numbers given to me before I left New York. Maxim was an artist, a friend of a New York acquaintance of mine named Richard who'd studied five years ago in Moscow. Maxim didn't speak English, and it took a lot of kopecks in a pay phone before we somehow managed to arrange to meet in front of a metro station at eight o'clock. The only words of description I understood were that he'd be wearing a black beret, apparently de rigeur for an unofficial, "underground" artist. I went off to my rendezvous nervously, figuring that at the least I'd get language practice. Anything seemed better than another night in my room.

Maxim turned out to be a small bearded man in his thirties who bore an unpleasant resemblance to Charles Manson. He declared scornfully that he hardly remembered "Reechard." When I gave him a book of Soviet avant-garde art of the twenties, a gift from Richard that I'd toted all the way from New York, Maxim complained that Reechard should have sent acrylic paints instead. Paints were very hard to find. He'd had a friend at the American Embassy who'd bought his work and given him paints. Did I know anyone at the embassy?

The embassy was a place I avoided after one brief visit. I had no interest in buying an American hamburger at the PX or dancing with marines, and the paranoia of the place was repellent.

Maxim and I traveled through miles of metro and a confusing jumble of trolleys. He insisted on carrying my bag and taking my hand every time I stepped on or off a trolley. I kept eyeing my bag nervously; it held my passport and visa as well as all of my rubles and dollars. I'd been warned that foreign passports were a valuable black-market commodity, and I kept waiting for Maxim to dart away into the crowd with my treasures slung over his shoulder.

Maxim lived and worked in a cold, filthy basement studio with a cement floor in a crumbling apartment building, an underground artist indeed. The ten-by-twelve room was filled with canvases, a cot, a small stove, paint, easels, and a table set with bottles of vodka and pickles and with chocolates. A friend of Maxim's named Dmitri was waiting there for us. Dmitri was a skinny computer programmer with lank, greasy hair and crudely made sneakers that looked like bowling shoes. He spoke about as much high school English as I spoke Russian. The three of us set about drinking toasts to Reechard, world peace, and art. Maxim's minimal charm diminished as the vodka disappeared, and sweat broke out on his forehead.

"You have many blacks in your country," Maxim stated authoritatively. "To us, blacks are like Martians."

Dmitri wanted to know what rock concerts I'd seen. He said that to see a rock concert was his lifelong dream. Maxim screamed at Dmitri to speak Russian. It took me some time to explain I needed to use the bathroom, and when I did I was sorry. It was a dank cubicle in the hall with dripping pipes and ripped-up pages of *Pravda* in place of toilet paper.

"I must to go home to hotel," I ventured in my pidgin Russian. "It is late."

"It is early," Maxim contradicted. "First you must look at my art. I am a great artist." Maxim pulled out stacks of watercolors, most of them hokey cosmic abstractions of whirling planets. "I am a great artist," Maxim repeated. "Do you like my work?"

"Very nice."

Maxim sat down beside me and began to stroke my hair as I flipped distractedly through the paintings.

"Do you like me?" Maxim asked.

"Friends," I said, edging away. I was desperate to leave, but I wasn't sure I could find my way home alone.

"Friends," Maxim scoffed. "Men and women are never friends. I am a man, you are a woman. So?" He grabbed me in a squashing embrace. I pushed him away hard and stood up, looking to Dmitri for help. Dmitri fiddled with his pack of Bulgarian cigarettes and looked away. Maybe this was some kind of conspiracy they'd worked out. Get me drunk, then the two of them would attack together. It was a mistake to have gone to an apartment with a strange man, two men. I should have met Maxim in some well-populated public place, where I could have left him as soon as I realized he was a creep, or I could have threatened to yell for one of the militiaman. I'd thought being foreign would protect me.

"I must return to hotel," I said firmly.

"You are so afraid. You think I am KGB, maybe?" Maxim laughed nastily and winked at Dmitri, who seemed embarrassed.

"Of course not." I didn't know how to say in Russian that I thought he was a pig.

"You do not want to stay here with me?" Maxim gestured toward the cot.

"No!"

"You want to buy a painting, maybe?"

"Next time!" I eagerly grasped this straw, hoping he realized that a raped woman wouldn't be likely to buy his paintings. "Now I have no money with me. Money in room. Next time I buy painting."

Maxim muttered something that sounded like curses.

"What number trolleybus to metro?" I begged.

Maxim was very offended. "You cannot go alone. I would not permit such a thing. I am a man as well as an artist! Dmitri will take you."

We left the great artist slumped drunkenly in his chair. On the trolley and metro ride Dmitri looked pained, either because of his friend's behavior or because he wanted to practice his English and I sullenly refused to speak. He also took my hand and offered to carry my bag—standard Soviet male courtesy, I surmised, like the automatic way men got up to give their seats to women on the bus. On the metro escalator, Dmitri reached out to smooth my brow. "Do not do that. Is no good. It makes . . ." he scrunched up his forehead in imitation of mine—wrinkles. "And next time, do not leave money in hotel room." He struggled for a word to indicate thieves. "Mafia!" he finally concluded.

At my station, Dmitri apologized that he couldn't walk me to my hotel. "It is for me dangerous to be seen with foreigner near hotel." He shrugged with embarrassment. "Many KGB there. My job they think secret. It is of course stupid. Everyone knows American computers thirty years ahead but . . ." Dmitri lifted his shoulders as though to say, "What can I do?" I felt sorry for him. He wasn't a bad guy, except for his choice of friend. Dmitri continued, "I am sorry I cannot to invite you to my home. I would play for you my records of Frank Zappa. Frank Zappa the best!" Dmitri pointed a thumb skyward.

A train came whooshing into the platform, pushing the air ahead of it in a roar and ruffling the hair of a drunk slumped dangerously close to the platform. I shook Dmitri's hand and hurried away toward the escalator, where only a few soldiers and teenagers now rode the steeply banked stairs. By the time I got back to the hotel they'd locked the door, and I had to bang and beg my way back in with my foreign passport.

I woke exhausted and depressed. Between Alexander Zakharich, Grisha, and Maxim, my prospects for contact looked dim. And then something occurred, changing everything. I was teaching Robert Frost to Grisha's classes using the Soviet texts. Alexander Zakharich was very fond of Frost, especially the poem "The Mending Wall," which he took for a parable of Soviet/American relations. He seemed under pressure to have me use their books for a certain portion of my lessons.

A few days earlier, I'd gotten into trouble for using immoral texts. I'd brought in a stack of *Scholastic* magazines. The kids had immediately zoomed in on the ads for audio tapes, Noxzema, and the New Army.

"Is it true, Miss Laurie, that you may buy tapes for only one penny?" They were awfully disappointed when I explained the meaning of fine print and advertising come-ons. We read a story together about a murder told from the point of view of a cat. The cat calmly describes the music on the stereo, the sound of footsteps, a window opening, a scream, his master falling to the floor, and then the wind flapping the curtains in the empty apartment. I assigned roles to the kids and asked them to play the cat, the victim, the murderer.

"What kind of music were you listening to when the murder occurred, Oleg?" I asked the boy I'd assigned the role of owner. Oleg looked down at his folded hands in embarrassment and blushed. "Okay, Masha, you're the cute little kitty. Did you like your owner?"

"No," Masha said, rising to the challenge. "I did not like him at all. Often he forgot to feed me the milk."

"Milk, not *the* milk," Grisha interrupted from the back of the room.

"Never mind, you're doing great!" I continued. "What about you, Vanya? Why did you murder this man? Was it personal, or a robbery? Do you know the word *robbery*?"

At the end of the class we held the first debate ever at School 45 on the innocuous topic of Cat Haters vs. Cat Lovers. Even the shyest students waxed eloquent on the subject of the loyalty of dogs versus the independence of cats. I felt thrilled by the success of the class, only to be reprimanded by Zakharich the next day. Murder stories were not appropriate for Soviet schoolchildren. Our duty was to teach them values, not merely to get them to talk, even in English. Grisha had used bad judgment in allowing me to proceed in that vein. So now I was droning on about two paths diverging in a yellow wood.

Grisha sat in the back of the room, flipping through the pages of a big color picture book of New York that I'd brought along to show the kids. We rarely had other visiting teachers in Grisha's classes, perhaps due to the fact that he was a man, or perhaps simply because his classes met the last periods of the day and everyone was already exhausted. When the bell rang and the room emptied, Grisha beckoned me aside. He had the tourist book open to a color photograph of two bicycle riders in Central Park.

"Is this truly permitted?" he asked.

"What?" I studied the picture. It seemed ordinary enough.

"To dress like this in the city?" I looked again. The man was shirtless, wearing shorts, and the girl wore a halter with her cutoffs.

"Of course, why not?"

Grisha put the book down and sighed. "It must be nice to live like that."

I was boggled.

"In our country," Grisha said, "if you were to dress like that in the city, the *babushki*—the grandmothers—would make a scandal. It is not permitted to wear shorts on city streets."

I laughed nervously, afraid to agree with his criticism. "I think the *babushki* are the true power in your country. Yesterday two of them yelled at me because I forgot my room key on the table in the hotel buffet."

"It isn't at all funny. It isn't nice to have people telling you what to do all the time."

"If someone did that at home, we'd tell them to mind their own business."

Grisha said quietly, "I envy you your life." Kids' voices wafted up from the street. A metal rake scraped on pavement. Grisha's hand on the book caught my attention: black hairs curling over his fingers, a gold wedding band. What if he was tricking me, trapping me with his confidence? I looked up into his eyes, searching for something that would tell me who he really was. Then I realized that he was the one taking the risk, exposing himself, if only with a few carefully chosen words, a minor criticism. I felt upended, out of equilibrium. Here was no provocateur, but a man desperate for contact. Someone knocked on the door. We both jumped up guiltily, as though caught in an illicit act: the crime of friendship. I gathered my papers as a fifteen-year-old girl came in with a bucket and mop, glanced at us, and started swabbing the floor. I watched the girl nervously. Was she listening? She was wearing heavy wool tights with her brown pinafore uniform, and like most of the children, she'd left her shoes in the coat closet and wore slippers on her feet. Why was it, I wondered, that the boys never stayed after school to clean the rooms?

"Would it be possible for us to talk again?" Grisha asked, suddenly stiff and formal.

"Sure. If you want to."

"I want to very much."

Children Stuffed Like Sausages

Grisha sat on his desk, one leg dangling. Behind his head a red poster with cartoon graphics invited students to apply to work at Asphalt Plant Number 209 after graduation. He was still wearing the Wimbledon sweater, and his synthetic trousers shone. Had he no other sweaters, I wondered, or did he wear his one piece of foreign clothing for my benefit? I disliked myself for judging his clothes. All of the Russian teachers wore the same outfit for days on end; they had no choice, here where an outfit cost a month's salary. But the American preference, if one had only three outfits, would be to alternate them—even the illusion of change has meaning for us.

"What do you think of our Soviet teaching methods?" Grisha asked.

"They are different from ours," I began carefully. Overnight, I'd begun to wonder if his admission of envy yesterday might be an aberration. Why should I trust him? Better to wait for him to make a move before showing my hand.

"I think they are awful," Grisha said, scattering his cards to the wind.

I glanced over at the half-open door in alarm. Grisha rose to close it. Now that I had what I'd craved, someone who spoke honestly, I half-wanted to ward off further revelations. Grisha was going to burden me with a responsibility I couldn't yet fathom.

"You know," he continued, pacing in front of the blackboard. "I find it painful to watch you teach. It shows me that we teach our children nothing. We do not allow them to think, we stuff them full of information like sausages, and they spit it back to please us. Not even information, so much of it is false. I am filled with shame when you ask them a question and they cannot answer."

"They are shy," I apologized for them, quoting the other Russian teachers.

"Yes, we make them shy, that is true. But that is not the only reason. They cannot answer if they have not first read it in a book."

I'd recently come around to what I thought was an admirably open-minded view of Soviet education, and here was Grisha voicing my original complaints. I sighed. "When I got here I didn't like the way you taught, but now that I've been here longer I see that your way is better suited to your society. Isn't it the job of schools to make good citizens? What use would it be for your children to go around asking why?" As soon as the words left my mouth I tasted their condescension.

Grisha smiled bitterly. "You are quite right. Here it is often better not to think."

The thrill of conspiracy ran through me. We were breaking some rule, I was sure. Grisha could lose his job for talking like this. It was ridiculous, nothing more than coworkers gossiping about a boss. But the Soviet State made such a convincing arbiter of right and wrong I felt guilty

"Grisha?"

"Yes?"

"How is it that you learned to think for yourself, if not in school? You must have learned somewhere. Was it at home?"

Grisha shook his head. "My father is a true believer. A real Communist. I learned nothing from him. Some people learn to think for themselves when they see that things are not as they have been told. Most people don't care." He walked over to the window. "It is always so stuffy in here. Would you care for some air?"

I shrugged. Grisha pushed aside the flimsy, pale green curtains and opened the line of double windows. Cool, damp air rushed into the room, carrying with it the odor of rotting leaves. Grisha came back and sat across from me.

"Why do you tell me these things?" I asked. "Why do you trust me? Aren't you afraid I might betray you?"

"I trust you because of the way you talk honestly, even to the children.

And because of your eyes. They are full of intelligence, and something more. Goodness, perhaps. And I trust you because of my own selfishness. I must tell someone what I truly think or I will burst!"

I was flattered. I preferred to think there was something he saw in me that made him open up, rather than simply his need to unburden himself of secret complaints.

"Remember that first day, Grisha? In the lunchroom? When I told you it didn't require documents to move from city to city at home? I thought you didn't believe me, you stared so strangely."

"I was probably jealous."

"What about your question about the CIA? I had you pegged as a provocateur."

"Who else could I ask? I was curious."

"Didn't you think of how it would sound to me? What if you were in my position, visiting America, and someone asked you about the KGB your first day?"

"I cannot imagine myself in your position," Grisha said stiffly.

"But you traveled to India. Natasha told me."

"You don't know how it is for us if we are permitted to travel. With every Soviet group there is KGB. We aren't allowed to go anywhere alone. And even without KGB, people inform on one another. I was stuck at a backwater construction project, translating commands to workers who spoke Pidgin English. We lived in barracks like soldiers, driving each other insane in the heat with talk of Moscow's snows and the sight of birch trees. I'm ashamed to think now how crazy I was to come home." Grisha paused. "No one but the most trusted diplomat can travel as you do."

"And I'm a nobody," I said as if to appease him, but in claiming my lack of importance I was adding insult to injury. In our country, nobodies were somebodies. For the first time I realized how easy it was to flaunt my privilege, to be tactless. Still, there was something basely satisfying in finding myself raised above the average that made me want to wave it in both our faces.

Grisha said in a near-whisper, "Tell me what it is like there, where you live."

There? I closed my eyes and saw color, the brightness of advertising, and the abundance in shop windows. Frivolity. The furred and jeweled costume parade up Madison Avenue sidewalks on Saturday afternoons, the painted smugness of couples on Columbus Avenue. Chinese restaurants, subway graffiti, bums eating out of the garbage. Roller skaters bopping to boom boxes in Central Park. Superhighways and supermarkets. Suburbs filled with houses, each with its two-car garage holding bicycles and leaf blowers and lawnmowers. Christopher Street gays. City restaurants with groups of women making the best of a Friday night. A city of single-occupancy dwellings and little dogs with rhinestone collars and knitted coats. How could I put into words such incomprehensible variety, such skewed wealth and loneliness?

I opened my eyes to the gray-green room with its dusty portraits of Pushkin and Lenin, the damp October air leaking in through the windows. Grisha leaned forward intently, his eyes behind his tinted glasses glittering. Where but in Russia would two people be drawn to each other out of a lust for information? There was something wrong in this, holding food out of the reach of a starving man. I wasn't even happy at home. But when I began to describe my life there, I heard the thrill in my voice, its homesick rhapsody.

It seemed as though one crack in the wall of my official isolation mysteriously made way for other breaches. In the lunchroom, I sat across from a buxom young blonde teacher who introduced herself as Tanya, English teacher of the fifth and sixth forms. Tanya had arched, plucked brows over mischievous blue eyes and a perfect round dimple in her chin; she was wearing a tight-fitting pink angora sweater that looked imported, and a watch hung from a chain over the dangerous precipice of her breasts like an unfortunate climber dangling on a rope.

Tanya smiled when I introduced myself in turn. "We all know who *you* are, Lora. May I call you Lora? Everyone talks about you constantly. I am so disappointed that you have not visited my classes. My children would like so much to meet you. It is quite a pity that Alexander Zakharich does not permit it."

"It's the fault of my bad Russian," I said, attempting diplomacy. "He doesn't want to waste me on the younger grades that wouldn't understand my English."

"My children speak very well," Tanya protested.

"You know, when I came here I didn't know which grades I'd be teaching, so I brought materials for every age. I'm not using the ones for the younger grades at all. If you like, I can bring you some textbooks and fairy tales. I've got *Tom Thumb*."

"Oi! *Malchik Palchik!* We have that too, in Russian. But you are serious? You do not mind?"

"Of course not. Somebody ought to use them. I'll bring them tomorrow."

"Oh, Lora, you are generous! But you must be lonely in your hotel?"

I shrugged. "It's alright."

"But the food there must be very bad."

"Like here." I looked down at the bowl of soup in front of me—fish-flavored potatoes in a broth topped by a grease slick.

Tanya wriggled her nose in sympathetic disgust. She'd been making her way through a plate heaped with pastries; she pushed it across the table toward me. "Here, eat these instead."

I waved them away. "I'm eating sweets all the time here. I must stop, or I'll be terribly fat by the time I go home." When had this imitation Russo-British inflection crept into my own English?

"Oh, but you have good figure, just like me, Lora. I eat and eat but I never gain weight. My husband even says my legs are too skinny, like a frog." Tanya grinned at the ridiculousness of this complaint. Obviously, she wasn't worried at all about her figure. She was built more like a Barbie doll than any woman I had ever seen. I would have to call my own figure ordinary, despite her compliments.

"I know," Tanya said brightly. "You must visit my home and eat a true Russian meal. I will ask my husband and Alexander Zakharich for permission, and if they say it is quite alright, I will invite you to come to my house for dinner. If you would like, of course."

"I'd love to! Do you think that's possible?"

"Well . . . Alexander Zakharich will be quite annoyed. He doesn't want me to meet you. Only his favorite, Natasha." Tanya leaned over the table. "Alexander Zakharich is very unfair. And Natasha keeps you all to herself as well. She is very powerful woman. Did you know that she is member of the Communist Party?"

"Oh?" I kept a blank face for that little gem.

"I will phone to my husband immediately," Tanya said, jumping up. "I will be so happy if you will be the guest in my flat. I am very good cook. And not at all modest!"

We left lunch very pleased with each other.

Grisha sat next to me in the auditorium to translate a student presentation of slides from a class trip to the Kremlin. A serious, bespectacled ninth former stood on stage and described the highlights while badly focused student snapshots clicked on and off the screen. A faint odor of stale sweat hovered above the heads of the uniformed students, who whispered together in the auditorium rows.

"The red stars were placed on the Kremlin towers in 1937," Grisha translated. Then, lowering his voice: "A good year, don't you think?" It was the year of Stalin's greatest purge. "The clock on the Kremlin tower is winded every twelve hours," he continued.

"Wound," I corrected.

"Damn! Of course, an irregular verb. Wind, wound. Grind, ground, find, found."

"That's the first mistake I've ever heard you make in English."

"And I wanted you to think I was perfect!"

"You almost are." Out of the corner of my eye, I saw Grisha's mustache lift in a wry smile. He began to translate again. "The Hall of Congresses was constructed . . . what a terrible bore."

"Shhh," I giggled. I felt the warmth from his leg radiating against mine. Down the row, Natasha frowned at the sound of our voices.

Natasha came into Alexander Zakharich's classroom just as we were finishing up a session with his tape. She leafed through a stack of spotty, badly printed photographs that one of the students had taken of me in front of a classroom. They'd been shot the morning after my visit to Maxim's, and I looked particularly dreadful.

"Yes," Natasha crooned. "You have the face of a very simple girl, but very clever. Yes . . . You know, there is something about you that isn't quite American. Where is it you said that your family was from?"

"Oh, mixed European," I answered with elaborate casualness. "Austria, Czechoslovakia, it's all jumbled up." Well, the Ukraine *was* part of the Austro-Hungarian empire at the time.

"You know," Natasha said, "you could even look a bit Jewish." She smiled slyly. "Isn't that so, Alexander Zakharich? We all know that Alexander Zakharich is no anti-Semite."

I shrugged as though I didn't get her drift.

"And what did you say your patronymic, your father's name was?" Zakharich leaped in. "Did you say Morris?"

"Murray."

Zakharich looked disappointed. Apparently he didn't know that Murray, like Stanley and Irving, were popular names for Jewish boys of my father's generation whose parents thought such names implied class. I had slipped out of his grasp, just as a phrase in his tape of *How to Steal a Million* eluded him. I sighed with the effort of it all, the lying. The deeper I got into it, the more impossible it became to reverse myself. To change the subject, I inquired about the possibility of hiring someone to give me private Russian lessons. Natasha and Zakharich exchanged unhappy glances.

Natasha said, "Private lessons are illegal in our country. It is a form of private enterprise, you understand. Nonetheless," she sighed heavily, "if you insist, we will find a solution. Perhaps a student—free of charge, of course. After all, you are our special guest." Clearly, I'd just added to her burden. I was turning out to be a very unsatisfactory guest all around.

Zakharich walked me to the metro station. The weight of our mutual dislike hung between us. "Tell me, how do you explain the word *frustration*?" Zakharich asked abruptly, just as we got to the platform. "We are very curious about psychological matters, you see, but we have so little opportunity to read Freud."

"Frustration? Feeling thwarted, I guess. When you want something you can't have."

"Ah, yes," Zakharich said, "I see."

In the hallway Tanya breathlessly announced that everything was quite okay; she'd been given permission for me to come to her house for dinner next Saturday. In addition, she and Grisha had been granted permission to give me Russian lessons after school. "We'll meet in Grisha's room after classes," Tanya said. "Grisha and I are *very* good friends."

"What about my tape sessions with Alexander Zakharich?"

"Don't worry, Lora, it is all arranged!"

So Grisha and Tanya had discussed my request. What else about me had they discussed? I felt unreasonably miffed. I had dropped the subject of Russian lessons since Natasha had seemed so put-upon, but I had told Grisha the story.

"Of course there are private lessons," he'd said. "I give them myself, although it's not allowed. I have to. My wife doesn't work, and teacher salaries are very low. I give lessons to the children of the rich, high party officials. The other day I was giving a private lesson, and when I left I realized I had mistakenly taken with me their American ballpoint pen. You see how ours are worthless." Grisha raised one of the flimsy, crude Soviet pens that rarely shared their meager supply of ink. "I was afraid they'd think I'd stolen it. I hurried back. When I told the mother why I'd returned she laughed and held out a jar filled with dozens of pens just like the one I'd taken. She was flaunting her connections."

"Maybe she just didn't want you to feel bad about taking it," I offered.

"How little you understand our people," Grisha said. "She wanted to humiliate me."

The Russian lesson turned out to be a farce. While Grisha struggled earnestly to conjugate verbs on the blackboard, Tanya wanted only to gossip about school. "And what do you think of Natasha, an old woman dressing like a girl? It is disgusting! Oh, but she is very, very powerful. And Alexander Zakharich with his . . . how do you say, those little white things falling from his hair?"

"Dandruff?"

"Dandruff." Tanya giggled. "And how is it that our Lora isn't married yet? If you lived in Russia, you would have been married twice already. Isn't that true, Grisha?"

"Certainly," Grisha said in exasperation. He turned back to write on the board, and Tanya leaned close to whisper. "Grisha is quite handsome, don't you think? And he speaks English very well, better even than Zakharich and Natasha."

"He sounds just like an Englishman," I said, avoiding the first half of her question. Grisha handsome? He still made me think of Groucho Marx with those brows and glasses and mustache, although he had a nice straight nose instead of Groucho's parrot beak. He'd begun to slide more into the Omar Sharif camp as I'd gotten to know him.

"I will cut my hair just like yours, Lora," Tanya said. "It is more fashionable short, I see." She whispered in my ear, "Do you know that I stain my hair?"

"Stain? You mean dye. People stain furniture, but they dye hair."

"Dye. Yes, you are right. That reminds me of an anecdote about Brezhnev at the barber. Grisha, forget your silly verbs for a moment."

Tanya jumped up and ran to the door, looked up and down the hall, then shut the door firmly. She told the anecdote, which had to do with Brezhnev's huge bushy eyebrows, with a look of delicious naughtiness, but I had to force a laugh.

"Perhaps Laurie doesn't share our Soviet love of anecdotes," Grisha said. "It is quite a sickness with us, an obsession."

"Well, you Russians have a different sense of humor," I apologized.

"I am not Russian," Grisha said.

"What?"

"I am a Jew."

I looked away to the blackboard, to the series of the form of the verb *derzheet*, to hold. My heart thumped in alarm—would I be forced into an equal admission? Tanya smirked as though listening to a dirty joke.

"I don't understand," I lied. "In America to be Jewish is a religion, like Catholic or Buddhist. They are Jews and Americans." *They*—the word buzzed shamefully in my head.

"Not here," Grisha said. "Have you seen our internal passports? There is a space for nationality. Jews are not Russians even if they've lived in Moscow for three hundred years. Our government thinks it very important to keep the races . . . in order."

"You see, it is very simple," Tanya said. "We are all Soviet people. *Oi*, but I am starving! Let us go somewhere to eat dinner together. Grisha and I must return to school tonight for the Komsomol meeting. It is quite boring, but what can we do? It is our system. Lora, aren't you hungry?"

I agreed, relieved that the question of nationality had been dropped without my having to lie further. So *Oi* was a Russian expression, not just Jewish, and Grisha was a Jew. . . . It wasn't all that surprising, given his darkness. And his dissatisfaction. It made me feel closer to him, yet oddly disappointed, as though his secret complaints were somehow Jewish in nature, and therefore shameful. He wasn't a *real* Russian.

We rode a trolley to the center. Tanya was in high spirits, filled with the excitement of breaking the rules, an unofficial outing with a foreigner. Grisha seemed uncomfortable. As much as I enjoyed Tanya, I would have preferred to be alone with Grisha, huddling in his classroom, sharing information. The first restaurant refused us entry, although we could plainly see empty tables behind the glass doors. We rode another trolley, and a second restaurant refused us. Grisha took the doorman aside and argued fiercely.

"What did you say to him?" I asked when the doorman finally waved us in.

"I told him that we had an American guest with us and it would not look good if we were refused twice. So, do you know the password yet?"

"What password?"

"Speak English!" Tanya and Grisha chorused.

"I don't get it. Why should they treat me better than you?"

Tanya said, "Well, you see, Lora, it is really for the good of our country. We need foreign currency, so we make things especially comfortable for our foreign guests."

"But that doesn't explain why they treat *you* badly. Those tables were empty."

"Why should they work?" Tanya snapped. "They receive their salaries all the same. I am afraid, Lora, that we are a very lazy people. Only I am not lazy. My husband calls me the dynamo because I am always busy scrubbing and cooking, I love my flat so. Soon you will be my guest and see it."

"And how do you feel when you go to the hard currency store?" Grisha asked me. "Does it make you feel powerful to be admitted where we cannot go?"

"No, it makes me feel rotten."

"I don't see why," Tanya said. "When my husband comes back from business trips abroad with coupons for foreign currency, I, too, shop in the *beriozka*. That is where I bought this beautiful skirt. Do you like it, Lora?"

"You are fortunate to have an important husband who can provide you with such treasures," Grisha said sharply. The glance that passed between them was wholly private. I was getting used to being the center of attention, and I didn't like being left out, despite my claim to be interested in equal treatment. In the ladies' room, where Tanya led me for a pre-meal primp, I was once again restored to my position of glory. Tanya admired my discount shoes, cheap street earrings, and half-priced T. J. Maxx sweater with flattery that was both oppressive and guileless. The ladies' room was cold, clinically unadorned, with the same shoddy plastic toilets as in my hotel. Why hadn't they figured out a way to build toilets that swallowed toilet paper, I bitched to myself, instead of keeping a basket of smelly wastepaper in each stall?

We headed back upstairs to the relative elegance of cloth napkins and generous place settings. Tanya and Grisha argued in rapid Russian about our dinner. They finally agreed on sturgeon appetizers, beet salads, Chicken Kiev, and fried potatoes. Tanya insisted we order wine and vodka. When the butter gushed out of her potato-shaped lump of Chicken Kiev, Tanya rolled her eyes heavenward and licked her knife with pleasure. "I do so love butter! It is the great treat for me; sometimes I eat it even without bread. I could eat half a kilo by myself; I am so wicked I forget to save it for my daughter. It is fortunate that I never grow fat. Alexander Zakharich is so disgustingly fat. But I would not wish to be as skinny as poor Nina Fedorovna. I don't see how her husband enjoys her at all!"

"We all admire your remarkable figure, Tanya. You needn't remind us of it constantly," Grisha said curtly. "And you know there is little danger of any of us growing fat from butter, when it is so difficult to find it in the shops."

Tanya glanced at Grisha and then at me, cocking a questioning eyebrow, then nodded her head knowingly as though to say, *Ah, so this is your game.* "And when was the last time you yourself visited the shops?" she countered. "After all, your wife must be a wonderful housekeeper, since she doesn't go to work."

"I'm sure Laurie is quite bored by our conversation," Grisha said, reaching for his wineglass.

"It is true, Lora," Tanya relented. "It is often quite difficult to find butter. When I hear that it is being sold in a store, I send my granny to stand in line for me!"

When the bill came, Tanya and Grisha refused to let me help pay, although I protested that I had few places to spend my ruble salary. The bill had to be shockingly high, judging by the prices on the menu.

"But you are our guest," Tanya insisted. "We know that if we came to visit you in America, you would do the same. Isn't that right, Grisha?" Tanya glanced at him with malice.

Grisha looked shaken as he forked over rubles. We walked the mile or so back to the school together in a light rain, stopping on the way at a photo salon. Tanya needed a new photo for her Komsomol ID. She decided that we must have a portrait made of the three of us together to commemorate our friendship. The photo salon resembled a larger version of a passport photo shop at Grand Central Station. The bare room held a line of waiting patrons and behind a curtain, a backdrop, a camera on a tripod, huge lights, and flash equipment. Grisha, Tanya, and I were shunted to the head of the line, perhaps due to my presence. The photographer, a pudgy man in a brown synthetic suit, seemed highly amused at the idea of photographing a man with two women, and kept insisting that we sit closer, until we were squashed together, Grisha in the middle, Tanya and I on either side, mashing our breasts against his arms. "The light and the dark!" the photographer shouted gleefully. The waiting customers chuckled and smirked.

"My Boris would kill me if he knew!" Tanya exulted, as she hid the receipt in her purse.

Back in the school courtyard, a woman stood by the school door, clutching the hand of a little boy. She looked up at us as we entered, her face full of terror.

"Grisha's wife," Tanya whispered, pulling me aside as Grisha strode over to her. "You see, she is jealous. She is always coming to school like this, saying the child is sick. She is so afraid she'll lose her husband. Grisha does not love her, and she is jealous. Now that she has seen you, she will be even more afraid." She wasn't unattractive—an even-featured woman wearing a sporty man's cap angled over her shoulder-length brown hair. It seemed a pathetic touch, this attempt to dress jauntily for such a depressing mission.

"Let's walk to the corner and have a cigarette," Tanya urged.

"But you don't smoke," I said in confusion, handing her my pack and lighter.

"I wish to be just like you, Lora. You know here they think it is bad if women smoke on the streets. They think you are prostitute!" Tanya lit up with defiant pleasure. I glanced back at Grisha, who was speaking urgently with his wife. I felt sorry for the poor woman, and guilty, as though I'd somehow done her a wrong.

Tanya's Lover

In the lunchroom, Alexander Zakharich sat down beside me. "You know what I call the new immigrants to America from our country?"
"What?"
"Refujews!"

At night Russian voices jumbled in my head, verbs tumbled over one another, adjectives danced in an aural hallucination. The voices plagued me constantly—fragmented pieces of conversation from the school lunchroom, the hotel maids and floor ladies, the people on the street. My neurons and synapses were firing madly in an enormous effort to rearrange my brain to accommodate an alien language, just as my essence—that of a truthful person—was being rearranged to suit my Soviet life.

It seemed as though a secret signal had gone out; one day, people were bareheaded, and overnight the subways were filled with silver fox, rabbit, beaver, and muskrat hats. I felt cozy and safe in the midst of all those large woolen- and fur-capped bodies on the metro. But standing on the platform, when the trains rushed in at precise two-minute intervals, each one with its single headlight shining, emblazoned with the hammer-and-sickle shield, I imagined that the whoosh of air was the sound of communism speeding to meet me, and I felt displaced and afraid.

It snowed even before the leaves fell off the trees; for one short day the trees in front of the Mayakovsky monument were laden with globs of heavy wet snow. The snow melted, but then it froze hard and snowed again, followed by miserable, damp, cold weather. I bought a cheap gray rabbit-fur *shapka* of which I was inordinately proud, although it was heavy and mashed my hair limply to my head. Natasha approved, "Now you look just like a real Russian girl."

Natasha offered to escort me to the Pushkin Museum, then canceled at the last moment. Her husband's sister had died, and there would be a service that afternoon. "It's something of a ritual from the old days, from the Orthodox religion," she apologized. "We're not religious, of course, but . . ." She confided that she was dreadfully worried about her husband, whose mother had died less than a year ago. He wasn't a strong man, really. . . . She'd found him weeping in the closet this morning.

Natasha's mascara-lined eyes welled with tears. I saw her then as she was in her complexity—not just the most official of women, but a maternal, middle-aged wife with a younger husband, a devoted, meddling teacher, and a tired woman forced to stand in lines, whose formidable will and faith in communism couldn't spare her from grief any more than it could keep the strands of gray from appearing in her long, girlish braid.

Tanya, chewing the ends of her blonde hair, told me sadly that her husband said her duty was at home tending her child after school, not staying late giving lessons to foreigners. She wouldn't be able to come to our meetings with Grisha anymore. But we would still see each other at her house in a few days. "What can I do?" she said. "I must do as he says." She winked. "He is very strict with me, but I need it."

"Zakharich asked why I give you Russian lessons," Grisha said after the last student had trooped out and I was gathering my things. "He wanted to know if you give me money. I suppose he cannot imagine any other reason anymore. I told him because you are a foreigner, and unmarried, and I wanted to do something about that."

"But I thought the password was 'speak English.'"

Grisha smiled. "Yes, that would certainly help you find a Soviet husband."

"I'm not looking for a husband," I said indignantly.

"I was only joking."

"Grisha, I have to tell you something," I said. "It's a confession."

"Oh?" Grisha pulled a chair close so that we were facing one another across a stack of pale blue student notebooks.

"You have to promise me that you'll never tell anyone. It could cause problems for me."

"I am not one to go telling everything I hear."

"Remember when you said you weren't a Russian the other day? Well, I always make such a big deal about being honest with you. I felt really bad because I didn't tell you that I'm Jewish too."

"Oh? Is that all?" Grisha smiled. "For a moment I thought you might be about to confess something really important. Pavel Viktorich, our idiotic teacher of political theory, believes you might understand more Russian than you let on in order to learn our secrets, as though a direct line exists from School 45 to the Politburo."

"It *is* important," I insisted. "You promise you won't tell?"

"Certainly, but why is it such a big secret?"

"I was told before I came that it would be better not to talk about it, in terms of visas and things . . . and people would treat me better. Anyway, I think that Alexander Zakharich is an anti-Semite."

Grisha laughed. "Don't you know that he himself is a Jew?"

"Alexander Zakharich? You're kidding! So that's why he's always trying to worm it out of me. But I still don't want you to tell anyone."

"If you wish. But it would be very interesting for him to know how you live there, as a Jew. We are all interested."

"It doesn't mean anything there!" I protested. "I live like anyone." As I said it, I wondered if it was really true. Until I was nine I'd lived in a dying New Hampshire mill town where I was called "kike" on the playground; even later, when we lived in suburban Boston, my mother always tried to keep me from talking too loud or wearing bright clothing. New York, the first place I'd lived where I wasn't a minority, was a relief; I didn't have to put a damper on myself to fit in.

"You know," Grisha said, "I used to be ashamed of it myself. It's quite unpleasant to have always to show it on your internal passport at the post office, or at a hotel, and have everyone know. They make rude comments, or they give you that look. . . . I was angry at my parents because they didn't prepare me. When I was a boy all I cared about was soccer, like any boy. At sixteen I got my passport and it said 'Jew.' It could have said 'Turk' for all it meant to me. But of course it determined my life."

"How?"

"I never wanted to teach. I wanted to travel with foreign delegations as a translator, play some part in the world. I always loved English. I learned it as a child, listening to the BBC on a shortwave radio. I was the best student in my language institute, but when I graduated, they tried to send me off to work in a school in some hellhole Siberian village. I only escaped because a friend, a girl with a Moscow residence permit, agreed to marry me."

"You mean the woman who came to school last night?"

"No, my first wife. After India, every time I tried to get an interpreting job they refused me. Sorry, but we don't need you. At first I was very hurt. I had abilities and could do nothing with them. And it has worsened. They say I can't travel again for my own safety. They will protect me from anti-Semitism abroad by keeping me behind our borders. International Zionism is, as always, to blame. It is, of course, a matter of the fifth question on my passport: Nationality. And strangely, I've become rather proud of being a Jew. Perhaps it is because I no longer want to be like *them*."

"What happened to her?"

"To whom?"

"Your first wife."

"Oh . . . she was a good girl. I liked her very much as a friend, but I didn't have feelings for her as a woman. We divorced . . . actually, she immigrated, to New York."

"To New York? But why didn't you go with her?"

"I don't know. . . . Well, now it's too late, isn't it? They aren't letting Jews out anymore. In any case, now I have accepted it. It is not so bad, teaching. Though I'm afraid I shall end up like Zakharich, hoarding a stack of Sinatra records and writing doggerel to commemorate our teachers' birthdays. He wanted to do more, of course. He is a very bright man."

So Zakharich, with his obsessive attempts to ferret out nuances of English, and his insistence that you can know a country without ever having seen it, was just as thwarted.

"You know, our school is considered a Jewish school because so many of the teachers here are Jewish. Our founder and director is Jewish, Leonid Isadorich. You haven't met him because he is away this semester in Italy with his Italian wife."

"But if he is a Jew, how can he travel?"

Grisha shrugged. "He has an important position on the City Soviet. It's why our school is more lenient than many others. But even so, Leonid Isadorich asked me to rein myself in. I was teaching Tolkien's *Lord of the Rings,* and every time we came to the description of Gandolf's bushy eyebrows, my class erupted into laughter. Eyebrows, you see, are a code word for Brezhnev. Leonid Isadorich heard about it. 'It isn't necessary,' he said, 'don't risk yourself.' Now I stick to proper texts." Grisha paused. "So, you are a Jew. You could just as easily be Ukrainian."

"You know, Grisha, it's the reason my grandparents left here. Because of the pograms, before the revolution."

"Left here?"

"Yes, the Ukraine, Odessa. It's another secret you can't tell."

"Odessa! Your grandparents came from Odessa? But it is my town, where my parents live, where I was raised. We could have been neighbors! You are a little Odessa *zhidovka.*" He wielded the disparaging term tenderly.

"Shhh!" I scanned the room anxiously as though someone might pop up from under a desk at any moment. "It's weird, isn't it," I whispered. "Like an accident. My family left, so I was born in America, but I could have been born where you were."

"You were the more fortunate."

"Who knows? I'm not really sure of anything anymore." I abruptly turned away toward the windows. Of course I was the more fortunate, but there was something here we lacked, something I wanted.

"Well, shall we begin our lesson?" Grisha asked.

I sighed. "Couldn't we just talk today?"

"Of course. Would you care to go somewhere to drink coffee?"

"Sure. I feel like we're always hiding or something here. It's kind of depressing." Grisha waited in the teachers' cloakroom while I retrieved my overcoat from Zakharich's closet. The janitress peered at us keenly as she stuffed hairpins back into a thin knot of dyed vermilion hair. Out on the chilly sidewalk I grew more cheerful. I reached up to stroke the black fur of Grisha's cap. "You look dashing in that," I said. "Like Doctor Zhivago in the movie. I don't suppose they showed it here."

"No. But I smuggled a copy of the book back from India, along with *1984.*"

Every café in walking distance was closed or had long lines. We finally had to drink our coffee standing up at an express bar, where tired workers and laden *babushki* gulped down sweets. Grisha bought us *kartoshki,* chocolate-flavored dough named for the potatoes they resembled in shape. "God they're sweet," I said. "They taste like raw cookie batter."

"I'm very fond of sweets," Grisha confessed. "Do you find that unmanly?"

I laughed into my glass of milky coffee. "I don't usually judge men by their sugar consumption."

"No? On what basis, then?" Grisha smiled.

"Oh, the usual. Intelligence, courage, strength. Looks. How they treat their women."

Grisha deflated. A white-coated *babushka* slopped coffee-milk into glasses at the serving counter and an overly bleached blonde cashier berated a palsied old man who couldn't find the kopecks in his pocket. "This must seem very primitive compared to New York," he said.

"New York seems pretty primitive a lot of the time."

"When I was a student, I worked as a guide with tourist groups in Moscow. I asked a group from Amsterdam if the tall new buildings on Kalinin Prospekt truly resembled the West, as some said. They laughed at the absurdity of my question."

I shrugged. The flat-fronted, even-height buildings on Kalinin Prospekt looked like all the newer Soviet buildings to me—massive, monstrous, monolithic. Just then a kitchen boy with a cigarette jutting out of the side of his mouth came out to deliver a mug full of cut-up pieces of wrapping paper "napkins" to the tables, and the cashier screeched at him for smoking.

"Shall we go?" Grisha suggested. "We could walk a bit," he added, letting me know he didn't want our meeting to end. It was already dark on the street, and the evening shoppers were woolen shapes trundling by. "If you don't mind a bit of a ride on the metro, I'd like to present you with something."

"All right."

"It's nothing, really, just a copy of a journal in which some of my translations appear. We can pick it up at the editorial office."

We pushed our way to the metro entrance at the old indoor tiered market, lush with imported goods in pre-revolutionary times and now offering a battle to get near enough to a counter to gaze on synthetic shirts, clunky watches, crudely painted plastic toys. We walked down the ramp past the machines selling the newspapers *Pravda, Izvestia,* and *Moskovski Komsomol,* heaved along by the crowds. It was peak hour, and the metro was mobbed. Grisha guided me by the elbow, insisted on carrying my bag. I gasped at the pummeling hordes. A warty grandmother knocked me aside with a thrust of her enormous icebreaker breasts.

"You know what's different at home?" I said. "No matter how crowded it gets at rush hour, Americans don't touch each other. I guess we've got a different sense of personal space."

"Russians enjoy smashing each other about in the metro," Grisha shouted above the din. "It's a way of expressing aggressions. You can't do anything about Brezhnev, but you can bash your neighbor at peak hour. Quite disgusting, don't you think?"

"Shhhh! Grisha."

"Don't worry, they don't speak English."

"How do you know?" I glanced about as though someone might leap out to arrest me.

"I don't care if they can hear," Grisha shouted recklessly. "If I don't speak my mind with you I'll go mad."

On the escalator, we rode facing one another, silenced for the moment by the closeness of our faces, our mingling breath. I looked down, embarrassed.

"You forgot your hat today," Grisha said. "You have no idea how to dress for our winter." He offered me his scarf, but I shook my head.

"You're a *babushka,*" I said, because his solicitousness, which I craved, made me uneasy. This is a married man, I had to remind myself. A twice-married man. We got off, and Grisha led me through the winding maze of streets until we came to the journal's office.

"Will you wait here for me while I run inside? It might be a bit awkward if you came in."

I nodded. I stood under a streetlight, then paced to the corner and back, as my toes and ears went numb. Grisha didn't reappear for twenty minutes. I'd grown anxious and unhappy, but he looked elated.

"Sorry to make you wait. It was a bit of a trial getting it," he said breathlessly. "This journal is strictly for foreign consumption, and they hold onto their copies like misers. They don't want to waste them on us. I had to threaten the secretary by saying we had a foreign visitor at our school and my director requested a copy of the *Gazeta* to present to her. When she wouldn't give in, I threatened to call him from her phone. I said he must be back from the meeting of the City Soviet by now. I was just bluffing, but she was scared, the old bitch."

I inspected the cover under the street lamp. The art reproduction wasn't bad, much better than the books I'd seen for domestic consumption. I flipped to the index, searching for his name. The door to the publishing building swung open, and we both instinctively hid our faces as a man in a raincoat came down the steps. When he'd passed I said, "Thank you," stuffing Grisha's prize in my bag. "I'll read it tonight." I turned toward the metro.

"Is something wrong?" Grisha asked.

I stopped and turned. "Grisha, doesn't it bother you?"

"What?"

"I could never live here."

"Fortunate for you that you needn't," he said, wounded. "Is the journal that unsophisticated to you?"

I waved an arm hopelessly at the street, the puddles, the office behind us. "It's not the journal. You can't take me into the office. They don't print copies for whoever wants them. We have to act like criminals and hide so no one will see us together. It's degrading."

"I suppose I've gotten used to it," Grisha said softly. "It's only when I see it through your eyes that I remember what I've learned to ignore."

"I'm sorry," I said. "I shouldn't say anything. I don't have any right."

"You have all the rights," Grisha said. "It is I who have no rights."

"Maybe this isn't good, these talks we have. I'm a bad influence."

"No, you are a good influence," Grisha said.

On the crowded train again, I was conscious of him standing behind me. I wanted to lean back into him, into his dark leather jacket that must have taken some wrangling to obtain. After he got out to take the train across the platform, I watched him watching me through the glass as my train pulled away, his eyes fastened on mine until we could no longer see each other. How different from the men I'd come to know at home, whose eyes seemed to go away before we'd left each other's sight; the ones who turned away before the door was closed. Except for Kim, the ones I'd slept with had been such strangers, hurrying to put on their clothes and reestablish the distance that had been disrupted by lust.

There was something wrong with us at home; something else wrong here. Grisha imagined that I was the more fortunate, but I was no longer sure.

I lay in my narrow, lumpy bed at the Pekin and fantasized that Grisha could come to my room. Of course he couldn't. In Russia, a citizen wasn't allowed to check into a hotel in his own city, under the premise that he couldn't be there for any good reason. Anyway, if anyone came, the *dezhurnaya,* the floor lady, would kick him out. I'd be exposed for immoral behavior. What was I thinking? He was married. And I didn't know if he was even attracted to me. Maybe he only thought of me as a fascinating foreigner, a source of information. Or like his first wife, as a friend, not a woman. Maybe it was my life he hungered for, not me. Anyway, Grisha wasn't a name I could imagine living with. It had about it a whiff of grit, grease, grief.

Tanya met me Saturday at a designated metro station and we rode a trolley to her region. We stood pressed together by the ticket dispenser; other passengers passed their change up and Tanya and I passed their tickets back to them. The honor system enforced by vigilant citizens. When a thick-featured laborer reached over Tanya's shoulder to turn the knob on the dispenser, Tanya squeezed his arm between her cheek and shoulder. "*Oi!* What a rude peasant," she exclaimed, flaunting her English, confident he wouldn't understand. "And he smells."

Tanya lived far from the center of Moscow in one of the sprawling complexes of boxy multistoried apartment buildings called suburbs. Tanya's region was new, and the buildings jutted up from a muddy field without landscaping, though across the street there was a deep, undeveloped forest. I wanted to explain about American suburbs, but to speak of private houses with two-car garages sounded like a fairy tale even to me now. When I said that my mother lived "in the country," Tanya probably imagined a peasant village like the one she said her husband, Boris, had escaped from.

The apartment had a black, diamond-quilted vinyl door, as did the others on her floor. For protection from the cold, I wondered, or for privacy? Boris wasn't home when we arrived. "All my girlfriends are afraid of him," Tanya informed me. Despite the fact that Boris's skill with language had landed him a trade position responsible for Tanya's Western clothes—he traveled frequently to Finland—they lived in a small one-bedroom apartment with a narrow balcony and a sofa bed, where their daughter slept. An enormous breakfront filled with crystal and china knickknacks dominated the living room. A few wooden inlay pictures of Moscow churches and the Kremlin, such as I'd seen in the souvenir stores, hung from nails. Beige paper of indeterminate print covered the walls. The kitchen was just large enough for a tiny table, but the walls sparkled with immaculate strawberry tiles that Tanya and Boris had put up themselves.

Tanya's meat patties stuffed with apples filled the kitchen with a wonderful aroma. I'd never minded not learning to cook—I'd thought of it as a measure of my independence from stereotypical female roles. But now I felt awkward and inadequately feminine, sitting idly at the table as Tanya bustled about slicing sausage and bread into decorative oblongs.

Boris came home. I was surprised to discover that this frightening man was tiny, far shorter than Tanya or me, and fifteen years older than his young wife. His small eyes glinted fiercely when he shook my hand. He spoke some English as well as Finnish, and Tanya translated whenever his English or my Russian didn't suffice. The dinner conversation was less a dialogue than a polite grilling. Could I explain, please, the role of the Ku Klux Klan in America? Why was it that the American police protected them when they demonstrated? I tried to explain the concept of civil liberties without much success.

"What kind of meat is this?" I asked to change the subject. "Is it pork?"

Boris peered at me intently. "You do not eat pork?"

"Yes, of course," I reassured him quickly. "I eat everything, though I hear that your Moslems in Central Asia do not."

Boris sliced firmly into his cutlet. "*Now* they do."

Tanya was oblivious. "I think it is quite unfair that I am stuck with the little children when Emma, whose English is no better than mine, gets to teach the upper form. I would lose my English if it weren't for you, Lora. It's such a shame; it's simply a matter of privilege."

Boris broke into a furious barrage of Russian. I understood enough to make out that he was chiding her for speaking of privilege in front of a foreigner. Tanya lowered her head like a chastened girl, but when Boris went into the kitchen to get more wine, she looked up impishly. "He's very strict with me. But he's a real man, not like someone else we know. . . ."

Boris returned, frowning. "Eat, Tanya, eat."

I was relieved when Tanya suggested we take a walk in the nearby forest while Boris went to pick up their daughter from her granny's. "We can smoke cigarettes," Tanya whispered. "Boris forbids me to smoke." She insisted that I borrow a pair of Boris's shoes in order to protect my already half-ruined suede pumps from the mud. I was humiliated to discover that my shoe size was nearer Boris's than Tanya's and tried to demur, but Tanya thought I was afraid of dirtying them. "Don't worry," she assured me, "I'll clean them when I get home. I always clean my husband's shoes. I am a good wife. Alexander Zakharich's wife must be awful. He always comes to school with such dirty shoes."

"That's enough," Tanya's husband warned.

We escaped into the cool, damp autumn air. Tanya's woods were full of crisscrossing, unpaved footpaths. We followed one path through firs and birches into a clearing set about with benches. Once seated, we lit up our illicit cigarettes. An old woman in a headscarf and a couple with a bounding collie strolled past.

"Boris likes you," Tanya said. "I can see it."

"I couldn't tell."

Tanya laughed. "He is a stern man, but I have no complaint with him really. Sometimes he beats me, but I need it. I am so bad. Perhaps I do not really love him, but then I am such a woman that I simply do not love anyone, not even my daughter, I'm afraid. She much prefers her Papa. Lora, did you know that Grisha is my lover?"

"Grisha?" I was swept with jealousy. Had the "lessons" and the dinner only been an excuse for them to meet one another? How could Tanya be his lover when I already thought of him—potentially, anyway—as my own?

"Yes, the whole school knows it, I'm afraid. Alexander Zakharich is forever making jokes about it. Grisha comes to see me in my classroom every chance he gets. It has been so for a year already. Of course I would never marry such a man. I do not respect him. He speaks English very well, of course, better even than Zakharich, but he is always complaining. You see, he does not like our country. He would like to leave. I cannot understand that. We have problems, but every country has problems. I could never ever leave. I'd miss my flat so!"

"I couldn't leave my country either," I said faintly.

"You see, Lora, Grisha is no patriot. It is because he is a Jew. They have no loyalty. I am like my husband, I suppose. He does not think highly of Jews. They are greedy, you see. But Grisha is wonderful in bed. So hot, like a Georgian. And he has hair all over his body!"

I flushed and stared down at Boris's shoes with their oversized, grommeted lace holes jutting out from the ends of my legs. I didn't know which was worse, Tanya's anti-Semitism or the fact that she was Grisha's lover.

"Poor Lora. I don't know how can you stand to be alone at night in your hotel. We must find you a nice Russian boy." Tanya giggled.

"Aren't you afraid that Boris will find out about Grisha?" With some satisfaction, I pictured Boris beating them both. He looked like a man who could kill.

"He goes away often on trips. I'm sure that he has his women when he goes to Central Asia, Kazakhstan, Armenia. So why shouldn't I have a man? You see, Lora, the problem is that Boris is too much of a man. When he is home he wants me all the time. Three times a day, like an animal. I must hide from him." She winked at me and threw her cigarette into the mud. "Well, we had better go back to the flat. Boris will be home with Anichka, and he'll accuse me of preferring you to my child."

I rose numbly and ground out my cigarette. Tanya probably expected me to share some matching confidence. What could I tell her, that I secretly lusted for Grisha and I too was a greedy Jew? Or that Grisha had invited me on an outing to Kolomenskoye, our little secret? Even if I wanted to confide in Tanya, I couldn't now because I'd let her say shameful things about Jews without speaking up. The strange thing was that I still liked her. Tanya didn't know what she was saying, parroting her husband's words.

Tanya grasped my arm. "Oh, I am so happy you are here. You are so good, Lora, far better than I. I want to be like you. Do you know the expression, *nash chelovyek*? It means our person, one of us. You are *nash chelovyek*, Lora. If only you lived in Moscow always, we would be such good friends!"

Cultural Enrichment

After school Natasha offered to accompany me to the Tretyakov Gallery. "We've done so little for your cultural enrichment," she said. "We simply exploit you, Lora." I'd made one trek alone to the ballet, tickets courtesy of the Ministry of Education. The ministry bulldog, Glebovna, had apologized for being unable to accompany me—her daughter was ill. Under her expensive fur hat, her face looked pale and worn. Even this highly placed woman was exhausted by her life. I gave the extra ticket she'd given me to a woman on the sidewalk in front of the Bolshoi, who was thrilled and tried repeatedly to pay me. *Les Sylphides* fluttered onstage while under the great gilt ceiling, in the best seats, stout women in glittering dresses sat beside bulky men in medal-laden army uniforms. Behind my balcony seat, students slid in to stand by the doors. They watched the dancers, rapt. What kids at home would stand for two hours through a performance of anything but rock music?

Since the Tretyakov Gallery, according to an office secretary, was under renovation, somehow it was decided that Natasha, Emma, Tanya, and another teacher, a lovely gentle-voiced girl named Marina who taught the youngest kids, would all go for coffee with me instead. "Grisha looked at us with those big sad eyes," Natasha joked as we hustled out into the cold. "He wanted to come on this outing, but Zakharich has work for him."

He wanted to be with Tanya, probably. "It's a woman's outing," I replied.

Tanya ran across the frozen puddles on the sidewalk, sliding and giggling like a kid. We overfilled a taxi, the fur hats taking up the room, Natasha in a fur-lined hood, looking like a Slavic pixie with her slanting blue eyes. Emma fretted that her silver fox hat would be crushed. Marina giggled in the front seat, beside the driver, who wanted to know whose harem we were.

In front of her apartment, Tanya gestured toward the padded door of her neighbor. "She's in there, the bitch. She's always snooping. Such a nosy one!"

I was about to shush her, then realized that the woman probably didn't speak English. As the others trooped in, Tanya whispered into my ear. "She's always sticking her nose out when I bring Grisha here."

"You bring him here?" I whispered back. "What about your husband?"

"When he's gone. We did it right in the bedroom while my granny drank tea at the table! Ah, but I'm a terrible person, aren't I? I'm not as good as you, Lora."

Tanya's oven wasn't working, and the heat was off. Undaunted, the women bustled about in the kitchen cooking on the stove burners. Still wearing our coats in the chilly room, we sat on the floor to eat delicious fried potatoes with onions straight from a pan. Tanya brought down her photograph album. Natasha held up a portrait of Boris taken at a trade conference in Paris. The camera had caught his eyes so that they glowed red. She shivered. "There is great cruelty in his face," she said, shaking her head. She examined pictures of Tanya's family, her grandparents. "So that is the one? You wouldn't know. He doesn't look at all . . ." her voice trailed off.

"You see," Tanya said to me. "I am very strange mixture of bloods. Some Russian, some Polish, Swedish, and even . . . something else."

Did she mean Jewish?

They began to chat about Zakharich, all but Natasha voicing complaints. She was Zakharich's confidante, according to Tanya. "He is in sorrow about his wife," Natasha said mysteriously, her face dreamy.

"Do you believe he is capable of a deep emotion?" little dark-haired Marina asked.

Natasha defended him. I was enchanted by the question, by Natasha's concern, her maternal bosom and tilted blue eyes, Tanya's winks, the feminine authority that was expressed by their tight-waisted dresses, their certainty in the kitchen. For all the deficits and hardships of this life, I suspected they knew who they were in ways that I didn't. I couldn't imagine a group of teachers at the Trinity School, my former employer, sitting on the floor to eat potatoes and discuss another colleague's depth of emotion. I couldn't even imagine Grisha doing it. Maybe it was better to sit on the floor with these women pondering questions of character than to share longing, impossible glances with a man who could do nothing about it, and had both a wife and a lover.

At the lunch table, eating cabbage soup, Alexander Zakharich insisted that 30 percent of Americans were unemployed. He wouldn't believe me when I disagreed with his statistics. He'd read it in *Newsweek,* he declared. There were hoboes everywhere in the U.S.

"Yes," I said, "there are homeless in our cities, but the unemployment rate isn't 30 percent. I doubt it's 10 percent."

"You are misinformed," Zakharich said, sliding a pastry between his steel teeth.

I nearly lost my temper. I didn't want Zakharich, who had never traveled, to tell me about *my* country. "Why would I lie now," I asked, "when I've been so honest with you?"

"Oh, yes, *very* honest," he said nastily.

I slopped soup from my bowl. Of course I'd lied, but only about being Jewish.

I ventured alone to the Intourist Hotel for the treat of real coffee. When I flashed my American passport to gain entry, the elderly door guard clasped his hands and begged me, "Please, no war! No war!" He was probably a veteran—this place could break your heart. Through the windows of the hard currency café on the twentieth floor, the city spread out dizzily below. Many Russians roamed this foreigners' hotel— I wondered how they got past the doors. There was so much I didn't understand about Moscow. They were dressed fashionably compared with most Muscovites, but in a peculiar way. Cowboy boots and jeans. A giant with a Baryshnikov face and bib overalls. A woman in tight bohemian black wearing a cross and too much makeup, speaking Russian. Who were they?

A thin, dark-haired Russian boy in a turtleneck sweater asked if he could join me. He said he knew I was American immediately. He couldn't explain why. He was openly critical of the USSR, said he was going to

France soon. I didn't know if he was about to emigrate or highly connected.

"I have no illusions about the West," he said, crushing out a Marlboro. He already had the attitude of the émigré who thinks he knows everything because he's lived on both sides. I remembered the warnings I'd been given about people who approach you speaking good English—black marketeers or worse. He wanted to talk literature—*The World According to Garp* and Thomas Pynchon. When he asked nervously if I sat alone in my hotel room all the time I became suspicious. Maybe he was fishing for American books or trying to pick me up. Something more nefarious? I didn't exchange numbers when he asked.

I had received no mail from home. If any ever arrived it would probably do so after I left for Leningrad. I dreamed of my brother Charlie, an uneasy dream in which he wore Grisha's black fur hat and spoke in a hoarse voice. I told Grisha that he reminded me of my brother.

"And you love him very much?" Grisha asked with a cryptic expression.

Was he flirting with me? Testing the depths of our friendship? Linking himself to my affection through my love for my brother? He was never *just* making conversation.

Tanya escorted me to dinner at the home of Yevgeniya, nicknamed Zhenya, a pretty young teacher of the youngest grades. She wore her auburn hair back in a clip, and her eyes were a beautiful gold-flecked green. "She is half-Jewish," Tanya informed me, "but she doesn't like that part of her family. It is why she could not marry a Russian. No Russian wants a woman who is even half-Jewish." Her skinny, dark-skinned husband, Eric, was Azerbaijani. "His real name was Anwar," Tanya whispered when Eric went into the kitchen to get more wine, "but you see, Anwar Sadat became an enemy of our people, so the name was impossible."

Eric/Anwar worked as a censor at Mosfilm and complained that Americans only exchanged stupid films for Mosfilm's good ones. He justified censorship, when I asked, by saying that they had to protect their citizens from Western decadence. He did like *Kramer vs. Kramer*, which was the rage now in Moscow. And he loved American music.

When I asked him about the famous Dean Reed, he said, "Dean Reed is garbage."

"Zhenya doesn't love him," Tanya told me as we rode a trolley after dinner. "She'd like to leave him, but what can she do?"

"She's so pretty," I said. "She'd find someone."

"She would lose everything," Tanya said. "I don't think her flat is quite as nice as mine, but even so . . ."

I went home with sweet-faced, delicate Marina, who was also Jewish and married to an Armenian, a dark little man with a mustache and a frown. They lived in only one room. He kept motioning to the walls when we spoke openly about Soviet problems, indicating we had to lower our voices so the neighbors wouldn't hear. Marina's two-year-old daughter was at her mother's house for the night. "I'm sorry, Lora, that you could not meet her. She is such a tender little girl," Marina said, her face suffused with a devotion that I recognized but didn't yet understand. In private, she confessed that she'd never been in love with her husband, but she'd wanted a child badly. The man she'd loved wouldn't have her.

With Tanya and Zhenya and Marina it was all hugs and "Lorichka" and *nash chelovyek* and admonitions to eat the caviar and the delicious *zakuski,* the snacks, that they'd gone to so much trouble to prepare. Too often these days I woke up hungover and bleary after toasts with vodka and wine. Yet I couldn't refuse the invitations. I feared how much I would miss these women—and Grisha—when I moved on to Leningrad. I'd be sent away before the five-day holiday—the Anniversary of the Great October Socialist Revolution, which occurred on November 7 by the new calendar. The fact that I would have five days off work and be separated from my Moscow friends struck me as either calculated or callous. But I could use the rest. I was so tired of talking, talking, talking. My voice was getting hoarse. Talking—all day in the classes, in the lunchroom, in Zakharich's office, with the teachers, even sometimes with the bravest of the kids, although teachers always monitored their questions.

"Would you like to see our school monument to Great Patriotic War for the Fatherland, Miss Laurie?" Dutifully, I toured a room off the first-floor hallway displaying war photos, helmets, shrapnel, and a Nazi Luger. "The children did it all themselves," Natasha informed me proudly.

Maybe they did, but was it right for children, born twenty years after the war ended, to be indoctrinated into memorializing their parents' losses? I knew the statistics, the twenty million dead, but I couldn't help seeing it as a perversion, institutionalizing fear of invasion, blinding the populace to the other twenty million dead in Stalin's purges, to the deprivations communism had imposed on them. But lying alone in my hotel bed, I could think only of our own deprivations, how disconnected we were compared to their stifling, yet reassuring, web of family and friends.

Glebovna from the ministry came to interview me in the hotel for some in-house ministry newsletter. She brought bread and raw cabbage—*vitaminki,* she insisted, and candies to munch on. She took off her imposing fur hat and leather coat and was transformed from a battle-ax into a pretty, vivacious woman. She talked, and another teacher translated. I noted but didn't mention Glebovna's ring—an inscribed Madonna's face graced her thick right hand. What aberration was that? I wondered.

Glebovna asked for my opinions of their educational system, but she put away her notebook when I complained that their English textbooks didn't teach the culture of English-speaking countries. Our Russian books are full of pictures of Russia, I added. She picked up her pen again when I mentioned that I had to purchase the materials for teaching in Russia myself—the sponsoring organization didn't pay. And she wrote down what plays and ballets I'd seen, what museums I'd been to. I mentioned the Rublev Museum, filled with the works of the medieval icon painter. I started to tell her that I'd seen the Tarkovsky movie *Andrei Rublev* at home, but I remembered that it had not been permitted to be shown here uncut. In the beginning scene a peasant floats over a field of carnage in a hot-air balloon made of skins. "I'm flying, I'm flying," he cries, enthralled, before crashing to earth. And near the end an invading Tatar chief tells the dismayed painter Rublev, who has lost his faith, "You don't need us to kill you. You'll do it yourselves." Even a seven-hundred-year-old tale was deemed too dangerous an allegory of current Russian life. I wondered what Glebovna's article would say. It pleased her when I praised the Russian dark bread, so much better than our own.

Tanya, Marina, and Zhenya devised an outing—a trip to a Finnish *banya* for me, a sauna with a dipping pool, in a tourist hotel. Hard currency was required, but somehow everyone managed to come up with the *valyuta*. We paddled naked in a small tiled rectangle with greenish water. No one seemed embarrassed by the male employee, Dmitry, Dima, who kept coming in to offer drinks and snacks, to give advice— "Don't burn your nipples in the sauna, girls"—and tell us a raunchy joke: A woman was married three times and was still a virgin. How could that be? Well, the first was a Frenchman, who used only his tongue. The second was a Georgian, who preferred the rear entry. And the third was a Communist—and here came the punch line—*who did nothing.* They all shrieked with laughter.

We scrubbed one another's backs with loofahs and an ease unknown at home. They ordered me to wrap my hair in a towel to protect it from the sauna's heat.

"I will tell you each your nationalities," Dima offered. Tanya was a Pole, he said, Marina a *Yevraika*—a Jewess, and Zhenya a Russian. "You are almost right," Tanya said, smiling at Zhenya.

"And what about Lora?" they wanted to know. Dima studied me carefully. "Italian?"

"He is good, but not perfect," I said, letting it go at that.

Tanya swam alongside me, her large breasts floating before her. When she climbed up the pool ladder, I saw the deep dimples over her butt and thought how Grisha must desire her. What man wouldn't? As though she read my thoughts, she again spoke gleefully of his hairy body and his passion.

In the sauna, cherubic Marina said, "My husband was shocked by my passion when we first met. We were in a taxi and he kissed me. I think I frightened him the way I kissed him back."

Zhenya observed of Marina, "You've grown so thin."

Marina looked down and rubbed her flat stomach ruefully. "Yes, I was ill. And what is a woman without a belly?"

Please, oh, please, couldn't we import that sentiment home? The only advertising visible in Moscow was for the Party, and Tanya and Grisha had assured me they didn't even see the banners and placards anymore.

How much easier it was to ignore such clumsy propaganda than our own barrage of marketing images. Only in its absence did I realize the overwhelming effects of magazines, newspapers, and television relentlessly telling us we were too fat or needed Oil of Olay. Here, without anorexic models and beauty products for hair, teeth, skin, figure, and sex appeal (not that these women wouldn't have been glad to snap them up if they could), I experienced a surprising freedom. It was nice to live without the tyranny of marketing, even if under the dictatorship of the proletariat.

Could I live here? I wondered. The red banners, the lies on the news, the children at school with their downcast eyes and massive feats of memorization, the anti-Semitism weighed against these generous, laughing women, easy in their flesh, and Grisha's searching dark eyes. Could I live here? I was, as they kept telling me, *nash chelovyek,* one of us. Of course, as a visiting American I was a star; I provided information as well as novelty; still, there was a warmth, an intensity of emotion, a way in which they seemed to matter to one another that moved me.

We stayed an extra hour. Marina's father and husband, who came to drive us home, waited outside in the car without complaint. Her father, who wore a beret on his head and a scarf wrapped around his throat, had the gentlest face, like somebody's kind old Jewish uncle. And more. He'd been a war hero and survived Stalin. When I whispered to Tanya that it might be better if they let me off a block from the hotel, she said, "Don't worry Lorichka. It is quite all right. Natasha and Zakharich know everything. We asked for permission, of course."

Grisha, too, appeared concerned with my cultural enrichment, though I suspected it was only an excuse for us to have more time to exchange information. He invited me to visit Kolomenskoye, a palace and park south of Moscow, on Saturday. We agreed to meet in a metro station in the center. The *fartsovchiki,* the black marketeers, peeled off the walls of the station lobby as I walked in. I could almost hear them calculating the value of my suede shoes, black canvas bag, Western overcoat and mocking my cheap gray rabbit hat. I knew it looked hokey to up-to-date Russians, but I liked it. Just as a skinny blond boy threw his cigarette into an urn and slithered close, Grisha materialized to grab my arm. He wore his leather jacket and jeans—the first I'd seen him in. "You make quite a sensation," he said, shepherding me past the control booth at the top of the escalators where the uniformed women checked our monthly passes and waved us on. "The *fartsovchiki* lust after your clothes."

"And I thought it was me they were after," I joked. "Am I so recognizably foreign?"

"Absolutely," Grisha said. He took the step below me on the escalator and pressed me against the rail so impatient travelers could run down the moving stairs.

"I'd rather just fit in," I said.

"You mean wear ugly shoes that hurt your feet as we do?" Grisha asked.

He'd caught me out. I glanced across the polished stone that separated us from the stern-faced, thickly bundled ascending passengers. No, I didn't want to live as they did.

"My wife wanted to come with us," Grisha said. "Would you have wanted that?"

"It wouldn't have mattered either way," I lied, not knowing the correct answer.

"We argued a long time about it. Well, I didn't want her to come actually. I wanted to be alone with you."

"Oh?"

"I told her it would be awkward, I would have to translate all day. She speaks no English. And for another reason . . ."

"What's that?"

"I don't know . . ." Grisha faltered. He began again. "You know, Laurie, there are some women a man thinks of only as a woman, and others that a man thinks of only as a friend . . . but to have both . . ."

"Let's not get too personal," I said, cutting him off, lurching forward as the escalator ended abruptly at the platform. What was the point of all this when I knew he was Tanya's lover? A train rushed in, and we were whisked with the crowd through its doors. I grabbed an open seat, and Grisha was left to hang suspended over me. I busied myself in my bag.

While we walked from the metro station, Grisha gave me a history lesson, vestige of his tour-guide days when he was a student at the language institute: Kolomenskoye was the residence of czars, including Ivan the Terrible and Peter the Great, a summer palace, displaying the first stone church of the Russian wooden-tent style, built in 1532. It was a departure from the Byzantine architecture that showed the influence of Italian masters, a return to old Russian forms. . . .

"Your feet must be quite cold," Grisha said suddenly. "Haven't you any boots?"

"I brought all the wrong clothes," I said. The Field Service had given me a list of clothes I'd need according to a former exchange participant, but they hadn't warned me that she was a nun, with no sense of vanity. I'd brought the suggested and meager two skirts, two slacks, three sweaters, flat shoes, and the clunky snow boots that I wouldn't wear yet. Only I sloshed through puddles in suede pumps. The *babushki* and peasants wore padded felt or rubber boots, while the more stylish city women now sported tall, sleek, high-heeled leather boots. How they got them was a mystery; they certainly weren't available in the shops. I'd already realized I wouldn't be able to replace my worn cashmere gloves with anything made of wool.

Inside the great gates a palace rose, and behind it white churches with blue starry domes stood. A few red Intourist busses waited for foreign groups in the otherwise empty parking lot outside the palace. At the palace entrance a bulky, sixtyish *babushka* blocked our way. The thin line of her lips matched the parallel creases on her forehead. Her nose formed a perfect bisect: a woman with a face like a grid. She crossed her arms over her breasts emphatically and gestured with her head toward a cardboard sign in the entrance window—closed. "Come back tomorrow, comrades," she said.

Grisha argued with her stubbornly. I caught only a few words—tomorrow was impossible, something about my being a special foreign guest.

"Grisha, just forget it," I begged.

"Just a minute," he said to me.

"No, I mean it, I don't want to go in."

"All right then," he said. He turned and said something to the woman too rapid for me to catch.

"*Khooligan,*" the guard screamed and spouted back more just as rapidly.

"Phew, that was nice," I said. "What did she say?"

"I told her she had immortalized the rudeness of the Russian people for you; she answered that I had no business with a foreigner anyway, and then she made the astute observation that I wasn't even a Russian."

"How did that come up?"

"It usually does, eventually. I'm awfully sorry about the palace."

"Don't worry about it. I don't even like palaces. I was just going along because I thought you wanted to. I'd rather walk around the park."

"But that's how I feel, exactly," Grisha said. "I no longer have much use for the 'riches of the people.'"

We walked the gravel paths through the trees, crossing a series of little wooden bridges spanning man-made streams. The leaves were gone, the trees bare, the sculptures boxed up, protected from the winter, the reflecting pools frozen; wind blew through the firs and birches. We found a little gazebo deep in the forest, spattered dead leaves stuck around its foundation. Graffiti had been scratched into the plaster: "Sasha loves Masha" and "No Bombs."

"Like at home," I said, excited, as though there were something special about spontaneous acts of vandalism, a form of stolen freedom here. We continued on around the palaces and outbuildings, finally stopping to sit on a wooden bench overlooking the Moscow River. Beyond it, fields stretched, and further, the dull concrete high rises and smoky stacks of the city "suburbs." Grisha picked up a scrap of *Pravda* that had caught on the bench leg.

"Shall we have a reading lesson, then?" he asked.

"You read. I can't read the papers, they're too hard. There's too much official language."

Grisha began, "At a congress of friendly Arab nations a resolution was passed decrying the recent actions of the bloodthirsty Israeli aggressors in which . . ."

"Stop! Forget it. I don't want to know."

"Here's something more cheery: General Secretary Brezhnev toasted the brotherhood of Socialist nations with Czech and Hungarian party leaders at a reception at the Palace of Congresses. . . ."

"Jesus," I said, "better toasts than tanks, I guess."

"Tanks first, then toasts, that's our way," Grisha said. "I don't suppose you are interested in soccer scores?"

I shook my head. Grisha let the scrap flutter to the ground.

"Grisha, do you think I look Jewish?"

"I wouldn't have thought it before, but now that you say it I can see. Something Jewish, and something very American too."

"I have a friend at home, a Soviet émigré. Don't tell anyone about that, either."

Grisha laughed. "You are so afraid, Laurie."

"You like seeing me afraid."

"Perhaps I do, a bit," he admitted.

"You think it makes us more alike."

"I can't believe how much alike we are."

I sighed. "Anyway, this woman told me that she could tell immediately that I was American by the stamp on my face, even though we have the same roots, the same genes. She said her little daughter had it already, although they have only been in America a year. Her daughter already looked more like me than like her."

"I see that stamp, yes, but I do not feel that you are a foreigner at all. I never believed that I would be able to feel so close to a foreigner, to understand one so well. Zakharich's favorite, Sandy, she was very friendly, with that big smile, but there was nothing behind it. She gave little gifts constantly—scarves for the women, records for Dmitrich's collection. A year later she returned with a group of touring school-children who presented their cast-off American jeans to our children. After she left, we teachers couldn't meet each other's eyes. We were insulted and shamed. We were envious of American children who traveled the globe, and envious of our own students who'd received such treasures. Yes, you and I come from such different worlds. But I have never felt as close with a woman. Often I feel that you read my mind."

I said, "It isn't a matter of countries. Sometimes people understand each other, that's all."

Grisha reached forward and pushed strands of my hair back under my heavy cap. I pulled back. "Grisha, is it true that you are Tanya's lover?"

"She told you that?"

"Yes. When I went to her house for dinner."

He sighed. "It is the joke of the whole school. She talks of it constantly. Yes, it is true. Now I am ashamed."

"Why? She's very attractive; it's easy to understand."

"You know what they say about Jews here, that they are greedy and unfaithful to their wives, that they have bad characters. . . ."

"But Tanya is also unfaithful, and she says her husband has women. Anyway, Tanya's an anti-Semite. You know that, don't you?"

"Yes, like her idiot husband."

"Grisha, how can you have a lover who hates Jews?"

"I can't explain. Do you think it is very awful? You know, I can't look at Tanya now that I know you. Tanya seems so silly to me, with her talk about her damned flat, and cleaning and cooking and gossip. But you are so different. I have never known such a woman. Here women think only of their families."

"And I think there is something wrong with me because I don't."

"There is nothing wrong with you."

"You don't know. . . ."

"Then tell me. I want you to tell me everything."

"Grisha, what are we doing this for?"

"Doing what?"

"That's just it. What are we doing?"

Grisha said, "I don't know."

I stood abruptly. "My toes are freezing. We'd better start moving, or they're going to fall off."

We didn't speak all the way back to the metro station. The small café next to it was closed for a "sanitary day." We rode the metro back to the city center.

"You must be very hungry," Grisha said. "Let me at least buy you something to eat."

We entered a *stolovaya,* a worker's cafeteria, where for a few kopecks they sold borscht and kasha and tea.

Grisha launched into an explanation of his affair with Tanya. "Things are very bad with my wife. She complains that at home I won't eat with her, but eat dinner in front of the television."

His indifference to his wife irritated me. I stirred sugar into my third glass of tea impatiently. "Why don't you leave her then?"

"How can I? I love my son."

"Are you sure that's all? Maybe you hang onto her because she makes you feel important. At least *she* needs you."

"I hadn't thought of it like that, but perhaps you are right. You see into me so much it is frightening. It is why I can't look at Tanya anymore."

I waved away his words. "It's just psychobabble, standard pop psychology. Don't give me too much credit."

"Psycho-babble." Grisha shaped the unfamiliar word, then shrugged. "I am stuck with my wife for the child's sake. I am trapped in the school. There is nothing else I can do. I'll never be allowed to go anywhere again, I'll never see anything!"

"Shhhh!" I warned. A young soldier balancing bread on a plate of kasha walked past.

"Laurie, if I couldn't talk to you like this I'd go insane."

"Then why didn't you apply to emigrate, when it was possible?"

"I was afraid. My parents . . . my father convinced me that I would never find a job in America, I'd be unhappy and never able to return. I let him convince me. . . ."

"Of course you'd get a job. Your English is perfect; you could teach Russian at a university."

"I am afraid that I wouldn't adjust. Your life is so different; I don't even know how to write a check."

I laughed. "Checks are pretty easy. Millions of people come, and they learn."

"Well, it's too late now, isn't it?"

"There are other ways, I suppose. I mean, if you weren't married, and you really wanted to leave, I could marry you so that you could."

Grisha's face paled. "For you it is just a joke. It means nothing to you to speak like that, but to me . . ."

"Well, anyway, you *are* married, so it doesn't really matter, does it?" I stood up, ashamed. I was tormenting him with the fact of his marriage because I was jealous of his affair with Tanya, and his lack of freedom in his marriage was somehow synonymous with his lack of political freedom. He couldn't leave; he couldn't come with me. I knew it was unfair, but his victimization by the state—and his acceptance of his limitations—struck me as a form of personal weakness.

We went through the metro turnstile and down the escalators, Grisha riding a step below and gazing into my eyes, just like the couples I'd envied. We pushed together into the train. A young man in a sportsman's wool hat yielded his seat to me immediately, and I took it, while Grisha held my bag of books.

I said, "I love the way Russian men give up their seats for women." In New York I would have lost all my credibility for such words, but it was true, I enjoyed it.

"You think it is manners? They wouldn't if they didn't have to. But if they did not, everyone would yell at them, so they do it."

"You mean you aren't really a gentleman? You only carry my bag because you are afraid of the *babushki*?"

"What gentleman would sleep with another man's wife?"

I smiled. "A good question."

When a seat opened up beside me, Grisha sat down. Across from us a middle-aged man sat with a large string bag propped between his feet. A two-foot-long sausage jutted up between his knees. I began to giggle, perhaps from the strain of the day.

"You think that it is humorous that we must always haul food around?" Grisha said in an offended tone.

"No, of course not. But just look at that thing between his legs. Haven't you ever heard of a phallic symbol before? God, you Russians are so full of symbolism, but you can be so blind."

Grisha touched my ear with his lips. "I'm not Russian, remember? You know, here, where sausage is such a rare find, when we look at phalluses we think of them as sausage symbols."

I almost fell off my seat laughing. Up and down the line of seats, passengers—whether or not they understood us—narrowed their eyes in uneasy distaste.

A Dose of Russian Soul

"And how many Russian lessons have you and Grisha had, hmmmm?" Tanya asked teasingly in the lunchroom.

"Not so many," I lied. I was scared that she knew about our outing, ashamed that I wanted to betray a friend, even if she was an anti-Semitic woman who'd betrayed her own husband. I was afraid of being caught and annoyed that Grisha had put me in this position for nothing. Still, we went on with our "lessons," our metro rides and soulful talks. He spoke frequently of when I'd come back. Back to Moscow, after my month in Leningrad, back to the Soviet Union after I left. *If,* I said, not when.

Erotic fantasies of Grisha disturbed my sleep, made me cranky and crazy with the desire for something to happen, for Grisha to take an action that would break this spell of frustration and ambiguity. For him to take an action to prove to me that he could. What right did I have to want that from him, to judge him for being afraid to emigrate, when I didn't even have the guts to admit I was Jewish? Yet I judged him. And wanted him. Judged him because I wanted him; didn't want him because he couldn't make a move. Though I tried to understand the pressures of Grisha's life, I wasn't large enough to keep from holding them against him.

I couldn't assess the depth of my feeling for him—my isolation, and his position as a source of truth in Moscow, colored everything, just as my being the one with whom he could speak openly, and my foreign "exoticism," influenced his interest in me. Would we have been drawn to each other if we had both lived in Odessa or New York? After all, it was Tanya, my physical and emotional opposite, whom he'd chosen as his lover. Though how opposite were we really? Tanya described herself as "the woman who does not love anyone," and I'd often wondered if that were true of me. My mother used to say, when I was a little girl, "You have an artistic temperament and are incapable of love." Who knew what she was projecting, but what good was an artistic temperament—whatever that was—if I couldn't stick to my "art?" And what did it matter if I was or wasn't capable of love, if there was no one with whom to attempt it?

My record with men wasn't very promising—I'd run from the ones who cared about me, mooned over those who didn't. Both behaviors served to keep me alone. Grisha provided a peculiar third variant, a man who cared about me but was unavailable because of where and how he lived.

I hated stasis, limbo, wanted everything to always be new, all doors to always be open. I was still in my twenties, impatient, impulsive, poorly suited to Soviet existence. I told myself it didn't matter what I felt for Grisha, because soon I would be gone.

Natasha invited me to her house for a preholiday dinner. She said she wanted to cheer her husband, who was still desolate over his sister's death. I suspected that Tanya's spontaneous offers had forced their hand; someone had deemed it improper that my official keepers had not yet invited me home. I had low expectations for this official gathering.

Natasha's apartment was located in the back courtyard of what must have once been a private mansion, now divided into apartments for the privileged, since Grisha had explained that most old private houses served as communal apartments for four or five families sharing one kitchen and one bathroom. An individual apartment in the center of the city, instead of in the boonies, was a plum, and further proof of her power.

Natasha's apartment wasn't particularly large—one bedroom with a tiny "study" converted for her son by her first marriage—but it had high ceilings, elaborate moldings, old-fashioned double windows like my hotel. The living room was furnished with an oversized breakfront filled with china and crystal behind glass panels; a couch; beige, patterned wallpaper; and beige, patterned drapes that slid on large rings on dowels—precisely the same fittings as Tanya's, and Zhenya's, perhaps the only ones available. But a large red Bukhara rug hung on the wall behind a table pushed up to a generously pillowed couch—Natasha's cozy bohemian touch.

The guests included Alexander Zakharich, Natasha's husband, Andrei, his Tatar brother-in-law Manser (husband of the deceased sister), Natasha's twenty-year-old son, Mitya, and fretful Emma, who had just that day accused me of calling Russians boring when I said, in response to a question about a picture of the Mickey Mouse float in the Macy's Thanksgiving Day Parade, Americans were often frivolous. I tried to avoid her as she bustled in and out of the kitchen with Natasha. Grisha and Tanya and the other young teachers were conspicuously absent. I thought it odd that Zakharich and Emma both came without spouses, adding to my sense that this was a put-up job, an official event staged for me.

I'd read that American booze made good presents for Russian hosts. I brought along a bottle of bourbon from the dollar store. When I drew out the bottle everyone looked disconcerted. None of them chose to try it, saying they preferred vodka, and the bottle went into the breakfront. I couldn't figure out my mistake. Was it that the cost of such a treat on the black market was so great that I'd brought an exorbitant and therefore vulgar gift? Maybe they just didn't like bourbon? But then, why the worried looks? I decided to bring only the much cheaper cognac, as I'd brought to Tanya's and Zhenya's and Marina's houses, in the future.

I stuck to polite topics, such as the upcoming November 7 holiday. Zakharich presided at one end of the table, and I was placed next to Natasha's husband, who spoke no English. Andrei appeared to be ten years younger than his wife, a handsome man with the softened, slightly blurred face of Marcello Mastroianni at forty. He kept my plate filled and too quickly refilled my vodka glass while Natasha looked on with the expression of an approving mother.

Natasha attempted to pry out of me the nature of my "English" classes with Grisha but I covered our tracks with lies about my "progress."

The women had outdone themselves to put on a good show. The table was laden with *zakuski*—herring, some kind of liver pâté, sausage, little slabs of pure, rendered fat that particularly entranced Alexander Zakharich, and salads with potatoes and beets in mayonnaise, followed by a main course of delicious garlicky pilaf made by Natasha's husband.

Given the quality of the produce, which must have come from the high-priced "free" markets, someone had laid out big bucks on my behalf. Vodka filled the glasses and we proceeded to toast friendship, women, cultural exchange, peace. The vodka hit me hard and I praised the meal madly, especially the pilaf, making Natasha beam on her husband's behalf. When the food was reduced to wreckage on plates, Natasha's husband and brother-in-law were prevailed upon to sing. Their voices rose in eerie, gorgeous counterpoint, a sobbing ancient Russian song of mourning. Then the chairs were pushed back and old American pop tunes—"Stop in the Name of Love" and "Poison Ivy"—blared. Natasha and her soft-faced husband twirled across the floor in unfeigned abandon, her long braid flying. I danced with Manser, who kissed my hand after each number. Even Emma kicked up her heels while Zakharich continued to load his plate.

"It's because of you," Natasha whispered. "Manser's barely spoken for weeks, and now look at him! I'm so pleased."

I ended up in the bedroom ensconced drunkenly in Natasha's bed. It was a charmingly arranged room with large, blown-up photographs of her family, fringed dangling scarves, a comfy stuffed armchair and an old bureau with a beveled mirror. We lay side by side on the layered quilts. Natasha showed me a wedding ring her son had found in the Black Sea when they were vacationing not long after her divorce from her first husband. "Somehow," she confided, "I knew when he found it that I could love another man. It was that week that I met Andrei."

She was a small child during the war, she told me. Her father had died in battle; she'd been evacuated to the Urals, losing her mother en route. She'd been taken into a state children's home. "So you can see how grateful I am to the state. And then I was rather adopted by my mother's dead sister's Jewish husband, who treated me as his own child. They were such loving people, Lora, you can't imagine."

She peered at me meaningfully, and I was just drunk enough to be tempted into spilling my own confession. My head was whirling with vodka and dance music, the echoing pure tones of the men's sorrowful voices. I wanted to tell this maternal, bosomy woman all my secrets, to unburden myself, but Tanya's warnings about Natasha's Party membership, her power, surfaced, and some vestigial caution kept me hushed. Besides, it would be embarrassing now to come clean after lying to them. I was being seduced by this warmth, more powerful than Grisha's complaints, our endless walks about the city, our metro rides. I was being seduced by eating potatoes on the floor of Tanya's apartment, by Natasha's whirling braid when she danced with her husband, by the men's haunting voices—by Russia.

Back in the living room, Alexander Zakharich offered his own confession. "Ever since you first came to us I couldn't stop seeing how much you look like my sister." I blushed, trying to imagine myself in any way related to this puff-cheeked pasha sliding bits of white rendered fat onto his fork.

The next day when I reported on the party to Grisha, he bristled. "So they gave you a dose of the famous Russian Soul, did they? I'm not so fond of the Russian Soul. Haven't you noticed it always comes accompanied by vodka?"

True, perhaps, but I resented his puncturing my romantic notions. I wanted to believe in the Russian Soul.

Tanya grabbed me outside of the teacher's cloakroom. She and Grisha had quarreled, she said, though she wouldn't say why. I felt the same rush of adrenaline, the panic in my chest as when Natasha first pried about my nationality. Had they quarreled because of me?

"It doesn't matter," Tanya said. "I do not respect him. You know, his wife is so unattractive. Her teeth are very bad, and she has enormous breasts. He'd like to hide his head in them, he is such a coward."

Grisha got up from his seat in the empty classroom. "Laurie, will you wait for me here? I must go across the street to the place where we have the food collection. It is my duty . . . one of the few benefits of teaching is that we are permitted to buy food through the school for the holidays. Items like butter, fish, sausage which are hard to find. Now I must go and collect it for the entire school. It is really quite unpleasant to be down in a wet cellar with smelly fish. Will you wait for me to ride the metro with you afterward?"

I agreed, but when he left I was overcome with a terrible dolor. The room was cool with the windows open. I went over and peeked outside. An old woman in a blue padded worker's jacket was sweeping the melted streets with a stiff, short broom three floors below. Across the layered roofs and chimneys the city droned on. I waited and waited until I began to wonder what I was waiting for. Grisha was Tanya's lover, yet she hated Jews. Tanya hated Jews, but I liked her. She was silly and impish and free in a way that I wasn't, just as she was satisfied in a way that I had never been, a way that Grisha wasn't. She praised me and hugged me constantly, and I couldn't even tell her who I really was. And Grisha, with his constant complaints about his wife, his worries about money . . . would a real Russian complain of the unpleasantness of smelly fish? Wasn't that somehow unmanly, to borrow his word? Or was Tanya poisoning me against him? Why didn't he do something? Why didn't he claim me?

By the time Grisha reappeared I was close to tears. Walking one of the little dirt paths through a wooded empty lot en route to the metro, Grisha turned to me.

"You look so sad now. You know, Laurie, you are the strangest woman. One moment you seem to know everything and to be so wise, and the next moment you look just like a helpless little girl."

"It's just a mood," I snapped. "I'm not *helpless*. Aren't I allowed to have moods?"

Grisha moved to put his arm on my shoulder, then dropped it. "Of course," he said.

"Tanya says you two have quarreled."

"Yes. I can't bear her anymore. But it isn't your fault. Well, in a way it is."

"Stop it! Don't do this to me anymore!"

"Do what?"

"You make me feel guilty when we aren't even having an affair. We're always sneaking around. We haven't done anything and I feel like an adulterer. I'm sick of feeling guilty for no reason."

Grisha grinned. "Let's have an affair then, so you will have a reason to feel guilty."

"Are you joking?" I turned to look at him. We'd made it to the metro entrance, in the midst of the gathering peak-hour crowds.

"Yes and no. Laurie, remember when we had that photograph taken together with Tanya? I was going crazy feeling you beside me. I want you. A man looks at a woman like Tanya and he wants her immediately; that is the kind of woman she is. But you, I thought when you arrived that you were nice to look at, but that was all. And now when I look at you, when I look into your eyes, the way you look at me sometimes, I think you are the most beautiful woman in the world."

But I didn't want to be a woman he'd come around to finding desirable, I wanted to be what Tanya was to him, a woman a man wanted immediately! And now, without a touch, he'd summarily decided we'd be lovers.

"What would we do?" I asked. "We can't go to your place and sleep in your wife's bed, and you aren't allowed in my hotel."

"I suppose you don't have such problems in your country."

"No. We have other problems."

"I have a friend with an apartment. I'll talk to him and work something out."

"But I'm leaving so soon."

"I will arrange something. I'll find a place. Laurie, I'm crazy for you."

I turned away.

"Now why do you look so unhappy?" Grisha implored.

"We're talking about logistics and we haven't even kissed," I whimpered.

Grisha grabbed my arm and yanked me out of the metro entrance, into an alley between apartment buildings. "Laurie," he said, grabbing me, pulling me hard against his leather coat. "*Sladkaya* Laurie." Sweet Laurie. His breath was hot, his voice husky. I felt dizzy in the presence of such sudden fervor.

"You're speaking Russian," I said. "You never speak Russian to me."

"I can't speak English *now*."

Then a door banged open and a *babushka* emerged to dump a bucket in the alley. We jumped back from each other like high school kids caught petting. I straightened my cockeyed *shapka* and drew away.

Grisha gripped my wrist fiercely. "I'll arrange something. I promise."

For some time now, enormous billboards with the faces of the Politburo—Brezhnev's portrait appearing much younger than his many years—had been erected on the streets and the lights strung across intersections blazed in star and hammer and sickle shapes. Festive, yet oppressive, decoration. Waiting for Grisha to arrange something began to oppress me too. It gave me too much time to think.

I rationalized that I couldn't hurt his wife because he was already cheating on her, and I was temporary, a foreigner who would be leaving soon. Whatever transpired between us would be ephemeral. Then what about Tanya, who had been so kind to me, the first to invite me home? It would be a betrayal of her, no matter that they'd broken off. I had never gone out with a friend's boyfriend or even a friend's former boyfriend. But here, like a Soviet, I'd come to see myself as entitled to whatever pleasure, whatever warmth, I might grasp from the gloom. No wonder adultery was epidemic.

Russia was changing me. I'd never been aware of my own anti-Semitism until it was shoved in my face here. Even the statue of Mayakovsky, beyond my hotel window, reminded me that the quintessential Bolshevik poet had been manipulated by his Jewish mistress, Lily Brik. Why did she have to be Jewish?

My parents possessed that brand of anti-Semitism peculiar to the New England Jew, who loathes his own kind while feeling secretly superior to gentiles. My father, an equal-opportunity racist, had told me that I couldn't go to the University of Chicago because it had too many blacks, and I couldn't go to Brandeis because it had too many Jews.

We lived in ethnic schizophrenia. We hung Christmas stockings but weren't allowed a tree. We received Hanukkah presents and were forced to attend eight years of Sabbath School ("so you'll know who you are when they say you killed Jesus," my mother explained), and Hebrew School as well, although only my brother was Bar Mitzvahed; we weren't Jewish enough for Bat Mitzvahs.

Part of Grisha's appeal, I supposed, was his Jewishness—the familiarity of his longing and sorrow and dark eyes. In him, I recognized myself. He reminded me of Isaac Babel's Jewish commissar in the *Red Army Stories* who had "spectacles on his nose and autumn in his heart." But I ascribed his failings—his complaints, his dissatisfactions—to his Jewishness as well. I'd rarely dated Jewish boys, considering them too namby-pamby, mamas' boys, more evidence of my own anti-Semitism.

I didn't love him. I couldn't love him when he was married, he lived here, he was stuck. (Marriage meant so little to me I might have married him to give him a shot at emigration, if he divorced. Though most Jews, including those married to Americans, weren't getting out anymore.) But there was something in the intensity of our connection—circumstantial, perhaps, heightened by the impossibility of it all—that felt more real than anything I'd had with a man since I'd fallen in love with Kim at age seventeen. But Kim was a drinker now and the other men I'd been drawn to possessed what I thought of as "dead eyes." Grisha had the opposite of dead eyes. They were vibrant with all sorts of yearning. If he couldn't do anything about his desire for freedom, why didn't he at least do something about me? Only days remained before I took the train to Leningrad.

At school Grisha, shamefaced, reported that he'd had no luck finding a place for a tryst yet; everyone was having guests for the holidays. Everyone was busy with preparations. "Give me time," he pleaded.

"It's sordid," I said, "trying to find someone's bed to use."

"At least I'll be giving you a true Soviet experience," he joked.

"A high point in cultural exchange."

"When you come back from Leningrad, surely I'll have something arranged by then."

But I'd have only five days when I came back from Leningrad. If he had really wanted me, wouldn't he have found a way for us to be together?

There is a scene in *Anna Karenina* in which two minor characters, Levin's brother and the unmarried Varenka, are picking mushrooms in a forest. The brother has made up his mind to propose to her, and she is willing to marry him. But at the moment when he might propose, they awkwardly speak of mushrooms instead, and the opportunity irretrievably passes. Both of them know it can't be regained. She remains a spinster, he a bachelor. Ours was the more prosaic Soviet version of that scene. The moment passed in fumbled arrangements, and I began to withdraw.

Tanya pulled me aside in the hall. "Lora, I missed you. I've quarreled again with Grisha. He told me that he made love to you."

I held my breath, feeling as though I'd been caught. Did intention count? "He lied."

"I told him I didn't believe him," Tanya said. "I knew that you wouldn't do that to me."

"He must want to make you jealous," I shook my head in fury. How could he have told her?

"I knew you wouldn't do that to me," Tanya repeated. "You are so good, Lora, you're a good person and would never hurt me that way."

"You told Tanya I slept with you," I accused Grisha after class as he walked me to the metro station.

"No, I didn't. I told her I'd *like* to."

I stopped, stamped my foot beside a puddle in the broken pavement. "One of you is lying. Grisha, why would you do that? Have you told my other secrets too?"

"Of course not."

"You wanted to make her jealous."

"Perhaps a bit, but mostly I wanted to explain to her why I could not sleep with her now."

"You must still desire her if you wanted to make her jealous. You only wanted me for titillation, the thrill of sleeping with a foreigner."

"It is terribly unfair of you to think that is the reason. I've quite fallen in love with you."

Just then a boy from our school passed our little drama, glancing over his shoulder with curiosity. Instinctively, we moved a step apart. "I don't know what to believe anymore," I said stonily, striding toward the metro. I was sick of other people's marital problems, their vulgar little affairs. And ashamed that I'd nearly taken part in one.

Tanya whispered in my ear at the cafeteria lunch table, "You know he and his wife share one pair of jeans? He wears them one day, she the next? Oi, and he is so stingy. That night we went out to dinner, he did not want me to order expensive food. He had no money. I had to pay for everything."

I knew in her hurt and fear she was trying to poison me against him, but it was working.

Still, I agreed to accompany Grisha on a good-bye outing, to Novodevichy Convent, a sixteenth-century fortress of white crenelated walls enclosing a cathedral from which five onion domes rose like pointed mushrooms. "It was here that czars and nobles once disposed of the wives they no longer wanted," Grisha intoned as we walked the paths. "Very convenient, don't you think?"

"The English just beheaded them," I said. "Even more convenient."

Grisha resumed his tour-guide voice: "Here too noblewomen took the veil after their husbands died. Peter the Great kept his rebellious sister Sophia inside for fifteen years. . . . Perhaps it's worse to be locked up," he added softly.

In the park, swans floated on a pond. Where did these swans spend the frozen Russian winter, I wondered. The early snows were gone now, the paths between the ancient white buildings rain-washed. A slanting late autumn light gilded the bare trees. We walked the paths nearly silent.

"Shall we get something to eat somewhere?" Grisha finally asked.

"All right." I had suitcases to pack back at the Pekin—I was leaving on an overnight train this evening—but I was in no rush to return to my room. We went to a restaurant in a foreigners' hotel using the pass-word—English—to get beyond the red–arm-banded guard. Though we could sneak in for a meal, there was no way we could get a room, not when both our passports would have to be handed in at the reception desk. Just as well I no longer really wanted to.

We sat across from one another waiting for our meal. I looked at Grisha more dispassionately than before. Yes, he was handsome, though his black hair was thinning already. Perhaps in twenty years he would resemble Zakharich, as he feared. And whom would I resemble? But I couldn't picture myself in twenty years. If I lived in this country I'd resemble Natasha or Emma, become thick-waisted and exhausted. At home we looked younger longer. We kept our hollow shine.

The waitress brought our meal, rudely thumping the plates on the table. "You aren't eating," I observed as I tucked into my *kutlyet*.

"I can't," Grisha said, gazing into my eyes. "Not when you are leaving."

I was embarrassed that I could—more proof that I wasn't in love. I was hungry and here was food, hot and available, when food was so hard to find. You waited too long, I wanted to chide him. You didn't claim me. You were afraid to emigrate; afraid to leave the wife you don't love. Didn't you understand I wanted romance, the feel of your skin under my hands when it might have meant something? Tanya's disparaging words came to mind—*I don't respect him, he's a coward.* I needed a fearless man, a man of action, to make up for all my fears.

"I can't bear that you're leaving," Grisha said. "You *will* come to the school when you get back from Leningrad, won't you?"

"Of course." He didn't say, "Call me when you get back." I couldn't call him at home and he couldn't call me at my as-yet-unknown hotel, wherever they might plunk me on my return. He couldn't take that chance.

"I will think of nothing else but you while you are gone." He reached across the table. "I've never felt this way about a woman."

"But what good is it?" I asked. "It's hopeless. You can't even come to the station to see me off." Whatever ministry official would be there to escort me to my train would surely report him if he did.

"Damn this place."

"Shhh." I averted my gaze from the anguish in his dark eyes. This romantic stalemate was, I thought, just one more in a lifetime of impossibilities for him; whatever he felt for me was only a symptom. Hampered by my own disappointment and need, I couldn't stretch myself enough to imagine how he might feel. "Now I must go back to my hotel and pack. Let me pay for dinner. I have all these rubles I've got to spend. They're just going to give me more in Leningrad."

Grisha said quietly, "Let me at least pretend to be a man."

Holiday

They sent me on the overnight train, a milk run that stopped in tiny villages. The station smelled of coal smoke—each train car had its own coal-fueled samovar. Porters wearing caps like working stiffs in a Preston Sturges movie ran overloaded carts up ramps to the outdoor platform. University students, heading home for the holiday, sang gaily and hugged one another in front of the train cars. Again, I was embarrassed by the amount of my luggage, which overflowed the four-passenger compartment to which I'd been assigned. My Russian bunkmates (we politely avoided one another's eyes) tucked away their plastic valises of apples and sausages, pulled out pajamas, turned their faces to the wall, and slept, while I pressed my nose to the cold glass and tried to make out the serpentine shimmer of streams cutting through broad fields of frozen grass in the darkness. The ghostly landscape sliding by filled me with an indecipherable longing, homesickness for a place I'd never seen. I dreamed—I thought it was a dream—of a train bearing down on us, about to crash, but then it passed beside us, the driver smiling and waving madly at me. I wished that Grisha could be in the train beside me, that we could be traveling through a romantic Zhivago dream together, but instead I had the snores of my bunkmates, the cold of the glass against my nose.

At dawn, an hour out of Leningrad, a smooth, professionally pleasant woman announcer's voice issued from the radio speaker, offering news. I only caught a few words, distressingly familiar: *Amerikanskii Imperialism, Izraelskii Zionisti.* The uniformed train matron brought glasses of tea in silvery holders with enormous wrapped lumps of sugar decorated with a picture of the olive drab train. People lined up for the bathrooms. In early morning light I watched in fascination as we passed villages of muddy streets, brightly painted wooden houses with carved shutters, fenced gardens, a man in black rubber boots leading a cow by a halter, uniformed schoolchildren trudging along with book bags strapped to their backs. Myriad footpaths wound in and out of the fields, crossing one another along the tracks. I'd seen such paths in Moscow, cutting through parks and vacant lots. There was something reassuring about their prevalence, a peculiar, stubborn order both ancient and simple, following a destination that had nothing to do with Five Year Plans.

I was met at the Leningrad station by two stocky middle-aged women and a young teacher named Galina—Galya—whom I soon identified as my "official friend." Galya held a bouquet of flowers, and her blonde hair was tucked up under a bristling cap of indeterminate origin—porcupine? She wore a coat with tanned hide strips separating fur panels that reminded me of the leathery chest of a gorilla. Her dark eyes, which never once met mine, remained focused in some middle distance of responsibility and prim reserve. Like the other English teachers, Galya spoke the correct but stilted British English of pedagogical institute texts. Galya, however, had added her own variant of pressed palms and skyward glances, as if she had modeled not only her speech, but her entire demeanor on the heroines of Jane Austen. "I do so love our beautiful city," she said, as I was shunted on a whirlwind car tour of Leningrad. I ached to change her words to "I really love," to loosen her idiom.

Still without sleep, I merely squinted at the glittering canals, the Neva, the gold Admiralty and ornate statuary on the roof of the Hermitage as they spun past. Leningrad's weary beauty was hard to absorb. The spires and bridges and canals, the vast slate of the Neva, the carved wild horses on the Anichkov Bridge were stunning, but everything looked bleak in November rain: the faded pastel buildings fronting Nevsky Prospekt seemed to be crumbling, their facades interrupted every twenty feet by corrugated tin drain spouts that ran down from the roofs to pour directly onto the sidewalk. Every block had a building covered with scaffolding, under *remont*—renovation. Female construction workers in padded jackets and head scarves hoisted buckets of plaster and cement while male overseers stood by smoking. The freshly renovated buildings were adorned with sculpted titans painted a historically accurate but unappealing mud green. Being at the edge of this continent, however, pleased me. The sight of water, a border not far away, made it somehow easier to breathe.

My hotel, the Baltiskaya, was well situated on Nevsky Prospekt, but dreary and stifling. Again, it wasn't an elaborate Intourist affair for foreigners, but a narrow, down-at-the-heels hotel filled with Soviet tourists and businesspeople from distant Soviet republics and Third World diplomats. The men wore dark suits, but the women dressed in their local costumes, yellow silky shifts over ballooning pants for the Central Asian Uzbeks, black for the Georgians, floral for the Azerbaijanians.

The Baltiskaya had a metal-grilled elevator that creaked its way up to my floor, where the *dezhurnaya* watched me come and go and took my key, and a restaurant in which I saw a roach climbing the dusty curtain. From the tiny balcony of my streetside room, I looked down on the lights and banners celebrating the Anniversary of the Great October Socialist Revolution. School was closed for five days, and here I was alone. Rather than welcoming the time away from my exhausting class schedule, as I thought I would, I regretted my isolation, the loss of Grisha and the School 45 "girls" now that I was far away. I couldn't contact any of them. I composed several letters addressed to Alexander Zakharovitch and "all of my friends at School 45" before settling on words I deemed suitably appreciative, yet vague enough that I wouldn't get anyone into trouble.

The next day, Sunday, I was sent with Galya on an officially sponsored outing, along with one of her powerful mother's pals from the Ministry of Education—a bulky, odiferous woman with the pale blue eyes and blunt features of a Siberian husky. Galya informed me that someday I would have the great honor of meeting her mother at the Pedagogical Institute. "I *do* so hope my mother will like you," she said. I *do* so hope I'll like her, I wanted to say. But it was inconceivable to Galya that I wouldn't be impressed and awed by her mother's eminence.

Escorting me through the chandeliered ballrooms and gallery halls of Petrodvoretz, the czar's summer palace, Galya confided that she was descended from nobility who had, of course, switched to the Communist cause immediately at the time of the Great October Socialist Revolution. Of course. This confidence amused me, especially since Galya repeated it twice. Nevertheless, I could believe it—Galya, slender and erect, honey-colored hair piled high, dancing through those parquet halls in a Tolstoyan romance. The guide announced that it had taken two workers ten years to restore the silk wall coverings to their former glory after the siege of Leningrad. Although I'd seen the palace at Kolomenskoye, Petrodvoretz dwarfed it. Our Rockefellers and Duponts had left us nothing to match such opulence and unfair wealth. No wonder there was a revolution.

Despite such lapses as her confession, Galya wore the drab browns of a girl with hopes of Party membership and the dream of foreign travel. I suspected that the responsibility of being assigned to me was both a plum and a terrible burden. She was the one who'd write reports on my activities. There wasn't a chance we'd be friends.

I hoped that there would be someone to chum with at school. If not, I had the number of another friend of Richard's, although the fiasco with Maxim in Moscow wasn't encouraging. I'd try calling Sasha Ivanov after the break; I assumed anyone with family would be busy on the holidays. At least Sasha, according to Richard, spoke English.

The Leningrad education officials were more organized and more formal than the Moscow officials. Being located away from the capital they had to be more careful, I guessed. No one in Moscow had provided me with an "official friend," though I didn't doubt someone had reported on me, Natasha probably. And School 45 with its director on the City Soviet was a model of leniency, Soviet style. It wasn't likely that I'd be so lucky twice. Certainly, the Leningrad officials had gone to much more effort to provide me with cultural opportunities. At one o'clock on the big holiday, Anna Maximovna, the woman with the eyes of a Siberian husky, came to escort me to the ballet. She provided me with a matinee ticket to the Kirov, although I would be on my own at the ballet since she had family duties. Galya would meet me after.

The streets between the hotel and the Kirov Theater were blocked off by military trucks to make a cordon for the enormous "demonstration" in honor of the seventh. A demonstration meant a show of military might and enforced marching of hundreds of thousands of Pioneers and Komsomols with red placards offering slogans about peace and pictures of the Politburo members. The demonstration in Moscow was even bigger, Maximovna assured me. We had to wend our way through the army trucks, even at one point climbing through the cab of one vehicle to exit out its other door while the soldiers looked on, amused. Maximovna negotiated well, using the leverage of Important American Guest more effectively than Grisha had at Kolomenskoye. She had more practice, I supposed.

The ballet was *Don Quixote,* not a favorite of mine. I'd seen a gorgeous *Koppelia* a day ago, and an odd version of the opera *Lucia di Lamamoor* the day before that, with the female lead singing Russian while the male lead answered her in Italian. All those kilts bobbing around the stage of the Kirov had blurred in my mind with the Spanish gypsies doing their alternating girl and boy show-off numbers. Although I knew I was blessed with cultural opportunities that most tourists, let alone the average Russian, couldn't hope for, I emerged from the Kirov dazed.

Galya stood waiting for me on the asphalt in front of the theater, holding red balloons that glowed in contrast to the late-afternoon Leningrad gloom. The changing of the Laurie guard had occurred while I was inside. Her husband, she said, was looking for a cab. A long line of people stood waiting patiently at the cab stop, while Galya's husband, Vladimir, a tall, skinny boy with longish hair, paced up and down the sidewalk to avoid meeting me.

"Isn't it strange," said Galya, "for a grown man to be as shy as a boy?"

A cab was finally found, and Galya gave directions to the house of a teacher, Aleksei, who was on medical leave for breaking his leg. How appropriate, I thought, that they'd send me to spend a holiday with someone with whom I wouldn't work rather than someone I might get close to at the school. (I would learn later that he was the only one who had been willing to invite me home.)

We slid through the Leningrad streets, Galya's balloons squashed behind our heads, her husband, Vladimir, up front with the driver. Big gray battleships lined the Neva. Across the river on Vasilevsky Island, the rostral column shot fire into the sky. The red banners, winking lights, and the illumination of the Peter and Paul fortress created an eerie anxious brilliance in the gloom. Meanwhile, Galya recounted for me the sufferings of her family during the Great Patriotic War for the Fatherland.

I frowned in annoyance. Why was it that the Russians thought they'd cornered the market on suffering? Had no one else ever lost family or friends? I'd been taken to Piskarovskoye Cemetery, I'd seen the graves, the museum to the war, the tiny piece of bread that was all the survivors ate each day for three years during the siege of Leningrad. Russia had lost twenty million, and another twenty million to Stalin's camps. But I'd also seen the Holocaust museum in Israel—Russia's number-one enemy besides America. Yes, yes, I agreed with Galya. It must have been awful.

"And that is why the Soviet people couldn't possibly want anything but peace, if only your country would let us," she concluded.

I'd had six weeks' practice in biting my tongue so I tried to ignore her. In the storage well behind our heads the bottle of French cognac from the dollar store—a gift for my unknown hosts—thumped at every speedy turn of the cab. We rushed out of the city proper and into "suburbs," high-rise developments like Tanya's.

Our host, Aleksei, opened the door. He was bulky, already balding, about my age, with a discomfitingly stern expression. He turned to bark at his small son, who was standing behind him, an admonishment to stop picking his nose.

The apartment belonged to Aleksei's mother, Galina Ivanovna, a short, stocky *babushka* wearing a floral house dress. She babbled at me in Russian too fast to catch and almost too loud to bear. I smiled back at her in dumb, shell-shocked goodwill.

"Galina Ivanovna was a children's gym teacher," Aleksei explained. "Don't worry, she always speaks too loudly."

His mother's blue eyes and gold-filled smile were clearly welcoming. How was it that this woman was consigned to the job of being my hostess?

Galina Ivanovna shunted us all into the living room/bedroom where an enormous television set was showing a Soviet western, set in Uzbekistan or Tadzhikistan or some such desert outpost. Aleksei's small son sat on the bed, entranced while the TV blared through the entire meal. The room was just big enough for the table, the bed, and the de rigeur breakfront with crystal. My bottle of cognac was deposited on a shelf behind glass. A museum piece? Aleksei's wife, Violetta, dark haired, with a heart-shaped, pale, pretty face, didn't speak English. She smiled at me shyly across the table.

After a few hits of vodka, Aleksei's stern demeanor gave way to winks and jokes. Aleksei became Alyosha, Violetta became Vyetta, Vladimir was Volodya, and I became Lorichka, Lorinka, Lora. Galina Ivanovna shrieked at me to eat more salad—*vitaminki,* she called it. Galya's formerly shy husband got quickly drunk and persistently tried to teach me complicated variants on "bottoms up" that I couldn't hope to remember. I felt like a smiling, nodding car ornament, trying to express mindless appreciation.

We moved to the kitchen in between courses to smoke cigarettes. Galya played with Galina Ivanovna's Siamese cat. Her wrists, I noticed, were covered in scratches, scars from her own kitten, a detail that fascinated me. I tried to imagine a playful Galya, Volodya, and a kitten crammed into the one-room apartment, which also served as Volodya's painting studio.

"I wish that I had jeans," Galya sighed, examining mine enviously. "I had a pair once, but they simply turned to rags and fell off my body. It was a shame, since they did so suit me."

A friend of Alyosha's appeared around dessert time, a short, wiry, curly-haired fellow in a brown velour suit who spoke no English. Kolya had been a seaman, Alyosha informed me. For the sake of conversation, I replied that I'd worked on fishing boats in Alaska some years before, letting Alyosha translate rather than struggling to find the words.

"*Molodyetz,*" Kolya said, "wonderful."

"Kolya says he liked you the moment he saw you," Alyosha said.

When we were suitably drunk—all but Kolya, who was driving and couldn't risk losing his license—it was decided that we would climb into Kolya's car to go visit friends of Vyetta's who lived in a dormitory at the design institute from which Vyetta had graduated. While we put on our coats, Alyosha's mother wanted to know my age. "Not married yet? We'll have to find you a Russian boy," she shrieked. We all traded ages—I twenty-nine, Alyosha thirty, Kolya thirty-three—like Christ, he said—Galya twenty-three, Vladimir twenty-five, but Vyetta put a hand over her mouth to whisper the deep, dark secret of twenty-eight years into my ear.

We wove around the city, six of us crammed into Kolya's car, finally parking at a collection of high rises. Kolya removed his windshield wipers before locking his car—an interesting precaution in the crimeless state. We had to lie to get past the guard at the dormitory door.

Vyetta's friends were a hospitable Siberian couple with Inuit faces who shared a tiny room. Chairs were squeezed around a table and more food appeared—sausages, cheese, mushroom casseroles. I could barely force myself to taste enough to avoid insulting my new hosts. Alyosha had brought along my cognac, I was pleased to see, and glasses were filled, then downed in a gulp. Kolya and Vyetta sat beside each other on the couch and whispered. I glanced at Alyosha to see if he was jealous, but he appeared unconcerned.

After a few toasts, it was decided that all of us but Kolya and the host couple would go downstairs to join a dance party in the student lounge. Old American pop tunes blared in a darkened room: "Baby Love" and "Heard It on the Grapevine." The only difference between this and any American high school dance was the rank odor of sweat wafting about the room.

Galya was disappointed that I couldn't teach them any hot new American dance steps—not my forte. I ended up in a clutch during a slow song with an amiable Siberian boy who couldn't believe that I was an *Amerikanka*.

Finally, near midnight, Kolya was prevailed upon to drive me back to the hotel before I got locked out for the night. He parked across the street rather than in front of the Baltiskaya. Galya was nervous again, overwhelmed by her responsibility for me. Walking me to the door, she said stiffly, "Of course, there's no need to mention to anyone at school about dancing at the dormitory. You understand."

"Of course," I said, amused by the transformation of the Russian disco queen back into Miss Priss. But I'd had fun, even if Grisha would have dismissed it all as another dose of Russian Soul.

School 185 in Leningrad was situated downtown not far from the Neva, a couple of trolley rides or a longish walk from my hotel. It was an old stone building with a courtyard, worn stone steps, a chilly teachers' lounge, due to the windows being open to release the roiling tobacco smoke, the omnipresent stinking, primitive toilets, and a lunch-room gaily painted, as in Moscow, with sheaves of wheat and girls in peasant costumes on the walls.

I had to do some taping after school ("You can't imagine how valu-able your accent is to us, Laurie"), and several lectures and talks at var-ious ministries. But my class load was lighter and my day shorter, which was just as well since it was getting dark by three-thirty in the afternoon at this high latitude. My new head teacher was a large woman with delicate features, small hands, and the mysterious, clever smile of the Cheshire cat. Tatiana Nikolaevna had no intention of working me as hard as they had in Moscow.

Although no one in Moscow had mentioned Leningrad, Leningraders seemed to be in a subtle rivalry with the capital, a mix of second-city inferiority complex and certainty that they were the more cultured and sophisticated. The Moscow accent was harsh, they said; they spoke a more pure Russian. Moscow was "a big village" while Leningrad was still Peter the Great's Window on the West. The teachers appreciated my exclamations over Leningrad's beauty and seemed pleased that they had planned for my cultural enrichment more than Moscow had. The classroom atmosphere was much the same, however. Teachers lined the back rows to observe me and critique their students.

"Who is fighting for peace, America or the Soviet Union?" a tall, thin boy with a wispy mustache stood to ask.

"Don't you know yourself?" cut in Yuri, the unctuous, Uriah Heap–like political theory teacher, sharply.

"Yes," the boy stood his ground, "but I wanted to hear it from an American."

So I trotted out my half-false tale of war protestation again, as though it would clear me of some national guilt, or, to those who cared, surreptitiously point out that there were places where protests were allowed. No Grisha appeared at School 185 to alleviate the formal friendliness and distance of my relations with the teachers and kids.

"Miss Laurie, is it true American students shoot their teachers?"

A workman came in to my hotel room to take the banner from my balcony. He seemed nervous and forgot his key and later his crowbar. Was I such a scary foreigner? Or was he nervous because he was there for other reasons?

I didn't know if it was Leningrad or the season, but everyone in the school seemed to suffer lingering coughs and other ailments. Teachers appeared in class with hands wrapped in gauze. Lip sores were omnipresent. The general complexion was pasty and unhealthy. Lack of sunshine and short daylight—it reminded me of winter in southeast Alaska, which was on a similar latitude. Sugary tea rather than milk for the kids, few fresh fruits and vegetables, and bad medicine kept many home with various ailments.

Although I never saw her in class, only in the teacher's lounge, Galya continued to gall me, lecturing me on my country's failings. Unlike School 45 in Moscow, School 185 had few young teachers, and Galya was the only beauty. One of my favorite teachers was a troll-like middle-aged woman under five feet tall who was enthusiastic and loving with her students. Another teacher, Anna Iosefevna, was a narrow-faced, freckled, plain woman of fifty or so with a stern demeanor whom I found intimidating. By some background arrangement, she offered to chaperone me on a tour of the Russian Museum after school.

Her knowledge of art history was impressive. We started with the earliest icons and moved through the great Russian landscape painters Levitan and Shishkin, pine forests pooled with light, Aivazovsky's remarkable seas, the soulful portraits by Serov. We came to the work of Alexander Ivanov, an enormous nineteenth-century canvas called "Christ Appearing before the People." Anna Iosefevna pointed at a hook-nosed, dark-haired, bearded John the Baptist and said, "He has a typical Jewish face, wouldn't you say?"

I had no idea how to answer; she was fishing for something, but I didn't know what, checking the waters, perhaps. I shrugged off her question.

We reached the revolutionary years and together admired the work of Kuzma Petrov-Vodkin, a still life with many-faceted silver teapot and tea glass, painted from an angle that made all the objects appear in danger of sliding off a tilted table. I remarked on the painting's disturbing energy.

"Yes," Anna Iosefevna said, "it was a time of great turmoil. No one knew what was up or down. All was out of balance. His paintings reflect that mood."

She tried to hurry me through the celebrated peasants and flag-waving partisans of the Socialist Realism phase that followed. "Unfortunately, there's not much of interest here," she said. Her intellectual rigor wouldn't allow her to lie in the face of such obvious mediocrity, all the more painful after our hours among real treasures.

Not a personal word passed between us, yet I sensed something stifled and lost, an unknowable suffering behind Anna Iosefevna's closed face.

I returned to my hotel after school, climbing under the covers to sleep a sleep that never refreshed. I was exhausted by confusion, the language, the grim, gray weather, the strange demands of this life. When I hurried to school in the morning, it was dark as night. And it was dark again before I got back to the hotel.

I wanted only to be done with my teaching, for this to be over. I began to dream of home. I'd wake, panicked, filled with inordinate fear that I'd never get home again. Each time I woke to find myself in a dark hotel room, in a narrow sagging bed. Through the grayish, opaque curtains on the French doors a streetlight glowed onto a street I knew to be wet and gritty and hopelessly drab, weak neon advertising dumplings and groceries—*pelmeni* and *gastronom*. I was in a place so alien I ached for the gentle folds of Vermont hillsides, even in drab November, when the Green Mountains became stark with bare maples and shivering birch trees.

I was sick of New York already, yet I couldn't imagine picking up and starting over again. In the past five years I'd lived in Vermont, Cambridge, Iowa, and New York, with additional stints in Alaska and now Russia. When I returned I would have no job, an unfinished novel. What would I find for work? I'd bombed as a prep school teacher. My rent was ridiculously small—$93 a month for two joined 7' x 12' maids' rooms and a shared bath on the roof of a building in the psychiatrist ghetto, the park block of East Sixty-eighty Street—a space I'd been offered by parents at the school from which I'd quit. With that rent, I didn't have to earn much, but I had to earn something.

I wanted a real apartment, a life with someone, I wanted to write, or at least to feel like writing. I tried to imagine Leningrad as the city of Nick, one of the characters in my novel, but his was a city of forty years earlier, in a country ruled by Stalin. Still, the angled northern light, when the clouds broke apart, must have looked the same.

One day, as I sat eating *solyanka*, a soup with olives and sausage, in the Baltiskaya restaurant, a *babushka* seated with a teenage boy at a nearby table got up to go. "Take the cheese," she admonished the boy. "Cheese is expensive." They were speaking Russian, and I'd understood as naturally as though I were eavesdropping in English. Weeks had gone by, weeks of total language confusion, and I'd woken up as though from a coma to suddenly comprehend.

I called Richard's friend Sasha. Although he too was an unofficial, "underground" artist, he turned out to be the opposite of creepy Maxim in every possible way. A slightly built, narrow-faced man in his early thirties who wore a bushy mustache, Sasha gently ushered me through the metro and a trolley ride, all the while asking eagerly about Richard, with whom he regularly corresponded. He spoke an idiomatic, slang-filled American English that he'd taught himself.

His apartment building on Prospekt Stachek was a model of Soviet incompetence; though only twelve years old, the walls were already dropping chunks of cement, the stairwells dank and filthy. Enormous stationary earth-moving equipment stood scattered about great swaths of scraped dirt. The wind from the Finnish Gulf whipped dust from the bulldozed plains over miles of stark concrete housing. In a rutted play yard, *babushki* sat on benches, and kids skirmished over a soccer ball.

"Don't speak English in elevator or hall," Sasha warned me.

In the elevator, a military man in uniform held the hand of a small beribboned girl as we rode up together.

Sasha's small apartment—a studio with a kitchen and the usual two cubicles separating toilet from bath—was warm and welcoming. He was thrilled by the Zappa record I'd carried from Rick, and eager to talk American music, movies, and books. I sank into his couch with relief as Sasha bustled about making tea and serving up cookies. He showed me a picture of a young, preppy Richard from his student days in Leningrad and numerous photos of Annie, the American girl with whom Sasha had fallen in love while she was on a semester abroad. He was planning for their wedding when she returned in the spring.

Though I had no doubt that Sasha was in love with the pretty girl who smiled from between his arms in the snapshots, he was also crazy to get out of Russia, and Annie could be his ticket. His sister had married an Englishman and immigrated to London several years ago; as a consequence, his father, a high-ranking professor at the Maritime Academy, had been prematurely "retired." This only added to Sasha's bitterness. He'd been disallowed from the artists' union because his paintings, while technically admired, were of the wrong subjects. He'd been advised to go to collective farms to paint proper "labor" themes. Instead, Sasha painted for himself, giving away his paintings to friends, and worked as a freelancer designing shoes, record covers, park benches—anything he could scrounge up for a measly 100 rubles a month. Though he'd started out with romantic themes, his paintings were growing increasingly dark and cynical, work that could get him arrested: a drunk grabbing for a ruble in the street, a hideous Brezhnev portrait, bleak cityscapes that reverberated with alienation.

Sasha, for all his bitterness, was a little mother. He tended to me as he did all his friends. His friends loved him. I could see it in the face of Zina, a plump, sweet artist who lived in a single, high-ceilinged room in a downtown communal apartment. She smiled tenderly at Sasha over a plate of dates and cakes and candies while we spoke of films and books and his love for Annie and the problem of trying to change professions in the Soviet system. On the sidewalk outside her door, Sasha said, "Her husband is a hopeless drunk. They put him in hospital, but always he drinks again. Therefore she lives alone.

"You smoke too much," he chided me. "And you smoke the worst cigarettes. Why don't you buy yourself some Marlboros at the dollar store?"

"I have rubles, not dollars," I answered as I drew in harsh Bulgarian tobacco and coughed. Sasha wouldn't let me smoke on the streets. "They'll think you're prostitute," he warned. "And watch out for *fartsovchiki*. What do you say if they bother you?"

"*Idi von! Ne khochu!*" (Get out of here.) I recited his lesson.

"We'll invite you to our wedding party in New York, Laurie. You, and Richard, and my sister from England. It will be big gas."

"What if you aren't given an exit visa?" I asked.

"I have great patience," Sasha said. "I will wait as long as necessary."

I hoped it would all come to pass.

In the teachers' lounge, over bad Kometa cigarettes, Galya harangued me about which American pop music records I owned and how much her husband, Volodya, longed to own some. The indirect request annoyed me. Galya was reeling off the names of Volodya's favorite groups when Yuri, the political theory teacher, came in.

"Have you told Laurie our sad news?" he asked Galya, rubbing his hands like Uriah.

Galya's face, animated by the hope of owning records, was transformed immediately into a mask of tragedy. Her mouth turned downward, and she stared down at her hands primly. "Not yet," she whispered.

"What news?" I demanded.

Yuri spoke in the unctuous tone of a funeral director. "Our leader, Brezhnev, has died." I wanted to laugh aloud at Galya's hypocrisy, but I was struck by the enormity of the situation. Brezhnev had been in power seventeen years. What sort of changes would this mean?

"And who will replace him?" I asked.

"We don't yet know," Yuri sighed. "I doubt you'll be teaching classes today."

I was sent back to my hotel. Leading me to the door, the assistant director, a dithery, sweet woman with a fuschia tint to her poorly dyed hair, confided that she'd cried and cried as a young student when Stalin died, but somehow she just didn't feel the same this time.

There was nothing in the news, no official reports. Just dirgelike classical music on all the television stations that went on for days. I imagined coups that would keep me from going home forever. I wished I could have talked it over with Grisha, but I didn't have his number, and calling him to talk politics was out of the question anyway. Finally it was announced that KGB boss Yuri Andropov had been chosen to replace Brezhnev. Everyone observed a five-minute public silence, stopping in the midst of work to come out on the streets. Soldiers, bakers in their big white hats, shoppers shouldered one another on the cold Nevsky Prospekt. The state funeral, broadcast on television, went on and on and on. And when I returned to school, it was as though nothing at all had happened.

Beachspeak

"We don't know what it means," Sasha told me. His narrow face was creased with worry. "We can only wait and see." I'd turned to him for an explanation of Brezhnev's death and Andropov's ascension. I'd managed to get a call to my father just to assure him, through the echoing, lagging connection, that I was fine, intimating through careful wording that no coup had occurred. I figured that Sasha, as an outsider, an unofficial artist, might have insight into the ramifications of a power shift in his country, but, like most Russians, he had no more access to the workings of his system than he did ours.

I'd been surprised that, although Sasha had made studying American culture his life's work, he misinterpreted the police protection of a group of American Nazis parading in Skokie, Illinois. I expected more sophistication from Sasha than from the schoolkids, but without a concept of civil liberties, he'd convinced himself that the police were actually putting the Fascist skinheads into buses to take them to prison, rather than protecting their free expression. I could tell that he disapproved when I insisted that even Nazis had the right to free speech under our constitution.

I was constantly reminded of the barriers to international understanding. At an officially required visit to *Dom Druzhba*—the House of Friendship—I was shown two movies, one about the Soviet republics and the other, rather pointedly, about the 1980 Olympics that we'd boycotted. I was impressed and a little frightened by all that synchronized Olympic flag waving, the huge audience in the stadium flipping banners; we'd do it out of order, I supposed. They had an official translator for me, and when the director, discussing the Soviets' interest in teaching their children science, said that the Russians were "the first on the moon," the translator switched it to "the first in space." They told me that they taught their kids to be peaceful, but when I was leaving they gave me anti-American tracts. I wasn't really insulted. If even Grisha admitted he couldn't imagine putting himself in my place, how could these *apparatchiki* be expected to understand my feelings?

Galya approached me in the hall. It had been decided that this weekend I would be taken on a trip up the Baltic to see more of their beautiful country. And, she added, smirking, Kolya would be coming too.

"Kolya?" I drew a blank.

"Alyosha's friend," Galya reminded me. "The one with the car."

I couldn't fathom her insinuating tone. "But will it be all right for me to go? I'm only registered for thirty kilometers outside of Leningrad."

"Don't worry," Galya reassured me haughtily, "Anna Maximovna knows everything. It is all arranged."

There were six of us crowded into the little white Zhiguli sedan, and in Russia it was illegal to drive with six in a car. Every time we saw the *gaii*—the car police—or neared a *gaii* checkpoint, Galya, who was seated on Volodya's lap in the back beside Vyetta and me, ducked to keep us legal. This was accomplished with a lot of giggling and slapping at Volodya, who pinched her under her coat.

We headed north from Leningrad, leaving behind the low blocks of stone buildings, the heavy-coated, floral-kerchiefed *babushki* gathered in front of food stores and trolley stops, awash in faint wintry light. I didn't know where we were going, and I didn't really care. All decisions were out of my hands. At least this excursion, with our illegal load of passengers, seemed less official than most for which Galya played chaperone. Even if I couldn't understand when they spoke a rapid slangy Russian to each other, I'd rather be riding along than left to a Sunday with spoiled fantasies of Grisha.

On the highway toward Vyborg, Finnish tour buses whizzed past us in the opposite direction. They were loaded with Finns coming into the Soviet Union for the weekend to drink. They had probably stopped right after the border; although it was only midmorning, flushed faces appeared in the bus windows, and young Finns leered and waved wildly as we passed.

"It is quite horrible," Galya pronounced, regaining her professional mien. "Even their little children drink. They lie about the hotels for days. They cannot drink in their own country. We call them vodka tourists."

Alyosha turned around in the front seat. His brown fur cap nearly grazed the ceiling. "This land once belonged to Finland," he explained, gesturing through the car window at the dark stands of fir and leafless birch.

Everything was so level—the Leningrad buildings, the land, the trees—it seemed that the people must have grown to match their landscape in the sixty-five years since the revolution. Unlike in Moscow, where the Stalin Gothic towers mocked the idea of a dictatorship of the proletariat, here along the highway to Vyborg and the Finnish border, the trees stretched on, dark and enduring, and nothing stood higher than the rest.

"The border was too close," Alyosha continued. "Of course, you understand. We asked them many times to move it back and we offered them a piece of land three times larger in exchange, but they would not agree. Naturally, we had to defend ourselves. Now we have very good relations with the Finns."

I suspected the Finns had a different interpretation, but it was not for me to say. I was unsure of Alyosha's stance in matters of dogma.

Kolya, driving, wanted to know what Alyosha had just said. Alyosha translated back into Russian.

"*Finniye khoroshiye rebyata,*" Kolya commented. The Finns are good guys.

By what mysterious arrangement had he consented to be our driver? Kolya made jokes as we drove, but I couldn't follow such rapid Russian, and I had no way of knowing if the jokes were funny. From time to time he threw back his head of curls and uttered an odd, gargling laugh. Alyosha translated something about Kolya getting drunk one night with his cousin the *gaii* captain and taking his car for a swim. I glanced through the window at the Finnish Gulf glittering between the trees. This was inconceivable—such recklessness with the *gaii* about, and everyone said it took years to save enough money for a car in Russia.

Because of my weak language I'd hardly spoken to Kolya, Vyetta, or Volodya. Vyetta and I were reduced to making amiable noises at one another in the back seat. I understood only that she admired my earrings. They were fake gold shell shapes, bought for two dollars on a New York sidewalk the day before I left home. Vyetta's own earrings were real gold and set with light blue semiprecious stones. Every woman on the metro wore a pair equally authentic. Walking home from classes once, I saw a female laborer pushing a barrow of rubble and joking with a male coworker. She was covered with masonry dust, but under her kerchief, diamond pendant earrings lit the damp street with an eerie light. Vyetta said she liked mine because they were "the new style."

Vyetta reached forward to wipe a smudge of grease from Kolya's cheek with a licked finger, a strangely intimate gesture for another man's wife. Alyosha didn't seem perturbed. When Galya and Alyosha had come to the hotel to pick me up, they said that Kolya's car had broken down a few blocks away. I wondered if he was faking, unwilling to pull his car up in front of my KGB-infested hotel.

We had stood around watching while Kolya worked over the engine. I tried to tell him in Russian that I used to have a car and even worked on it myself (well, I had changed the oil once), but the car died. Kolya laughed at my idiomatic use of the word "died," impossible for a machine in Russian. I couldn't understand a word of his reply; all that registered was Kolya's strong-boned face, that smudge of grease, something eager in his eyes, and the wall of language between us. Now I was left to discussing points of English usage with Galya in the back seat. When I leaned forward, attempting to join the Russian conversation, Galya impatiently demanded, "Speak English please."

We bumped off the highway onto a dirt road lined with small pastel-hued wooden houses with elaborate carved trim. We stopped in front of one; no explanations. Alyosha and Kolya exited and disappeared around the corner of the house. Vyetta, Volodya, Galya, and I got out to stretch our cramped legs. Both Galya and Vyetta were wearing dresses—Galya in her typical dull browns, Vyetta in a smart red plaid jumper she'd sewn herself from *importivnii* wool. We lit cigarettes, and Volodya removed a box of chocolates that had been rattling behind our heads in the storage well. Across the dirt road a small spotted dog barked frantically in a yard. I tried to make a dumb joke about the dog sensing a capitalist invader. A calico cat ran out and crouched under the ticking Zhighuli, in the universal language of cats seeking warmth.

I liked it there on the dirt road in the midst of trees, away from the orderly rows of stone facades and courtyards and the blocks of postwar housing complexes. It reminded me of the slightly run-down clusters of wooden "camps" and cottages that line the shores of Maine and New Hampshire lakes. There were no troops of soldiers walking by, no gaggles of long-coated policemen on corners. Just a solitary *babushka* in rubber boots who scolded us in passing for talking too loud, for being young and laughing in the quiet street.

The men reappeared, and we piled back into the car. Perhaps they'd stopped to pick up batteries; a large boom box emerged from between Alyosha's feet, and soon we were zipping along on the highway again, beating time to Western tunes. I leaned forward and tried to translate the lyrics of American and British pop into my bad Russian. What a sense of power! Even Galya and Alyosha, with their years of language institutes, could not decipher the words.

Mick Jagger wailed, and I translated, "I am not satisfied."

"Speak English!" Galya commanded. "And I will tell them in Russian."

The Finnish Gulf curved in and out of the trees on our left. Again I felt that sense of burgeoning freedom at the sight of open water, the diminishing of the Soviet boundaries. I couldn't say that, but I wanted to share something of what I felt, so I addressed Kolya, the seaman.

"*Ya lyublyu morye*—I love the sea. That's why I love Leningrad, because there's water everywhere. Kolya, did I tell you that I worked on boats too?"

I had at the drunken party on November 7, but I'd forgotten.

"We are both seamen," Kolya said, and laughed. As if in response to my rhapsody, Kolya turned the car off the road and parked in a sandy opening between fir trees. We piled out and walked down to the beach. I dipped my booted toe in the dark water, suddenly elated. Was that Finland visible across the water, so close, or merely a bank of clouds? It looked like Maine, the dark firs and gray water, and I felt, for the first time in months, at home. A couple of *babushki* appeared, marching energetically along the beach, gripping the mittened hands of bundled children. But it was cold, and we had seen the gulf, so it was back into the car again.

Our next stop took us off the main road, up a hill through dachas in what looked like a health resort. Joggers huffed by, serious in their royal blue warm-up suits. Kolya stopped to ask directions, backed the car and made another turn. We parked in the midst of birch trees in front of a small wooden A-frame with a deck. The weak sun had disappeared into general overcast. Inside it was dark but cozy. A bar stretched along the back wall. A few wooden tables filled the small room. The only other customers were a pair of men in dark turtlenecks and broad-visored caps, the kind that workmen wore at home during the thirties. They sipped cognac and looked relaxed in a way I hadn't seen in the crowded city cafés.

Over our table hung a moth-eaten stag's head. The legendary gravel-voiced balladeer Vysotsky filled the café with a lament; one wall was a shrine of Vysotsky portraits. "He spoke for us," Alyosha said. "He spoke the truth. Thousands of people went to his funeral." Alyosha and Kolya and Volodya returned from the bar with coffee and snifters of cognac for us. The chocolates reappeared on the table. Only Kolya didn't drink; as our driver, Galya explained, he had to remain sober because the penalties for drinking and driving were stiff. I wasn't ready to drink so early in the day, but I acquiesced, made agreeably passive by my passenger status, by the fact that this trip had its own mysterious itinerary and I was clearly along for the ride. The cognac burned my throat.

"This song," Galya said, "is about the horrors of war. All Russians, you know, are against war, we've suffered so."

The cognac soured in my mouth. Galya had cornered the market on suffering once again.

"In my institute," she said, "we had one girl from Vietnam. She could not bear the sound of the English language because of the terrible things the Americans did to her country." Galya looked skyward with that infuriating gesture.

"It was a very bad time and a very bad war," I intoned. "Many people in my country protested that war, including me." Damn her, putting me in the position of defending something I had no desire to defend.

"Drink your cognac," Alyosha urged, reading the dismay on my face.

Across the wooden plank table, Kolya sipped his coffee silently, listening to the incomprehensible English attentively, head cocked.

I reminded myself that Galya was only twenty-three, had never been out of her country, and must have no idea how she sounded. To change the subject and perhaps to taunt her, I offered that my brother and his wife now lived in England and that I intended to visit them on my way home. The idea of flitting from Russia to England to America sounded alien even to me.

"I do so wish to travel," Galya said wistfully. "To London perhaps. In our school we once had a visiting teacher from Britain. Unfortunately he was a *fascist*." Galya hissed the horrible, fascinating word. "Of course, our director saw this immediately and warned us not to listen to a word he said."

I sighed and tried to pick up the thread of the conversation shuttling back and forth between Alyosha, Volodya, Kolya, and Vyetta. I wondered what the two men in caps at the table behind ours thought of the English running between me and Galya. Did they understand, or was it foreign mumbo jumbo? So many times I'd swung around at the sound of foreign voices on New York streets, galvanized by curiosity. I saw the same reaction when I walked through Russian streets speaking English. Often I was only discussing my metro stop or where I'd eat; maybe the foreigners I'd heard at home were speaking of laundry or taxis. When I thought about this, I experienced a weird, fun-house feeling of disorientation: I was the foreigner inside the mystery of language/I was outside listening in. There was no solid ground, and the slippery change of perspective made my head swim. Maybe it was only the cognac working on my empty stomach.

When we left Kolya paid our bill. Outside the little café, a golden retriever puppy frolicked, nipping at my ankles and Vyetta's dress. Vyetta laughed at its antics. Why should I have been surprised that Russian puppies were as exuberant as the ones we had at home?

The road cut through the woods like a gash. Sandy raw banks, forks, dark trees. "*Kak doma*," I said, like at home. Like a college trip in an overcrowded car to someone's parent's summer home up north. Vyetta's shoulder touched mine. Galya giggled on Volodya's lap. Damp wool and warm breath, the incongruity of the Russian voices, the Rolling Stones on the tape player. The trees thinned out, and the land opened. We passed a collective farm: long wooden barns, pigs milling in mud, small wooden shacklike houses with pretty carved trim.

"What is life like here?" I asked Galya.

"Quite all right," she answered quickly. "The people have everything they need, even television."

Along with TV antennae, the houses were blessed with outhouses—so they had no running water. Grisha had told me that everyone wanted to live in the city; the village people had to travel long distances to shop in Moscow or Leningrad. I didn't press the point.

We passed through more New England forest, then the trees broke open, revealing an expanse of lawn, substantial stone buildings and a train depot. Kolya pulled into the parking lot of a large rectangular box of a modern restaurant. There were no cars in the lot save ours and one Finnish tour bus.

"Now we will have something to eat," Galya said. "But first Kolya will go inside to make arrangements."

Why Kolya? Kolya traded his olive drab army jacket for a brown corduroy sport coat—very collegiate. I was pleased by this bit of wizardry and asked him where he'd hid it.

Underneath, he gestured. When he hurried inside, I complimented his Western jacket to Galya, who replied dismissively, "Each to his own taste." Kolya returned. All was okay. Knowing how hard it was to get into Soviet restaurants, I wondered what influence or rubles he'd wielded. We trooped in and relinquished our overcoats, as required, at the checkroom. I was sorry that I'd dressed so casually in jeans. The women primped in front of the floor-length mirror in the entry. I hadn't gotten used to this Russian custom of public grooming—I was the sort who felt ashamed if another woman came into the ladies' room and caught me inspecting my face in the mirror.

The restaurant was cavernous and empty save for two tables of towheaded Finns, who stared as we came in. There was a major consultation over our seating arrangements, and then I was placed beside Kolya. Each woman, Galya explained, must have a man beside her to attend to the filling and refilling of glasses and plates.

Kolya ordered for us, bear meat all around, but he said he preferred beef as he'd had too much bear lately.

The vodka arrived in a glass carafe, to be washed down with a pale, pinkish juice. We toasted women, friendship, and the soul of the bear that had sacrificed for us. We began with *vitiminki*—cabbage salad—and thin slices of tongue, followed by the bear, which arrived in little metal casseroles laced with onion. It didn't taste wild, as I'd expected, but sweet and greasy and good. Kolya kept refilling my plate. I proposed a toast to Russian men, who were so charmingly attentive. I knew that the women did all the housework, but my feminism was sliding away to unregenerate romance. With Grisha I'd learned to like having doors opened for me, someone to carry my bag, to help me on with my coat, and to hold my elbow when crossing streets.

Volodya wanted to know if I remembered the hundred different Russian variants of "bottoms up" he'd tried to teach me at Alyosha's dinner. I'd forgotten them all and couldn't keep up when each one required that a glass of vodka be downed in one gulp.

"Don't listen to him," Galya warned. "He is soooo vulgar." She seemed pleased.

I pointed out that Russians and Americans ate bread in different styles. Even now, at our table, they each gripped a piece in their left hands, holding it aloft while eating.

"You are right," Alyosha said. "It was a means of identifying spies during the war. We love our bread," he added with a smile.

"And it is very good bread, much better than ours," I assured them.

The conversation turned to school, and I offered horror stories of wild New York city schoolkids who sat with their feet on the desks and even attacked their teachers.

"It is the same here," Alyosha asserted. "You have seen only the best students in the best school, but in the village is a different story. The students get up and walk out of class."

Surprised by his honesty, I wondered if Galya might not report this indiscretion. I could feel Kolya beside me, alert but cut off by our English. Since we were discussing schools, I registered my one complaint. A teacher named Irina was driving me mad with her belligerent questions. The same kinds of questions Galya would have been asking if I worked with her classes at School 185.

Irina was a troublesome, attractive woman who wore her blonde hair in a French twist, a Doris Day lookalike. But she had no "que sera" attitude. She often cornered me during the breaks between classes to harangue me, accusing me of calling on all the kids in the class in an attempt to expose Soviet weakness.

"Don't worry about her," Alyosha instructed. "She is that way with everyone. It is nothing about you. She makes us miserable at school. She is even more bad-tempered now since she must take half my classes."

Alyosha's broken leg kept him from working, but it didn't seem to stop him from getting around on these outings. Russia's employee benefits system was hard to understand—excessively long sick leaves but no substitute teachers when one fell ill, just other workers doing double shifts.

My words about Irina would probably get back to school, and perhaps the woman would be reprimanded for making a bad impression, but at the moment I didn't care. My first denunciation! The vodka was having its way. At some point, when I hadn't been watching, the Finns had disappeared. Everything seemed to be occurring in an old movie—a series of jerky scenes. We were at the table, we were getting our coats, we were back in the car. Kolya remained behind to pay. What was the source of his endless funds? Would Alyosha and Volodya settle with him later? Why was he our host?

We were driving south at a good pace, cheerful, an open bottle passing between the front and back seats, when suddenly Kolya veered off the road and bumped to a stop.

"*Gaii*," Galya said.

Alyosha turned off the tape player and hid the bottle.

Kolya got out and walked back to the police car. I panicked, sober immediately. I imagined myself caught in some breach of law, yanked out of the car, my documents examined, dragged away. This wasn't a joke. These were *Soviet* police.

"What's the matter?" I whispered.

"Don't worry," Alyosha said. "You worry too much."

Kolya returned. He was laughing. He turned the key, and we drove away.

"What happened? What was it?" I begged, craning around to see the *gaii* car pull away in the other direction.

"Galya forgot to hide," Alyosha said. "Kolya gave him three rubles, and it was all settled."

Galya stared out the car window. "We do not have bribes in the Soviet Union," she intoned, "but sometimes a little something helps."

We stopped at the beach we'd visited before lunch. We finished the vodka bottle, Kolya still abstaining, and Alyosha planted it in sand. The wind was blowing stronger now, and only a few hardy beach walkers remained. I was numb to the cold, thoroughly drunk. Volodya pulled my floppy maroon cashmere beret over my eyes and laughed. I displayed the holes in the fingertips of my matching cashmere gloves. The holes amazed me. I should have chosen sturdier wool. Kolya wandered away to the edge of the gray water while the rest of us began to dance. Soon we were dancing in a circle around the vodka bottle. Winded from months of too many cigarettes, I flopped in the sand.

Alyosha grinned above me. "What do you think of such behavior? Responsible teachers dancing on a beach? Remember the night you came to our house? After you went home, Vyetta and I stayed up all night drinking at the dormitory and on through the next day too."

What I thought was: Grisha wouldn't be doing this. He'd copied his beloved Brits too well. Only in regard to sex did he play like a Russian.

Kolya came back and looked into my face—a wordless measuring—but said nothing. Someone was chiding me for sitting on the cold sand, so I sat on my tote bag, squashing the private stash of toilet paper that I carried with me everywhere in Russia. My shoes and coat pockets were full of sand. I could have sat on this windy beach staring out over the gulf and never gone home. I didn't want to go home anymore. In New York I was always in the company of women, rarely men. New York men and women didn't know how to be with each other anymore. They didn't know how to have fun, not like Russians. To hell with Grisha and his contempt for the Russian Soul. I wanted this.

We were back in the car, waiting for Kolya to buy juice at a store in the village where we'd stopped earlier in the day; we had to have juice to wash down more vodka. Several vodka bottles appeared out of Kolya's trunk. We drove to what looked like a deserted boatyard, bumped down a rutted dirt road and came to a stop at the edge of a river. There was no wind here, just silence and dark placid water lined by leafless trees, a tiny spit of a beach. Alyosha set the tape player on the dead brown grass. Kolya handed me shots of vodka followed by over-sweet Bulgarian tomato juice. The red juice ran over my sticky gloves, in through the holes at the tips. Kolya proffered a blue glass jar of tiny salted fish. They looked like minnows, or bait, and I shook my head, unwilling to taste them. Galya chided me for refusing a delicacy.

"You know what I love most in the world?" Alyosha asked me.

"What?"

"Tomato juice!"

We drank so many shots I felt dizzy and sat down on the embankment. Kolya appeared with the back seat of his car; he'd removed it for me to sit on. It was an act of chivalry of the highest order, and I started to laugh. Galya sat down beside me and sidled close.

"Is it true that in your country the women only receive 60 percent of the salaries of men?"

Oh, god, yes, it might be so in certain cases. How could I explain something so complicated as no central planning? "It isn't a policy," I explained, "but employers set salaries as they wish beyond the minimum wage." Really, this was too much to bear now, and I broke my rule of never pointing a finger back. "You know, this is a problem of women everywhere," I proclaimed. "Everywhere men have more power than women. On the Anniversary of the Great October Socialist Revolution, I saw so many placards of Politburo members, and not one woman's face!"

"But we have many directors of institutes that are women," Galya countered.

"So do we. But everywhere men have more power than women. Alyosha, isn't that true?"

Alyosha was dancing with a vodka bottle. "You women will have to settle this yourselves," he said.

Nothing would be settled with Galya. I got up to dance with Alyosha and Volodya. It had begun to rain, but nobody cared. The silence settled in with the rain. Only the tinny taped music disturbed the peace. My shoes sucked mud, and my hat soaked through. Volodya bent me back, pretending he was going to push me into the river.

When I sat down again Galya informed me that Kolya had suffered all day watching us drink. He wanted us to go to his house, where he could join us, and we could take the train back to the city.

Kolya's house turned out to be the place where we'd stopped for batteries this morning. This morning? It felt like days ago. I'd never been in a Russian house before, just apartments. At Kolya's there was a rickety gate, junk piled in the yard, a sailboat under a tarp. I saw people through a window as we passed the main porch stairs and went around to a side entrance. Galya helped me over the mud.

"You see, Laurie, Volodya is my second husband," she confided. (How could this be, when she was only twenty-three?) "My first husband, well, it did not work out. We were both virgins, and it was not good for us in bed. But Volodya. I fell in love with him on a train to Riga. I knew I loved him the moment he made me laugh."

I supposed the vodka had prompted this sudden confession, this un-characteristic girl talk. I nodded dumbly.

We climbed wooden stairs and passed through a heavy door covered in the ubiquitous black, quilted vinyl. I was given worn slippers to wear when I removed my wet shoes. Inside there was an anteroom and a small chamber that had been converted into a dining room for our ar-rival. Clearly we'd been expected: a long table filled the narrow space, pulled up in front of a couch. I couldn't believe we'd have to eat again, but the table was laden with baskets of *piroshki,* plates of bread dotted with caviar, sausage, and metal pans of horrible-looking jellied meat in aspic.

I examined the room: the same print beige wallpaper I'd seen at Natasha's and Tanya's. The requisite breakfront and wardrobe. A calen-dar with a nude pin-up from Italy. Carvings of boats, a pirate's face. An icon hung, surprisingly, over the couch/bed. On a desk in a corner stood a portrait of an angelic child with folded hands: Kolya's son, Anatoly.

"Kolya is a good father," Vyetta assured me. "He visits his son often and brings him everything."

"What do you bring him?" I addressed Kolya.

"Caviar, sausage," Kolya replied.

"Caviar?" I knew how hard it could be to obtain such goods. "You bring him caviar? At home, the parents eat the special food and the children eat the rest. Why caviar?"

"He likes it," Kolya said.

What a remarkable idea—to give children the best!

I sat down at the couch. Between the plates of food a small slide viewer and box of slides had been set out for perusal. I began to realize what all this was about as I flipped through the slides: Kolya on his sail-boat, arms stretched raising a sail, standing on deck against a back-ground of firs and sea. The slides didn't seem so much an act of vanity as Kolya, knowing he had little time and few chances, presenting him-self.

"*Kracivii paren*—a handsome fellow," I commented politely to Galya, offering her the box of slides. Galya shrugged.

Kolya stood beside me, distracted, checking to see that we had everything we needed, that all the bottles of vodka and champagne were in place. He looked comically worried—the good host.

"*Sadees,*" I offered. Have a seat.

"And who will do everything?" Kolya asked.

"Everything is fine. Sit."

Kolya sat beside me. "My mama made the *piroshki* fresh. Do you like them?"

In answer, I nibbled one and proclaimed its deliciousness.

Alyosha put a record on the stereo. After toasts, we got up to dance. Everyone urged me to eat and drink.

"I love red caviar," I demurred, "but I just can't eat anymore."

"But you must," Galya insisted. "How can you refuse caviar? At least lick it off the bread!"

The table was already a ruin of half-eaten piroshki, bread crusts, overturned glasses, and dirty plates. Kolya had been drinking quickly to catch up with us. Soon he was standing with an arm around Alyosha. "My brother Alyosha," he declared in English. His voice sounded strange and awkward in a foreign tongue. "Alyosha *bolshoi* bandeet," Kolya exclaimed, squeezing Alyosha's neck. "Beeg bandeet!"

"You speak English, Kolya?" I inquired.

"No, no. Only beachspeak."

"What?"

"Beachspeak." He switched back into Russian. "The words a sailor learns on the beach." Then heavily accented English: "Viskey. Vooman. My love."

I laughed. "Kolya, did I tell you I worked on a fishing boat?" Somewhere, far away I knew I was repeating myself but couldn't help it.

"What kind of work is that for a woman?" Alyosha complained. "A woman is not strong enough for such work."

"But I am strong," I insisted, flexing a bicep to prove it, though I knew it was a ridiculous gesture. When I'd told Grisha that I'd fished and done construction work he had been shocked. "You must have terrible parents to let you work like that," he said. The intelligentsia held themselves above labor, which was for peasants. There was no way to explain that in a country where women my mother's age and social station often didn't work at all, construction work had seemed like an accomplishment. Of course, it made no sense here where women regularly swept the streets and hauled cement.

Galya stage-whispered, "We really are stronger than the men but we pretend not to be for their sake."

"The women are talking too much," Alyosha pronounced.

"Kolya says that intelligent women are dangerous because they attract like a magnet," Galya translated.

The record played gypsy music, a whirl of violins and then a sobbing, crooning voice.

"Kolya says he has gypsy blood," Galya translated.

"*Ya tsigan*—I am gypsy! I see everything!" Kolya shouted drunkenly.

I realized that he reminded me of Neal Cassidy, the model for Dean Moriarty in Kerouac's *On the Road*. He was slighter and had moments of silence, unlike Cassidy, but they shared the same Adonis profile, quick movements, rapid banter, and driving skills.

The women headed to the outhouse together. The air smelled fresh: firs and a whiff of the gulf. But Vyetta was too drunk and stumbled and fell. Galya and I had to support her back to the house.

"Alyosha!" we shouted. "Come take care of your wife!" Alyosha put Vyetta into Kolya's car to sleep off the booze in the cold. Volodya was making incomprehensible speeches. The only word I could catch was *Kommunisti*. He was shouting epithets at Communists, while Galya kept trying to shush him. Alyosha held the bottle to his lips. Kolya pulled me off the couch and danced me into another room. Then he was kissing my hair, my throat, my mouth. Surprised, I felt nothing but confusion. Where was Galya? Had she seen? Why was he kissing me when we'd hardly spoken five words to each other all day?

"Am I pleasing to you?" Kolya inquired, the Russian construction for "do you like me?"

"*Koneshno.*" Of course.

"Why of course?" He sounded disappointed.

Of course, because he'd been such a good host, but I couldn't think of the word for host in Russian. Of course, because I didn't know what else to say. I could've said, "as a friend," but I didn't want to insult him. I didn't even know him. He was just some wild man with a car who called his friend a "*bolshoi* bandeet" and spent a lot of money on us. But I could feel the imprint of his hand on my hair, the vodka I'd been drinking for hours and hours, and I knew I could fall into his touch— the touch that Grisha had prepared me for. But where was Galya? Wouldn't she write some kind of report? I was a guest in her country; I had an official reputation to maintain.

Kolya grabbed my hand, led me to a book-laden desk. "See? My books." He simplified his Russian to make me understand. "I read all the time. I love to read." He gestured to the wall, where books ran floor to ceiling on shelves. His voice was full of urgency. In between the volumes of Pushkin, Chekhov, Hemingway, Twain, there were shells, driftwood, African carvings, curios from his seaman's trips. "Everything here I did for you today. My mama made the food for you. For *my girl*." The last two words were in English and jarred. His girl?

"At Alyosha's house I liked you the moment I saw you. I wanted to see you again, but what could I do? It took time to arrange an opportunity. I had to ask Alyosha to help."

Galya peered in through the door. Kolya stopped midsentence. Chastened, we headed back into the other room. I danced with Volodya, then Alyosha, while Kolya and Galya whispered together furiously in the anteroom. They were dancing now, but something looked wrong. They didn't move together. Kolya pushed her about like a wheelbarrow; Galya's back was stiff. Vyetta reappeared, sober and moaning that her hands had frozen. Kolya wrapped her in a sheepskin yanked off a chair. Volodya, who'd been dancing with Alyosha because I wouldn't dance with him anymore, stumbled against the stereo. The record squawked.

"Vladimir!" Galya shrieked. "Oi!"

Volodya tried to pull her up to dance, but she slapped away his hands. He stumbled against the dressing table, knocking bottles of cologne to the floor with a crash. A horrible wave of imported cologne filled the room. Galya was furious.

"Earlier you were praising our men," she said to me, "but now I am afraid they are proving you wrong."

Kolya grinned happily, waving it all away. He sat next to me on the couch, his fingers trailing under the neckline of my sweater. I was so drunk, so sleepy, at that moment I no longer cared about Galya or Grisha. I slid down and lay my head in Kolya's lap. From that angle, his nose looked fat and funny.

"Sleep," he crooned to me in Russian. "Sleep."

He leaned down to kiss me, and I could taste on his tongue the peculiar flavor of jellied meat from the aspics his mother had made. Perhaps I did sleep for a moment. I woke to hear Vyetta and Galya worrying over our train. We'd miss the last train to Leningrad if we didn't hurry. Galya looked frightened. Here I was, her responsibility, and everything was sliding out of her control. The thought amused me, then I remembered that I was slated to give a lecture to 150 teachers at Galya's mother's pedagogical institute in the morning. It was so late now, and I'd had so much to drink I was sure I'd be sick in the morning and botch it. I sat up fast and reached for a pitcher of water. Galya and Vyetta were drinking water too but Alyosha and Volodya were drunk beyond recall. They danced with each other, shouting and stumbling.

It seemed like another hour before Volodya and Alyosha were bundled back into their hats and coats. Galya and I waited outside in the sobering cold. "There is something wrong with Kolya," Galya remarked, turning her eyes to the overcast night sky.

"What do you mean?" I begged, contrite. "Something wrong in general, or just now?"

"In general."

"What do you mean?"

"I don't know." Galya sighed meaningfully. "I only know that there is something very wrong with Kolya."

"Maybe he is just lonely." I wanted to disassociate myself from what had taken place—the image of me lying in Kolya's lap, his fingers under my sweater—to make myself innocent again in her eyes.

Then Vyetta, Alyosha, and Kolya appeared. Kolya took my arm and led me ahead of the others. I couldn't see anything but the ruts in front of my feet.

"All of these houses," Kolya said, but I couldn't understand what he was saying. "They will not be here. There will be big houses. . . ."

I mistook the word for houses, *doma,* for lady, *dama.* I thought he was speaking of big ladies.

Kolya said, "You know what means *bulldozer*?"

Then I got it. All of these hand-built wooden houses, with their many-paned windows, their decorative trim, would be bulldozed to make way for new high rises. But why here, on top of these beautiful houses, when there was so much open land between here and Leningrad?

"Where will you live, Kolya?"

"In my car."

"You can't live in your car."

"I will live in my car."

Behind us we heard yelps and cursing. Alyosha had fallen and pulled Vyetta down with him into the mud. Rolling Stones tapes and imported wool aside, they had a Russian affinity for mud. It called to them, and they answered. The station lay ahead. I could see the lights of the *elek-*

trichka, the electric train, platform. Alyosha and Vyetta arrived, smeared with earth. Kolya pulled me under the light of a lamppost and scribbled his number.

"You will call me," he commanded.

"Kolya, I don't even know you. We haven't even talked."

"I know you. I am *Tsigan*—gypsy. I can tell everything from your face."

"No. It takes a long time to know someone."

"I know you. You are intelligent, good, pretty. I see everything in your face. You will call."

"But aren't you afraid?" I glanced around for Galya.

"I'm afraid of nothing. Fear is worse than death."

"Kolya, my Russian is so bad we won't be able to talk."

"One week with me and you will speak. I'll be your teacher. Call me. The night time is best."

"Yes," I said, to hush him, but I didn't mean it. The train was coming. Kolya tore the paper with his number out of a notebook and stuffed it into my coat pocket. He kissed me as the train pulled in. Alyosha, Vyetta, Galya, Volodya, and I bumbled into the train car. The door snapped shut, and we left Kolya behind.

The nearly empty train glittered with fluorescent lights and chrome. We took seats on facing benches, Alyosha and Volodya on the ends. Twice Volodya fell off the bench onto the floor.

"Oi, Volodya," Galya cautioned, but she no longer sounded angry. I was on my way back to the city, safe from danger, and she was back in control. Now she spoke to her drunken husband with the annoyed but forgiving tone of a mother indulging a naughty child. Vyetta slept peacefully with her head against the window, her pretty plaid jumper covered in mud. As Galya's mood improved, mine soured. I didn't want to lean against Alyosha's spattered parka. I grew angry when Alyosha and Volodya insisted on lighting cigarettes in the no-smoking section. I feared the appearance of a guard. In a few hours I'd have to get up to organize my lecture and I felt terrible already.

Alyosha turned to me. "Why didn't you talk to me when I came to school last week?" His voice was petulant.

"I couldn't. I waved to you through the door, but the ministry lady came to observe my class that day and I couldn't just jump up and leave her and run out in the hall. I thought I'd see you after she left, but she took me out for pastries."

"I understand," Alyosha said, but a moment later he began again. "Why didn't you talk to me when I came to school?"

Why was he harping on it? Then I realized he'd probably wanted to give me a message from Kolya, and failing that, Kolya had to arrange this outing, including Galya. I fingered Kolya's number in my pocket. I wouldn't call. What was the point? Who needed such problems? Wasn't it enough that I'd been through all that with Grisha? Kolya wasn't married, but what was the point when we didn't even speak the same language? I wasn't particularly attracted to him, and anyway, I would be leaving in a matter of weeks. To hell with them both, I thought grumpily, my hangover already beginning to take shape.

Everything Is Possible

My lecture to Galya's mother's institute was laughable. After what I considered a reasonably competent forty-minute presentation about current American literature, rescued from the dregs of my hangover, there was only one question from the mass of plump female students with unwashed hair: "Are you married?" Galya's mother, an imposing battleship blonde (how did slender Galya ever emerge from that piece of unbronzed Socialist Realist sculpture?), pronounced me "charming."

The next morning I hurried into the dreary little teachers' room for a quick between-class smoke. The single window was opened to drain the clouds of foul smoke from the men's *papirosi*—unfiltered harsh tobacco in cardboard holders they clamped between their teeth, the cigarettes Alyosha favored. Galya came in and sat beside me on the battered couch. "Alyosha left his fur hat in Kolya's car," Galya said, looking skyward. "And today we had seven degrees of frost."

"Oh, no," I said sympathetically.

"No? You know that he did not?" Galya turned to me quickly.

"No. I don't know if he did or didn't. It's just an expression. You say "oh, no" when you hear something unpleasant or unfortunate. It doesn't mean anything."

Galya sat quietly, smoking her cigarette. "And guess who now has a broken heart?"

"Who?"

"Our Kolya." Galya waited for my response.

"That can't be helped," I said. Two other teachers came in, ending our conversation. She's sweating it, I thought. But I simply wanted the whole embarrassing picture of that evening at Kolya's to evaporate. Blame it on vodka, and forget it. I finished my fourth class and headed for another smoke in the teacher's lounge before facing the dreary streets. My chest already ached, and my teeth were developing dark stains near the gums from the rotten tobacco, but I couldn't stop.

The benches against the walls in the entry were filled with the afternoon's assortment of *babushki,* parents, and grandfathers come to pick up the smallest children after school. I saw them every day, waiting patiently while the children bundled back into their puffy coats and drew on their boots. There was a smell of damp wool, something like the odor of mushrooms, the solidity of the bodies filling the hall. Striding past, I noticed one man who glanced up at me with a serious, thoughtful expression. Nice-looking, I thought, and hurried on into the lounge. When I came out again he rose from the bench, and I recognized Kolya.

"You didn't call," he said reproachfully, "so I came."

"What about Galya?" I glanced around nervously.

Kolya waved a hand dismissively. "Forget Galya."

After an entire day of teaching English, I could barely summon Russian words to respond. "*Palto,*" I said, overcoat, meaning let me get my coat.

"I'll be waiting," Kolya said.

I stumbled over good-byes to Tatiana Nikolaevna's secretary while I nabbed my coat and hat as quickly as I could. I wanted us to get out of there, to someplace safer, where I could figure out what this meant. He'd come for me, risked making his intentions public, here where such connections were dangerous.

Kolya took my elbow and led me past the pensioners, past the stairwell. I glanced up in time to see Galya, stopped in midflight, watching us, mouth opened in a startled "O."

Outside, in the autumn drizzle, two soldiers walked down the sidewalk, a pail of red paint suspended between them from a broom handle. I imagined the pail tipping, the paint spreading over the sidewalk, a crimson Soviet tide marking our passage. Nothing happened. One of the soldiers threw a cigarette butt onto the wet sidewalk. Kolya unlocked the door to his car, and I got in.

"This is crazy," I said in my stilted Russian. "I can't even speak your language."

"No problem. I will be your teacher."

Out of the corner of my eye I saw Kolya's square red hands on the leather-wrapped steering wheel, and dangling from the ignition a key chain with tacky plastic American dollars. I could smell his cologne, sense the shape of his shoulder beside mine, the hard angle of his cheek. Who was he? What did he want?

Maybe this was all some kind of setup? Yet there was a relief to his simple sureness; unlike Grisha, he didn't talk endlessly about what he wanted, he took control. Exhausted, I was ready to be led.

"Where are we going?" I asked.

"*Pryamo.* Straight ahead."

Kolya pulled out into the afternoon traffic: little white and black Zhiguli and Moskvich sedans (there seemed no other colors), green army trucks, and rusty orange produce vans. I sensed that if I looked hard enough through the car window, I would see myself moving among the shoppers, following my lone route to my hotel past the bleak windows filled with cans and fading political posters. I saw myself wandering at the edge of the crowds, safe and correct, while another incarnation sat beside Kolya, about to be swept away. When we turned a corner, the first Laurie kept walking.

"I have to return to work," Kolya said, enunciating his Russian words slowly and clearly. "What are you doing tonight?"

"I don't know." I fumbled for another cigarette. Kolya's ashtray was filled with coins—he was the rare Russian who didn't smoke.

"On the floor," Kolya said, indicating my ashes. "You smoke too much. Tonight, I want to see you. I work until nineteen."

"When?"

"Seven. Seven in the evening. I will come for you at seven-thirty, okay?"

I shrugged. We approached my hotel. Kolya didn't pull up in front but turned the corner and parked. "There," he said, pointing to a corner. "Wait for me there. Seven-thirty." He traced the numbers on his dashboard clock. I nodded, and Kolya leaned across the seat to kiss my cheek. Then I was standing on the sidewalk. Shoppers pushed by, intent on their search. I wasn't eager for this meeting, but it was as though I had no choice. My will had become a small, weak thing in the face of Kolya's decision. I didn't want to make decisions anymore.

At seven-thirty I was shivering on the corner. I felt guilty and afraid, as though my mind were readable and everyone, or at least one of the stone-faced guards at my hotel, knew I was a foreigner standing there waiting for a Russian man. At seven-forty I crossed the street. Maybe I'd misunderstood his Russian and this wasn't the right corner? Or he'd changed his mind? Soldiers lingered. People lined up in front of the pay phones. Shoppers carrying their eternal plastic bags trudged by. I watched a couple meet, embrace. Women gripped the arms of their men. I started back across the wide Nevsky on the crosswalk, nervous now, uncertain. How much easier it would have been to just stay inside, out of this cold and dark. But I'd just spent forty-five minutes trying on my meager supply of sweaters, skirts, and pants, fussing in front of the mirror in my room.

I moved along with the rest of the surging crowds. Halfway across Nevsky a man addressed me in unintelligible Russian. I turned to see a grinning Kolya. There he was, following me, making a joke of my fears. I felt instantly charmed. His was the only smiling face in the midst of grim shoppers.

Kolya took my arm and led me to his car, parked on the opposite side, two wheels up on the curb. I felt like some large package, being moved about, drawn into the machine and into the stream of traffic.

"Eleven," I said. What was that, twenty-three hours? I pointed to the dashboard clock. "I must be back by eleven."

"No problem."

"Where are we going?"

"Whatever you wish. A film? A café?"

"I will not understand a film. The language. . . . We could walk around."

"First we will drive. We will see the city."

"I must make a phone call at eight-thirty." I'd promised to call Sasha Ivanov to set up our next meeting.

"There are phones everywhere," Kolya said.

"I brought you a gift." I pulled a paperback Russian/English dictionary out of my bag. "So we can talk. We will not be two, but three. You, me, and the dictionary."

Kolya laughed and kissed my cheek. "*Molodyetz.*"

"How is your work?" I didn't know exactly what it was he did for a living.

"Good," Kolya said flatly. "It is necessary to say good, even when things are not good."

"I don't agree," I said, an American Pollyanna, self-righteous and put off by his sentiment. "It is better to be honest."

Kolya shrugged.

I didn't know where we were. Streets, crowds, light on damp pavement flashed by. We crossed several of the city's innumerable bridges, over canals with wrought iron lampposts and carved statuary, past the magnificent grillwork on the gates of the Summer Gardens, where Kolya said he liked to read during his lunch breaks. Then we veered into a side street.

"I've got to stop," Kolya said. "Just for a minute, to bring some things to my son. I'll be very quick." He parked and left me sitting in the car. Somewhere above me, in a warm, lit apartment, Kolya was greeting his son who lived with his *babushka*. And, perhaps, his ex-wife. Alone in the car I felt uneasy. What was I doing there? What would *they* think, whoever *they* were, if they knew I was sitting down here, the other woman, the American?

Kolya jogged toward me. I wondered if his son cried, if he begged him to stay.

"How is he?" I asked when Kolya climbed in.

"Cheerful," Kolya said. "He is always cheerful. I bring him a big sausage, and by the end of the day he has eaten the whole thing. A piece here, there, and it is gone."

Again we were on the road. Whenever I wanted to find a word in the dictionary, Kolya pulled over to open the door for the light. Each time he took out a pencil and seriously, carefully underlined the word and its explanation. I offered my pen.

"I use only pencil," Kolya said. "I was a navigator. Navigators use only pencils." He underlined a word he said was very important: *gorizant*—horizon. I grew seasick from the jerky stop and go. We stopped once more to fill a container with gasoline for a friend of his, and again to buy me cigarettes. Kolya paid for them.

"Kolya," I said, shaping the Russian words with difficulty, imagining how stilted I must sound, "there is one thing I don't understand. Why people cannot travel freely from your country." False naïveté—I wanted to sound him out.

Kolya pulled over. "Look. I was a seaman. I have been everywhere, and I know that life is hard everywhere. But there are young people who do not know this, who think life is better somewhere else." He opened his palms. "So."

"But if they were allowed to go see for themselves that life is hard elsewhere, they would come back," I dissembled. "So why not let them see?"

Kolya shook his head. "I don't like to discuss politics. I like to be cheerful."

"Cheerful? Then you have the wrong woman. I am very serious. At home I am more cheerful, but here everything is new, and I want to understand."

Kolya veered back onto the road. "That is natural. When I traveled, I never drank in other countries. I was careful." I remembered Grisha's words about the KGB always accompanying them when they traveled, and how people informed on one another. That was probably true for seamen too. The discussion was closed, and I was dissatisfied with Kolya's answer, although he had no reason to trust me with his views.

It was time to make my call. Kolya parked before a pay phone, gave me a two-kopeck piece from his pocket. He sat in the car reading while I dialed Sasha and set up a meeting for the next night. When I came back to the car, Kolya said he had to make a call too. There were two phones, but Kolya used the one I'd used, and I was struck by paranoia. Perhaps he was tracing my call? Sasha was nervous about our contact and made me promise I'd call only from pay phones, something I already knew, just as I'd been warned not to tell one Russian friend about another. I glanced at the book Kolya was reading: *Mallarme* in Russian translation. Was that his usual reading, or something he'd brought along to impress me? Who was he, appearing in my life all of a sudden? What kind of a setup might this be? When he returned to the car I was stiff, distant.

"You are afraid of me," Kolya said.

"Why did you call when I called?"

Kolya laughed. "I called my mama to tell her I would not be home until late. She said I should sleep at my grandmother's tonight. My grandmother lives in the center. You're so afraid."

"Yes, of everything. I don't know who you are."

"I am a man." Kolya grinned. "A *leetle* one," he added, using the English word. "Nobody." He kissed my cheek. We drove across another bridge and parked near the Neva embankment, where a schooner, the *Kronverk*, had been converted to a nightclub. Two drunks reeled in front of the tethered ship.

"*Piyaniye*," I said, showing off my knowledge of the word for "drunks."

"I worked on a ship like this when I was training," Kolya said.

"I saw the photograph on your wall."

"You see everything."

It was cold out on the walkway that led across another bridge to the Peter-Paul Fortress. Kolya put his arm around me and led me alongside the tall brick walls that had held cells for pre-revolutionary prisoners. The tall golden spire was lit by floodlights, but the place looked abandoned.

"Is it all right to go in at night?" I fretted.

"We'll see."

We peered through windows. Again I was being led, pushed, shown, just as I was when gripped by large official women who led me on cultural tours. I liked the feel of Kolya's grip on my arm, although it felt awkward to be walking along with this strange little rooster of a man no taller than I. Nobody came to chase us away. Maybe he was just as he said, a man. A man who liked me, who wanted to see me, nothing more. Why did I have to turn everything into a problem, into a KGB thriller? But he wasn't that simple—one moment he'd be grinning, the next moment remote and serious, as though lost in some private calculation.

Back in the car Kolya asked, "Have you seen the Hermitage?"

"Not yet."

"Oh, they are bad at your school. They make you work and show you nothing. I will show you everything. Do you know where we are now?"

I identified the streets correctly.

"You see a lot; you remember," Kolya said. He started the engine.

"Now where?" I asked.

"Come to my place, come to me until morning," he whispered, the words soft and seductive in Russian: *Priyezhai kmne do ootra.*

"I can't."

Kolya parked the car beside a lovely canal, the Fontanka. A slight drizzle fell against the windshield. When a pedestrian passed close, I froze with apprehension, guilty as a teenager in a lover's lane.

"Kolya, remember when we went to dance on the night of Alyosha's dinner?"

"Of course I remember."

"I saw you take the . . ." but I didn't know the word for windshield wipers and had to point and pantomime. "I saw you take those things when we parked. Why, if there is no crime in the Soviet Union? At home, of course, we have terrible crime," I added quickly, "but here?" I vaguely realized that I must sound like Galya, like Irina, with their quarrelsome questions.

Kolya smiled. "Ah, you see everything. Of course we have crime. You are so clever; you see and understand without language. You know, Laurie, it is why I like you. There are very few intelligent women."

"How can you say that? There are very few intelligent people!" I was annoyed but flattered that he thought me intelligent, despite my baby language.

Kolya laughed. Stalemate. How could I expect him to share a more egalitarian American view? I resented and forgave him.

"What about your clothes and money?" I began again, much like the nagging Galya, but I needed to know who he was. "I do not believe it is from your job. You work in a store now. I know the salary of teachers. I don't believe you could have such clothes, jeans, caviar, a car on such a salary. How is it possible? Did you bring things back from seamen's trips to sell?"

Kolya smiled again, a close-mouthed smile. I was asking him to trust me far more than he'd asked me. I was asking him to tell who he really was. Kolya leaned back against the car door and turned to look at me. "I know you will not speak to anyone of such things," he said.

"Of course not."

He didn't explain further. "It is nice to see you without Galya," I offered.

"You don't like Galya?"

"I hate Galya."

Kolya laughed. "Galya is evil."

"Do you think she'll write a report about us?"

"She already did. Forget about Galya."

"You aren't afraid?"

"It's better to live one day well than a whole life badly."

An admirable sentiment, but his use of such fortune-cookie philosophy bothered me. Did he always speak in clichés and it was only my weak command of Russian that made me unable to tell?

"Why are *you* afraid?" Kolya asked.

"American propaganda," I said. "We're taught that the KGB is everywhere, following."

"*Erunda*," Kolya said.

"What?" We had to search for the word in the dictionary: Nonsense.

Kolya pointed to the dashboard clock. It had reached the eleven mark.

"Another hour will be okay," I relented.

Kolya said, "The day after the dinner at Alyosha's, I went to him. I couldn't call you. It took time to arrange. I thought only of you, Lora. When you didn't call, I came." Kolya kissed me, and I kissed back. I wanted this; I didn't know if I wanted him, but this, this warm giving in. When we drew apart I saw on the windshield that our breaths had condensed. He had a small cold sore on his lip, and I worried that it might be something I could catch. So many Russians had these sores, maybe the result of the communal glasses at the soda-water machines.

"You are *laskovaya*," he sighed.

"What?"

"Ah, another very important word." Kolya thrust the car door open with his foot to shed light and hunted for *laskovaya*. I imagined it meant something embarrassing, like passionate, hot-blooded.

"Don't show me; at hotel I will find."

At ten to midnight, Kolya dropped me off around the corner from the Baltiskaya so I could get in the door before they locked up.

"When can I see you?" he asked. "Tomorrow?"

"Tomorrow I'm busy." I'd arranged to meet Sasha Ivanov.

"Thursday?"

"Thursday is a big American holiday. Thanksgiving. I'm going to the American consulate for dinner."

"You have no time for me?"

"Friday."

"Friday. Seven." Kolya pointed to the clock, and then across the street. "That corner. You understand?"

Back in my room I found the word *laskovaya* in the back of a small Russian language text I'd brought with me. It meant affectionate. But lying in bed with the pleasant, modulated reassuring voice of the radio broadcaster droning on about American atrocities and Israeli murder in Lebanon, the Soviet Union's fight for peace, I felt anxious again. I weighed

the flavor of jellied meat in Kolya's mouth when we kissed the night of
the Baltic trip, and the cold sore on his lip, his ridiculous velour suit at
Alyosha's against the charm of his coming to school for me, his following me on the street. I didn't want Kolya to complicate my life. But I
craved his certainty, his joyful energy. The balance swung back and
forth like the creaking traffic lights strung across the street beyond my
balcony.

I walked Nevsky Prospekt in heartbreaking, oblique northern light.
Saint Isaac's Cathedral was on *remont,* though its gilded dome was visible through a web of scaffolding. The admiralty glittered with gold.
Russians took photos of each other beside the glorious bronze statues
of the taming of the wild horses on the Anichkov Bridge. This city was
undeniably beautiful, even if the former Kazan Cathedral now served
as the Museum of Religion and Atheism and displayed torture instru-
ments used by the Inquisition. Everywhere was *nyetu* (we don't have it)
and *nyelzya* (it's not allowed) and *defisitni* (deficit goods) and, I was beginning to discover, ways around them.

At a gathering at Sasha's, a sulky American exchange student reported of her mandatory group visit to Kiev, "I hated my trip, being
with Americans all the time. I'm always with Russians." I detected a
weird competitiveness, an attempt to assert her dominance in the number of Russian friends she possessed, the amount of language she knew.
I was too tired to speak Russian, annoyed by her *znayoo*—I know—in
response to everything I said. Sasha had invited two buddies, a short,
bearded troll named Petya, who was an engineer (like everyone, he
said), and Igor, a skinny chemist. Igor wanted to speak English with me,
but Petya drunkenly insisted, "Speak our language!" I was tired of
drunken men leaning on me. I was tired, period, but I had to wait for
the party to end before Sasha could accompany me back to my metro
stop. He wouldn't hear of my traveling alone.

"Here's your wallet, don't lose it," Sasha urged Petya tenderly before
Petya stumbled from the apartment. "Don't forget your hat."

The consulate served American turkey, flown in, for Thanksgiving
dinner. Russians raised their own turkeys on fish and thought it a food
unfit for human consumption. The consulate didn't *smell* like Russia,

an indefinable mustiness that collected in the hotel hallways and school halls and elevators, it smelled American, but I didn't want to be there in the plush, glossy dining room with its myriad electronic bugs and career bureaucrats.

A reporter seated across from me said, "We envy you because you can really get to know the people. We are always watched; we'd endanger people if we went to their houses. We don't get to know half of what you do."

I thought of the American student and her *znayoo*. I didn't want to spend my time with Americans either.

I took a stack of proscribed *Time* and *Newsweek* for Sasha Ivanov when I left. "You won't disseminate these to Russians," a consulate employee warned me. "Of course not." I was getting used to lying to everyone.

"How quickly you forget the Russian language," Kolya sighed.

After three days apart, dinner at the consulate, and a day of English classes, I couldn't make it through a Russian sentence. I sighed in frustration.

"Then let's speak my language!" I said in English. Kolya laughed.

"Where are we going?" I managed.

"*Pryamo.*" Straight ahead. We rode along in silence, beyond the edges of the center, heading north out of town. I knew he was taking me to his house, and that he wanted to make love to me, and that although I didn't particularly want to, I wouldn't resist. It felt the same as the official excursions: somehow it was already out of my hands. Even to shape a Russian sentence now was as much as I could handle. We rode in silence. If I tried to say something in Russian, Kolya would have to wait for me to get the words out, and then he'd correct me. Kolya pulled the car off the road in a sudden swerve. A car that had been running on our tail rushed past.

"Was he following us?" I asked.

"KGB," Kolya said. I didn't know if he was joking. My mistrust flared up again. Maybe this was all some elaborate arrangement to keep an eye on me: arrange a boyfriend, let me start talking freely. I had no secrets that anyone would care about, but that hadn't mattered in the stories I'd been told.

"You are so afraid," Kolya said, shaking his head. We were stopped at the *gaii* checkpoint. I waited while Kolya showed his papers, settled his accounts. "My friend," Kolya said, tilting his head in the direction of the fat, uniformed car policeman. "Three rubles."

Ten minutes later we pulled into a small village. Kolya told me to wait while he went inside to buy juice. Why wait? Why couldn't I come in with him? Disgruntled, I watched him enter the store and thought, does he look short in comparison to the men coming out now? How high on the door frame does his head reach? Kolya returned empty-handed.

"Ah, *Rossiya*," he said, turning the key in the ignition.

"What?"

"*Sovietskii Soyuz*." Soviet Union. "Empty." He was shamed to not be able to buy the juice for me. Who needed juice? We pulled into the driveway by his house. A *babushka* stood on the porch. "Hello," I said to her in Russian as we passed the porch. She didn't acknowledge my greeting but turned and went back into the house.

"She didn't hear you," Kolya said. I didn't believe him. I'd been inches from her. Kolya led me around the house to his entrance. Already the junk in the yard, the boat under the tarp, a derelict car seemed familiar. It was a real house, comforting. Somewhere not far away was the river where we'd danced, fir trees, the Gulf of Finland. I pushed past the quilted vinyl outer door into the entry, where Kolya removed my coat and hung it for me, offered me a pair of battered slippers. The inner room still stank of cologne.

"Three days I couldn't sleep here after Volodya broke the bottles," Kolya said.

The table where we'd feasted was gone, and the divan was opened into a bed. It offended me that Kolya hadn't bothered to fold it up into a couch for me. Did he know that he'd bring me here, that I'd yield so easily? All of this was happening too fast; I was too passive, too ambivalent to make it not happen, except to say, when Kolya sat down beside me on the bed and slid a hand under my sweater, "So soon?"

"We don't have much time. What difference does it make, a day, a year?"

Under other circumstances I would have argued with his sentiment, but the logic was inescapable given that I would leave Russia in several weeks. It wasn't that I wanted this to happen, but I didn't want this not to happen, either. Kolya's will was stronger than mine. It had taken me six weeks *not* to sleep with Grisha, and two dates to go to bed with Kolya. I leaned back, and Kolya slid my sweater off, exclaiming softly, that two-toned falling Russian "Ohhh—ohhh." A sound I later came to recognize as meaning appreciation, agreement, rue. He felt too unfamiliar, his slim back, wiry white arms, face pressed close, his curls touching my forehead. His cold sore had healed, I noticed. Because he was short he seemed closer than a tall man would, face to face.

"*Ostorozhno,*" I whispered, "be careful." I knew the word from the recording on the metro: "Be careful, the doors are closing." I hadn't brought my diaphragm with me, not wanting to show I expected anything to happen, not even knowing if a Russian knew what a diaphragm was. So I could only think that I didn't know this man, didn't trust him to think of me. I didn't know the word for pregnant. "I don't want to have a child," I said.

Kolya stopped and looked into my face. "You don't want a child?"

"Not tonight," I amended. A woman who didn't want a child wasn't a woman here.

"Don't worry, don't worry," he reassured me, moving inside me. I moved to meet him, a beat behind, trying to keep up, but distant. *Laskovaya,* but not passionate, I thought. The Kolya who held himself above me seemed so thin, insubstantial, shoulders no larger than my own. My mind drifted away somewhere. I felt reconciled to an act that had no meaning. Kolya pulled out before he came, and curled beside me.

"You've been alone a long time?" he asked.

"Yes," I said, wondering if Grisha counted. Was I lying? But it seemed as though I'd been alone my whole life. A loneliness deeper than hotel rooms and foreign streets bereft of the familiar flash of advertising, a loneliness going back so far—

"Why alone?" Kolya asked.

"I'm waiting for a man on a white horse."

"A *knight,*" Kolya said in English, surprising me.

"And you?"

"Also alone."

"Why?"

"I was waiting for you."

I cringed at the line. Kolya reached behind our heads. He opened a bottle of vodka with the back of a knife and poured out two glasses. "If you drink, how will you drive me back to my hotel?" I asked.

"Don't worry, my cousin will drive us."

In the soft light, Kolya lay his head on my breasts. "A child would be very comfortable here," he said. "Our child."

I didn't expect such words, didn't trust them. Maybe they were what a Russian man thought he must say when he slept with a woman. What American would say such a thing, and so quickly? Yet Kolya spoke so naturally the idea struck me as a revelation.

"It will not be," I said.

"Why not?"

I didn't have the words in my bad Russian then, not even in English, if Kolya could have understood my language. I gestured at the softly lit room with its beige print wallpaper, at the enormity of the dark Leningrad night and everything about it that confused and frightened me, like the *gaii* who stopped us at the checkpoint to examine Kolya's papers. I could have just as well been gesturing at my purse on the floor and in it my visa, its expiration date clearly marked. "Because you live here and I live there," I concluded.

"We will be together. I know. We will live here and there."

"It isn't possible."

"It is. There are such people who live this way."

"Famous people. Diplomats," I argued.

"Everything is possible if you want it very much. I want, and it will be. Everything can be arranged." He rubbed his thumb and forefinger together in that universal sign for money. "*Ya khochu dolgo,*" he muttered, "I want time." When Kolya threw his head back and gulped his vodka, I saw something there, strange and desperate.

I sat up to take my glass. "Kolya, we don't even know each other. I speak Russian so badly, when you were telling jokes and everyone was laughing, I didn't even know if your jokes were funny."

"Of course, funny. I have very *gipkii* mind."

"*Gipkii?* What does this word mean?"

"*Gipkii, gipkii.*" Kolya reached for the Russian-English dictionary. Carefully he underlined the word in pencil, with all of its meanings: Flexible. Agile. Such a shameless declaration made me laugh. "Kolya, you are proud," I said, because I didn't know the word for bragging. "You have a *gipkii* mind and I have *gipkii* body." Sitting heels together, I leaned over and touched my forehead to my toes to demonstrate. Kolya ran a finger down my naked spine, kissed me between the shoulder blades.

"You were a gymnast?" he asked.

"No."

"And I was."

"Show me."

Kolya downed his vodka in a gulp, stood naked and tested his weight on a chair.

"No, please, Kolya, it isn't necessary. Only a joke." I didn't have the idiom to dissuade him—you'll break your neck, I was only kidding, if you kill yourself, who will drive me back to my hotel before they lock the door?

Slowly, breathing deeply, Kolya placed both hands on the chair. He kicked upward and hung, jackknife position, balanced horizontally over his hands. His slender body looked beautiful, every muscle tensed, and a single drop of sweat ran down the side of his face. Slowly, trembling, he raised his legs overhead in a perfect arch. The chair wobbled under his weight. Seconds ticked by. Kolya dropped down lightly, slid beneath the covers with me, and grinned.

"*Vsyo mozhno,*" he said. Everything is possible.

A Candle for Saint Nikolai

While the wind rattled the windows, I drew a map with pencil in Kolya's notebook, under the soft golden light of the bedside lamp. I drew America, making Florida too big, forgetting Texas. "And here is where I live," I said, marking New York, "and here is where my mother and father live," X-ing Vermont and Massachusetts. Kolya exclaimed as though I possessed some marvelous talent, creating this map of America without proportion.

He took the pencil and drew on another sheet a coastline, the mouth of a river. "Here," he wrote in my name, Alyosha's, Vyetta's, Galya's, Volodya's, his own. He sketched in his car, the circles of headlights. "This is where we danced on the beach." On his little map Kolya drew an island, a clearing, a small tent, and a rowboat. "This is where I like to go in summer." Over the drawing he wrote: Kolya's Island. "In the summer, when you come back. . . ."

"*If* I come back," I corrected.

"*When* you come back, I will take you there."

I'd brought Alaska photographs to show Kolya, imagining he'd enjoy the sight of the fishing boats. Kolya studied the pictures of me raising a salmon on a gaff hook, hoisting an anchor, then pushed them away.

"Who took these pictures of you? Someone who knew you very well."

"No one special. Just a man I worked for." It was a lie, but what did it matter that I'd had a brief affair with a skipper that amounted to nothing?

"Yes, a man who knew you very well." He shook his head unhappily.

"Well, of course I've known men," I said in exasperation.

"How many? Ten? A hundred?"

"Kolya, it isn't necessary to talk like that. Besides, you were a seaman. I know how seamen are. You must have known many girls."

"There was no one but you."

I grimaced at this stupid line. "Don't lie to me. What about your wife?"

"Listen," Kolya said. "You think you want to know, but you don't want to know. If I tell you, it will make you unhappy. So why do you ask? There is no one but you. There was no one before you."

He was right! What was that American compulsion to make everything clear, the confession that reduced each lover to a number on a list, after the last, before the next? No wonder American men and women were so suspicious of each other, so incapable of sustaining contact. Better to believe there was no one but me.

Now when we made love I was avid, eager. We moved together easily, and afterward Kolya never fell asleep but held me, talked. He asked me to stay the night, and I consented, but later he roused me, told me to dress.

"You don't want me to stay?"

"I want you to stay, but I want to see you again, and if you stay without your hotel key, I know I won't be able to see you again."

"What do you mean, you know?"

"I just know."

"Then how is it possible to arrange so that everything will be okay?"

Kolya waved my words away. "We don't need problems now. There will be enough problems when the time comes."

The next night I brought the key, with its big attached metal cone weighting my pocket. It took some effort of will to sneak it out, and I hoisted it in front of Kolya with pride.

"*Molodetz*," he said, embracing me. Terrific.

"Careful, careful," I warned when we made love, but this time Kolya didn't pull out fast enough. I hadn't been careful either, wanting too much to watch his face when he came, as though all his strength were gathered there, the way it tensed and darkened.

"I'm sorry," Kolya said. "I forgot. I was thinking Lora, Lora, Lora, and I forgot."

"You forgot?" I reached to gulp from a glass of water by the bed.

"What about me? What will I do if I become pregnant? I won't even know until I get home, and you'll still be here."

"I'm sorry," Kolya said.

"Easy for you to say, but I am the one who will have to pay."

Kolya corrected my usage of the verb *to pay,* an action so infuriating, given the circumstances, that I took the cup of water I was holding and dashed it on his head, surprising both of us.

Kolya said nothing, only turned his head as if to measure me anew. Silently he got up to get a towel and wipe his dripping curls. "You are not afraid," he said. "That is good."

"Afraid of what? That you would . . ." I didn't know the word for hit, so I pantomimed his hitting me.

"We will be good together," Kolya said, smiling. "Sometimes you'll throw water, sometimes vodka, sometimes milk."

I don't remember exactly when it changed, when my indifference to Kolya slid away to eagerness, and then to joy. Maybe it had already started when he came for me at school, or when he did a handstand on a chair, convincing me that anything was possible. I began to wonder what would happen to us. Weeks piled up, and suddenly time that had dragged became precious. The ritual of Kolya waiting on our corner shaped my days. Kolya kissing me as I got into his car, his sighing complaint, "How quickly you forget the Russian language." His patient corrections of my mangled speech. The darkness and cold, the long drive to his house, and the warmth of his room, which made school fade away, a protection against the stern faces of the hotel doormen and floor ladies, the unsmiling waiters in my hotel restaurant, the bundled shapes shoving me in the food lines, Galya's accusing face across a lunchroom table. Kolya and I made love again and again, never having to ask or wonder, but simply moving toward each other, clinging, holding, while the gypsy record played over and over my favorite song: *Forgive me for everything.*

Outside, ice formed on the windows. Kolya brought me caviar, cooked me meat and kasha. I bit into buttered circles of bread dotted with the sticky globules that popped and melted between my teeth.

"Caviar! Kolya, you've found the path to my heart."

Kolya grinned. "I very much want to find the path to your heart."

"You are wonderful."

"I try."

In Kolya's room there were no distinctions, no time. I no longer knew when we finished making love, began again. We relied less and less on the dictionary as I began to speak.

"Only here I feel at home," I said.

"It is your home."

"*Ya tebya lyublyu*," he said, suspended above me. "I love you. I love you. I love you." He kissed me tenderly: neck, face, eyes. "Good, good, good," he murmured, moving inside me. "Lora, *this* is very important."

"Kolya," I laughed, "whoever said it wasn't?"

"We are alike," Kolya said in the simplified Russian he used for me. "We think alike. We both love the water, boats, books. If you lived here we would have been married long ago."

But when the *gaii* stopped us for the umpteenth time at the checkpoint en route to Kolya's, I had a tantrum. "Why, why is it necessary?"

"It is necessary," Kolya said. "The border is close."

"So what? The border is close to Vermont, but we don't have *gaii*." We were on the road again, driving a darkened highway past dark firs, the gulf glinting between them, the road banked with snow. In my mind's eye I saw Kolya's laughing face when he got out to show his papers, a mask. And the *gaii* laughing too. Oh, he knew how to do everything here. Always the three-ruble bribe. He was at home, and I would never be at home here. Home, home, home. I missed my home suddenly with a fierceness that made me want to cry out. "I could never live here," I said. "I want to be home. I want to be driving now in Vermont."

Kolya shifted gears fiercely, laughed. "Lora, sometimes you are a strong woman, and sometimes you are like a little girl who wants her mother. It's all right; a man likes it when a woman is like a little girl sometimes."

The same words that Grisha had said, a Russian sentiment. "I do not miss my mother," I said with annoyance. "I miss my land. I never think about the people there, but the land, the way it looks . . ." I was afraid that I would never see that land again, that I would somehow be suspended on this road, stripped of my freedom, stopped by *gaii*, forever.

"Here it is also very beautiful," Kolya said, touching my knee. "Not so much in winter, but in the summer . . ." he gestured toward the leafless birch. "Very beautiful. Like Lukamora, the Pushkin fairy tale. When you come back you will see. I'll show you everything, we'll sail. . . ."

"But I miss *my* home."

"Of course," Kolya said softly. "Your homeland. That I understand."

His mother came out to open the gate for us when we drove up. She pushed it wide, but it swung shut again. Kolya laughed and laughed until I hated him, the same face I'd seen at the *gaii* checkpoint. Why didn't he get out to help her? He was suddenly alien to me, as alien as his voice on the phone, barking, brutal, answering mysterious calls that he never explained. And why was it that I never met his parents? And why, whenever we went anywhere, did I have to wait for him in the car? He was the one who ran into stores, or ran up to Alyosha's mother's apartment to gather up Alyosha and Vyetta. When I asked, he always had answers, but they didn't satisfy me.

"Alyosha's mother talks too much, if you come up we'll never get away."

Perhaps he feared she'd talk about us to someone. I didn't push him further. Maybe I didn't want to know Kolya's limitations. Or diminish him by asking him to admit them. He was the man who said *vsyo mozhno*—everything is possible. But if I was Kolya's secret, how could everything be arranged?

"I could live anywhere," Kolya said. "To me it doesn't matter where. I want to build a house for myself like my father did." Kolya's father had been awarded the use of a plot of land for being a hero of Soviet labor, and he, with Kolya's help, scraping together materials, using only hand tools, had built this house over the course of years. "I want to build but here it is not possible," Kolya said. "See this room? I did everything myself, even the foundation."

I pictured him digging a hole, mixing cement, loading a wheelbarrow. "And soon your house won't be here."

"It will all be gone. Lora, I'll build you a house on your land in Vermont."

I had described for him the twelve acres of pasture and woods I'd purchased years ago with a small settlement from my parents' divorce, but the land lay vacant since I'd never had the money to build on it.

"When a man wants to build a house it is for a woman," Kolya added. "I want to build for you."

"Don't speak like that," I argued. "You know it isn't possible. What about your son?"

"The years go fast. When he is older he will join us if he wishes.

Everything is possible. When I meet a roadblock, I go around. We will be together, I know. I love you, Lora."

"You don't know me. We're just playing a game. I can't say I love you. I don't want to love you. I don't want to love a man who lives here. I don't know if I'll ever come back."

"If you don't come back I'll come for you. I'll defect. In New York I could find you in two days."

It was a ridiculous idea, Kolya ferreting me out in a city of eight million, but I believed him.

"Only I could have done that," he would say, after driving us on a perilous route over ditches and along a cliff edge to arrive at his cousin's house without encountering the *gaii*. I'd grip the dashboard, wanting to jump out when we teetered on a sandy embankment, but he would whip the car back onto hard ground.

"I hate to travel the same route," Kolya said. "I like to go a different way every time. When something gets in my way I go around it."

In another mood he'd say, "I am *malenkii*, leetle. I am no one."

Still, Kolya was the only untamed Russian, speeding down highways, unafraid.

"You are beautiful," I said one morning, watching him dress for work.

"I? No, my face is very ordinary. A thousand people have my face. Only my eyes are my own."

"To me you are beautiful." And it was true. Somehow his funny, angular, expressive face had become beautiful to me. His eyes always remained strange though. They were blue-green and darted away if I looked at them too long.

"How can I trust you if you don't meet my eyes?" I asked.

"It is my work," Kolya said. "The habit I get from my terrible work."

"Tell me about your work." Whatever illegal work he did that provided all the money and goods, that prompted those late-night barking calls.

"There is nothing to tell."

I asked to borrow his blue terry cloth bathrobe to go to the outhouse. When I returned Kolya looked at me. "Ooh-ooh. Very pretty. Your hair, the colors." He untied the belt to the robe. "Very pretty. It is American, the bathrobe. *Malenkaya maya.* My little one. *Lyagushka.*"

Lyagushka, frog, was what he had named me when I joked that he lived a frog's life, hopping from work in Leningrad, to his house half an hour away, back to the city apartment where his son lived, or to pick me up near my hotel.

"Lyagushinka," I said, adding the diminutive ending.

"That's a word that doesn't exist in Russian," Kolya said. "It is very, very tender. Very tender, *malenkaya maya. Lyagushinka.*" He slipped his hands into the robe, against my chilled flesh. He was excited, insistent that I understand how tender was this word. It was a word in our own language, the language we invented here in this room where we made love.

In the mornings we spoke little, moving about with the exhaustion of lovers who have been up all night talking, making love. Kolya insisted on eating meat in the morning, which I couldn't stomach. I nursed my cup of tea and watched him put together a lunch in the kitchen he shared with his parents. Their rooms lay behind a bolted door. There was no running water in the house, and I had to splash cold water from the metal reservoir that stood above the sink. He took his showers at the public pool where he swam daily. Sometimes Kolya waited in the car while I dashed into the Baltiskaya, showered, dressed, and ran back out so that he could give me a ride to school. Leningrad would be thick with morning traffic, full of drab trucks, overcast and dark. It seemed we were always in darkness, so that the short daylight hours, my time at school, were only something to dream through until night fell and Kolya and I were together again. Then he would be waiting for me on a corner, ready to drive me away to my real life, with him.

Home began to seem farther and farther away, and when I dreamed of home I dreamed of Vermont, not New York. New York disappeared as though I'd never lived there. It was the place I showed the kids at school in pictures: the Statue of Liberty—they called it the "Monument of Freedom"—and the Empire State Building. I looked at those pictures as amazed as they did, as though my year and a half in that city was nothing but a two-week tour. What had I been doing, living there?

Lying in bed I began to relate an event in school. "I want to explain . . ."

"*Obyasnit,*" Kolya corrected my mispronunciation of the verb *to explain.*

"*Obnyasit*," I repeated, incorrectly.

Kolya laughed indulgently. "*Kak Yevrei*," he said. Like a Jew. The stereotyped Jew had a comical lisp in Russian.

I rolled away, a crimp of panic in my chest.

Kolya wanted me to light a candle at the icon of Saint Nikolai, patron saint of travelers and seamen, in order to ensure my return. We went to the church with Alyosha and Vyetta. A whole excursion had been planned for me: church, the Palace of Weddings, lunch in a restaurant, evening at a club. We'd driven around the city for half an hour while they'd argued out our plans. Vyetta seemed anxious that I see everything and be pleased, that they make a good impression.

I'd been in an Orthodox church already. Anna Maximovna, the education official, had taken me to see the Alexander Nevsky Monastery, quite a cultural coup. We were accompanied by two of her cronies, thick-waisted, middle-aged education officials in synthetic dresses that needed a good washing. Apparently, it was very difficult to get admission to the monastery, and this outing was as much an adventure for them as for me. We'd been met by a heart-stoppingly handsome young priest, with long Jesus hair and beard, named Father Markel. Father Markel had given us a tour of the library where religious scholars hunched over books in carrels, and the cemetery where many famous Russian writers were buried. Who were these priests and monks, I had wondered, immune in some mysterious way to the demands of the Socialist State. Why was it that some degree of religious freedom existed within these walls? To become a priest, I imagined, was one path out of the *Komsomol* and the army, a means of escaping false communist pieties. Perhaps it was a safety valve permitted by the authorities.

Father Markel had led us to the monastery cafeteria for lunch. He wasn't eating, as it was a fast day, but lunch had been promised as part of the tour, and lunch we'd have. My chaperones had dug into their *kasha,* happily stuffing apples into their bags for later. Anna Maximovna said, "Imagine, Father Markel is just your age, Laurie! Oh, what a shame he's taken a vow of celibacy."

"Perhaps he'll change his mind?" one of the other official women said, with a wink and a guffaw. I had looked back and forth at the tittering women there in their odiferous synthetic *shmatas,* then to this beautiful, ascetic priest, and understood his choice. When I'd told Kolya the story he had had a good laugh.

Now Kolya guided me past dirty patches of snow and crusts of ice and frozen mud outside the beautiful blue onion-domed church. I couldn't help glancing around to see if there were KGB taking pictures of this forbidden activity, but no one seemed to be watching those streaming in and out of church. Inside, everyone wore bulky winter coats. The interior of the church was dark, smoky, and filled with murmuring voices. Kolya bought two narrow tapers from an old woman behind a counter and led me to the icon. A coffin stood open in the middle of the church, a corpse's beaked nose jutting up. I turned away from it, my face into Kolya's shoulder. "Don't worry," he said, "It is good luck, a good sign." I placed my candle beside a guttering dish of oil while Saint Nikolai looked down from his frame of beaten silver. I didn't feel the picture speak to me, but I wanted to believe in Kolya's magic. When Kolya took my hand, a *babushka* began to scold us: "It is not permitted! Holding hands in church!"

Kolya led me back to Alyosha and Vyetta, who stood on the edge of a cluster of parents and grandparents watching a bearded priest baptizing crying children. Alyosha said that Vyetta felt bad because they'd never had their child baptized.

"Do you believe?" I asked Alyosha.

"No."

"Does she?"

"No."

"Then why?" I remembered the icon hanging over Kolya's bed. When I asked, he'd said he believed in fate. All sailors did.

Alyosha watched my face. "Lora doesn't like it here," he pronounced.

"I like it," I said, "it's just a little strange. At home our churches are different." But it wasn't just a matter of spare New England churches with their simple white spires and barren pews, their oblique, streaming light. "I'm surprised," I finally said. "I didn't know churches were . . . allowed." I knew that many churches had been destroyed or turned into warehouses, that various believers had been persecuted.

"Why not?" Alyosha asked. Was it all propaganda then? They weren't afraid to be seen with me here. What did it mean, then, that Kolya always met me on designated corners, none of them came to call on me at the hotel? I was afraid: afraid of the maid who would find my bed unslept in if I spent a night at Kolya's house, afraid that the guard at the desk would see me slip out without returning my key, afraid of saying or doing the wrong thing without knowing what the wrong thing was. I couldn't ask for an explanation, couldn't decipher the logic of what was or wasn't allowed—*mozhno* or *nyelzya*.

Outside again, Kolya seemed too slight beside me, no match for my shapeless fears. When we walked along the stone embankment beside the Neva River, still filled with battleships brought in for the holiday, I shivered at the sight of Soviet might. Gray against gray, majestic and forbidding.

"Lora, see that ship there?" Alyosha pointed, grinning. "It has a bomb on it, just for you."

Kolya hunched his shoulders under his army jacket and walked away from the sound of our English words.

In the Palace of Weddings, a converted stone mansion, we followed a wedding party up the curving staircase after checking our coats. Was this supposed to be some kind of preview, a rehearsal? Alyosha and Vyetta made a handsome couple: he tall and imposing in his furry cap, Vyetta lovely in another one of the woolen dresses she'd sewn herself. As usual, I was inappropriately dressed. I hadn't known where we were headed this morning and felt awkward now in blazer and jeans. The women here wore frills and lots of makeup, high heels, hair piled high. In the marriage hall the bride and groom stood solemn before a woman official in a long velvet gown draped with a sash and medallion. A three-piece band on a balcony played a few strains of the wedding march. I'd heard the same three stanzas played in the last wedding while we were down below checking our coats. These weddings took only minutes, and the line was long. All that I deciphered from the official's speech was something about the couple doing a service to their country. I felt odd, standing at the back of the room beside Kolya, an uninvited guest. When the bride and groom kissed, a photographer leaped out to snap a picture. As we were leaving, I whispered to Kolya, "I was in the picture."

"I was too."

So we'd been joined, unknown faces appearing in a stranger's wedding album. What would they think, poring over it years from now, unable to decipher who we were? We would be bound there forever, maybe longer than their marriage would last.

Kolya waited in the car while I ran up to my hotel to change. We had reservations for a night on the *Kronverk*, the schooner-turned-nightclub that Kolya and I had passed on our first date. We met Alyosha and Vyetta outside the club, trooped down a spiral staircase into the ship's hold. It must have been difficult to get in, but I didn't ask how the arrangements were made. As usual, Kolya took care of everything. I was sorry that I had no nightclub clothes, just an angora sweater over a school skirt. Vyetta wore a swirly gold gown with spaghetti straps and the street earrings I had given her, the fake gold shells. She liked them because they matched the glittery dress she'd sewn. Alyosha wore a hairpiece for the occasion, one that traded his baldness for a premature gray.

"In the West you must have some very nice ones for men, in nice styles," Vyetta said. I suspected she'd made him wear the wig.

I tried to ignore the fact that I hated the shirt Kolya wore—brown rectangles on a white background. The white glowed purple from a black light, as did the lint on his brown velour suit, the one he'd worn to the November 7 holiday. Kolya shrugged and laughed about it with us.

Vyetta complained that we were seated too far from the floor show, but when the music began I was just as glad. As with all Russian bands, the music was deafening. Kolya, of course, couldn't join us in drinking since he was our chauffeur. He sipped mineral water while we toasted with vodka and champagne, and we all ate eggs stuffed with caviar, slices of tongue. The waiter had been told that I was an American guest and made a great production out of satisfying my needs. I peered around, trying to figure out who these people might be, overdressed women, affluent men.

The floor show began, its theme a trip around the world. The dancers came out in skimpy costumes, dressed first like Parisians, in stripes and berets, then in Flamenco getups.

"*Strashno,*" Kolya said, shaking his head. Awful. "Such women frighten me."

"Why?" I asked.

"They lead a hard life."

"How?" I persisted. Were they prostitutes as well as dancers?

"They stay up late drinking vodka. A hard life."

"Look," I said, gesturing toward a dancer wearing a gown cut into open diamond shapes over what must have been a flesh-toned body stocking. "She has no belly button." Since I didn't know the word for navel, I asked Alyosha to translate.

"You know why?" Alyosha asked, laughing. "She has worn it away with too much use." He launched into a series of what he called "police jokes," which were exactly the same as "Polish jokes" at home.

Vyetta chided Kolya for not attending to my needs: "Lora has no tongue on her plate, no vodka."

"You do fine," I whispered to him. "You do everything."

Kolya kissed my cheek.

Alyosha and Vyetta complained that we weren't talking to them, just whispering to each other. Alyosha led me onto the small, crowded dance floor for a slow number. "Do you like Kolya?" he asked.

"Yes," I answered cautiously, "but what is the point? I'll be leaving soon."

"But you can take him with you," Alyosha crooned.

I went rigid in his arms. Was this all some elaborate plan they'd cooked up to get Kolya an exit visa?

"Maybe he likes me because I'm American," I ventured.

"No, no. He likes you because you are you. He's had too many women already. We all like you." Alyosha was getting drunk. He pulled me closer. "We like you and want to do everything for you because you are our friend. Don't think that if I wasn't married I wouldn't want to change places with him." The song ended. Shaken, I headed back to our table quickly. Kolya and Vyetta were deep in an intense conversation. I remembered the first night at Alyosha's party when I thought there was something between them. But it must have been me they were discussing. Vyetta got up to dance with her husband.

Kolya said, "When you were dancing with Alyosha, Vyetta asked me how you and I could understand each other, without language. I told her we understand everything. We think alike. We are alike." It was true, he talked to me in such simple Russian I understood him, and he translated their Russian into simpler Russian words for me. But Alyosha's words had put me on edge. It had been weeks before I noticed that Kolya had a missing finger, cut off at the knuckle, he kept it so neatly hidden. What else had he hidden from me?

Later that night at Kolya's I told him Alyosha's words, omitting the part about Alyosha wishing to trade places with him.

"Alyosha's a fool," Kolya said. "I'll have to teach him a lesson. I don't want to leave. If I wanted to leave, I would have left. I was a seaman. I had many chances to escape. I love my country. I love you. We will live here and there. Everything will be all right."

"How do I know you don't simply like me because I'm American, something new?"

"If you were Russian we would have been married a long time ago. Because you are American there are a lot of problems for me. For Alyosha and Vyetta you're like a holiday. For me it is very, very serious, do you understand? Do you understand? I love you."

"Don't say it."

"Why? It is true. I love you. I love you. I love you. You are my *malenkaya*, my little one. We will be together."

"I don't want to love a man who lives here," I said.

We made love, but I couldn't sleep afterward. I tossed for hours and woke sour and distant. Silently I watched Kolya wash and dress. Everything I did seemed wrong. I wiped my face with the dish towel in the kitchen. Kolya handed me a face towel, and I felt I'd made some stupid mistake. I remembered rather drunkenly putting out a cigarette in an open box of candy before bed and flushed with shame. How wastefully American.

"When will we see each other? You need to sleep alone tonight," Kolya said. I wasn't sure if he was being understanding or rejecting. Tomorrow I couldn't see him because I had plans with Sasha, and the night after that he couldn't see me because he had to attend a mandatory political meeting. He wanted me to change my plans so I could see him tomorrow and we'd both be busy on the same night. We argued about it. I finally consented but felt disgruntled and unhappy. We drove back to Leningrad in near silence. It was still dark. Kolya parked on a corner, and we sat in the car. A tall, bareheaded African student crossed the street before us, followed by a second.

"*Chyornii*," Kolya said musingly. A black. "Two."

"You're racist," I said, picking the fight. "What does it matter, if they're black?"

"I am not a racist," Kolya protested. "Let everyone live as they want to. My friend Noel in Cuba, I've been to his house many times. I am not against blacks. Only, they don't like to work."

"That is racist. And what did you mean the other night when I mispronounced *obyasnit* and you said, "Like a Jew?"

"Jews no good," he said in English, shaking his head.

"My grandmother was from Odessa," I announced shakily. To say Odessa was as good as saying Jew, since the ones who'd immigrated to America from Odessa were nearly all Jews.

"It is nothing, a grandmother," Kolya said, waving it away. I didn't correct him, tell him about the other three grandparents, admitting only to a quarter of this tainted blood.

"I don't want to talk about this," Kolya continued. "It is a small problem, and I have big problems. All day long, I think Lora, Lora, Lora. I think how I will arrange for us. Lora, you are tired. You haven't slept. Now you will go back to your hotel and rest. You will change your plans, and I will see you tomorrow."

I clattered away across the frozen puddles without looking back. The chambermaid was in my room when I entered, guiltily, still wearing the angora sweater, my nightclub getup. It was clear that I hadn't slept in my room since my bed was as neatly, tightly made as when I'd left. Ordinarily I rumpled the sheets before I went out in the evening. What a fool to forget.

"You've been on an excursion?" the maid asked sweetly, looking me up and down.

"No, no, I'm sick," I said, hoping to distract her. "I can't go to work. I must call and tell them, my stomach." I did feel sick, exhausted and sick from my conversation with Kolya. The maid turned all sympathy and instructions. Russians respected illness. I was confused and scared and gave her a magazine for her son, a small bribe for complicity. I called in sick, and the maid brought me tea. I sat on my bed in my nightgown while the day grew light outside the curtains and the shoppers began their grim parade down Nevsky. My mind whirled with Alyosha's words, "You can take him with you." And Kolya's, "Jews no good."

In the afternoon I walked down Nevsky to the Hotel Astoria, a charming pre-revolutionary building across the street from St. Isaac's Cathedral—there was a ruble buffet where American graduate students on fellowships congregated for a good cheap meal. Sometimes I went there to spend my ruble salary and to give myself a break from the cabbage soup and the beef and kasha at the school's two o'clock luncheon. I sat alone, thinking of Kolya, who could not enter. I tried to picture him sitting there, among the American students with their little wire-rim glasses and their talk of their doctoral theses, their complaints about the

Soviet dorms and their attempts to one-up each other with their Russian friends and command of the language.

How would Kolya fit in? The truth was that I didn't know how Kolya sounded in his own language. Always he tailored his language for me, shortening his sentences, using the small working vocabulary I'd developed in the past weeks, speaking slower than slow for me. On the phone his Russian was a totally different language, so fast and harsh I couldn't follow it. Did he have an accent, I wondered, the way a Brooklyn accent is so detectable at home? Did he speak with subtlety and nuance, or was he crude? He repeated certain expressions frequently, but then it seemed that most Russians loved such little sayings, familiar phrases that in anyone else irked me, they smacked so much of received ideas. If I knew the language better, would he seem less marvelous to me? I knew he was bright and that he read classics constantly, but how would he sound at home?

From time to time he would try a word of English on me and I would cringe at his accent, the fumbling sound of someone swimming out of his depth. "Leetle," Kolya would say, and I immediately corrected him, harshly. "Lit-uhl. Lit-uhl." Kolya grinned and repeated, "Leetle." I was a terrible teacher. I had no patience for Kolya's mistakes. I only wanted the Kolya who knew everything. How to get us into restaurants, how to drive with one wheel over the edge of a cliff, how to manage to live without waiting in lines, how to bribe the *gaii*. Who would he be in America, without language, without a job, dependent on me? I wondered if it would crush him, but more than that I suspected that I wouldn't be able to stand an uncertain Kolya. It was his certainty I loved.

One of Us

A week before my departure for Moscow and then home, they moved me from the ratty old Baltiskaya Hotel to the Hotel Leningrad, a shiny new Intourist high rise for Westerners. The excuse was that my Baltiskaya room was needed for a convention of African socialists. I figured they wanted me to remember my stay in terms of palatial banquet halls, beige sound tiles, and glossy picture-window views of the Neva rather than the Baltiskaya's threadbare carpets and stuttering iron elevator. But my room at the Baltiskaya, with its double French doors and parquet floor and tiny balcony, possessed more charm than the wall-to-wall carpeted cell they stuck me in at the Hotel Leningrad. Having to pack up all my clothes and toiletries and teaching materials was merely a nuisance, another surrender to the all-powerful "they" at a time when I was losing my voice to laryngitis, coughing a deep bronchial bray, running a low-grade fever, and frantically counting down my days with Kolya. I moved through my classes as if in a dream, waiting only for Kolya's car, that ride back to the haven of his house, where we clutched and clung to each other.

"They" also decided, at the eleventh hour, to do a story about me in the propaganda magazine *Soviet Life,* a badly printed, large-format, Western-export "glossy" that appeared at occasional American newsstands and high school libraries. It would be a "Laurie Goes to Leningrad" story of international peace and goodwill. This meant that for five days I was tailed by a personal photographer. Another nuisance, although my vanity was touched. Where else but in Russia could I be a model and star?

Andrushka, the photographer from Moscow, was kissy, fussy, and viewed himself as an artiste. He swept his longish hair back from his forehead in a Russian pompadour and waved his arms about dramatically as he described each brilliant shot. Unfortunately, the effect was ruined by a speech impediment that distorted his words into nearly incomprehensible baby talk. In Andrushka's Russian, *khorosho,* good, became *khorotho,* and *kracivi,* beautiful, became *kwathivi.* He spoke no English. Tatiana Nikolaevna, who had come in to observe, rolled her eyes as Andrushka flitted about my classrooms, snapping rolls of film while I smiled idiotically at the kids. After school, Andrushka and his driver transported me about the city in a black Volga sedan, searching out scenic spots where I could pose with bouquets of flowers.

We drove to Smolny Institute on Proletarian Dictatorship Square. Formerly a school for noble young ladies, it had housed the headquarters of the October Revolution and was now a sacred shrine. Andrushka artfully placed me before a statue of Lenin raising his arm forcefully toward the future. I smiled artificially. Andrushka squinted at me through the viewfinder, then shook his head and waved me toward him.

"Pewhaps this picthure would not be tho good for you in your countwee?" he asked. Extrapolating from Soviet realities, he feared that a photo of me in front of Lenin might be construed as a vote for communism, something that could harm my career. I appreciated his tact. He decided to shoot me on Anichkov *Most,* my favorite bridge, crossing the Fontanka Canal, with the statues of the wild horses on each corner.

"Yeth, bewtiful, bewtiful," he coaxed me toward him as traffic whizzed over the bridge in clouds of repulsive black exhaust. No EPA standards here. It was a dreary, cold, gray day, and I was wearing my tall Russian cap for glamour. I sucked in my cheeks and soulfully concentrated on Kolya, our imminent separation. If this article ever came out I could study my own expression to see what I'd felt for him. Just then cars screeched and a little brown dog went flying into the air. It landed, four legs up, rigid, before me. Judging it an omen, I burst into hysterical tears.

"Vewy thad," Andrushka pronounced, putting a consoling arm around me before he bundled me back into the black Volga.

Andrushka wanted to round out his story with pictures of a typical evening of me relaxing with my Soviet friends. I balked. No way Kolya or Sasha would want our relationships publicized. Pale-eyed Anna Maximovna was brought in to convince me. *Soviet Life* was a Moscow-based magazine, apparently more powerful than her Leningrad education office, and she was clearly under pressure, fearful of not delivering what had been requested from on high.

"Maybe my friends don't want their pictures taken," I argued when we gathered in Tatiana Nikolaevna's office for a showdown. "I have my own life, you know."

"You have no right to your own life," Maximovna snapped. "You are our guest! We've provided you with everything."

"It's true, you gave me wonderful ballet tickets and I'm thankful, but you also provided me with people who have to ask permission to invite me to their houses. Did you expect me to sit in my room the rest of the time?" Maximovna and Nikolaevna exchanged glances.

Maximovna snapped her purse shut menacingly. "I shall have to write in my report that you are terribly ungrateful."

I wanted to stamp my foot. I was sick, feverish, exhausted. Why didn't they leave me alone? And now I was ungrateful. I was a bad exchange teacher. I'd made Anna Maximovna's job difficult, I hadn't pleased Zakharich back in Moscow, I'd lied about my nationality, I had my own criminally private social life. What difference would her idiotic report mean to me when I was home? But of course, I needed another visa to come back to see Kolya. Maximovna might be able to nix my return. I had to be a good girl, a good guest, cooperative. I had to be a Friend of the State.

We compromised. They would arrange an official good-bye party/ photo opportunity for me in a restaurant with the teachers. Alyosha would be there, Maximovna assured me, apparently as a concession. But what did she know of my friendship with Alyosha? What was the basis of *his* quasi-official status? After all, they'd sent me to him for the holidays. An icky wave of paranoia rose within me as it had that night on the Kronverk when Alyosha said, "You can take Kolya with you." Perhaps she knew all about Kolya already?

The official party was held right after classes on my last day of teaching, in a downtown restaurant with a hokey, Old Russia theme. The waiters wore peasant blouses and trousers tucked into boots. Enormous samovars, balalaikas, and *matrioshki*—nesting dolls—lined the walls. It was like a party inside a souvenir stand. Andrushka bustled about making everyone nervous with his light stands and thrusting camera. I was clamped in a seat next to a purse-lipped Anna Maximovna who wore her expensive silver fox fur cap throughout the meal, either as a mark of her status above ordinary teachers or to hide her unwashed hair. The English teachers spoke to one another in rapid Russian, leaving me out of the conversation and refusing to meet my eyes. Even though I hadn't wanted this party, I was insulted. Here was a party in my honor, and no one but Maximovna was speaking to me! Galya was in her element, the perfect priss, carefully raising her glass to her lips and smoothing her napkin: a five-year-old at a grown-up's tea party. When the food arrived, everyone dug into the appetizers frenziedly, eager to escape the need for conversation. It was a command performance and we were all playing our roles, I no less than they, without a bit of natural feeling in the room. From the moment I'd arrived at this school, I'd never escaped my position as foreigner, an alien, a cause for caution and alarm whenever an official was about. Kolya and Sasha Ivanov were my only respite. I'd already said my good-byes to Sasha, packed away gifts for his Annie and Richard, toasted his upcoming marriage.

"Did you enjoy your party?" Alyosha asked as we hurried along the sidewalk. He'd arranged with Anna Maximovna to escort me "home."

"It was insulting. No one even talked to me. They all spoke Russian to each other, even though I was supposedly the guest."

"But my colleagues were providing you with a last opportunity to learn the Russian language!" Alyosha joked. "Never mind, Laurie. It wasn't to exclude you; they were simply terrified to speak English in front of one another."

"They acted like they were afraid of showing that they even *knew* me. Afraid it would get recorded somewhere." How irritable and unfair I'd grown. In Stalin's time, people had gone to camps or their deaths for simply writing letters to foreigners. If these women were afraid, they had their reasons and I had no right to judge. Over the months my attempt to understand had been swamped by exhaustion and annoyance.

Alyosha waved my words away. "What do you care? It isn't important. Kolya is waiting for us now. Everything will be quite all right."

Everything would be all right. Even now I didn't know what to make of Alyosha's graceful slide between the worlds of Anna Maximovna and Kolya, his role in all this. In a few days none of this would even matter. Saturday night I'd be put on the midnight train, the Red Arrow, to Moscow. And then, a few days later, home.

Kolya got out to open the car door for me as Alyosha climbed in the back. He kissed my cheek and laughed at my stuttering description in

Russian of the party, the photographer. We drove to Alyosha's apartment. Apparently I was permitted to come in this time because it was Alyosha's own apartment and not his mother's, so we wouldn't have to deal with the garrulous Galina Ivanovna. I caught a quick glimpse of dark rooms, a plastic beaded curtain à la the sixties, and a giggling Vyetta in the midst of doing home permanents with a girlfriend, before we trudged out again. Kolya, Alyosha, and I drove to a distant neighborhood, indistinguishable from any other new region, and parked in a lot in front of a long, low cement grocery store at the base of an apartment complex.

"A supermarket," Kolya said in English, nodding at the plate glass windows steamy in the evening frost.

"Just like at home," I exclaimed, once we'd entered and I saw the multiple checkout lines, a novelty here, where shopping required many visits to many stores, each with its double lines, one for getting a receipt for the goods to present to the nasty salesgirls behind the counters, the second line for paying.

"But there is one difference." Kolya nodded at the empty shelves and shook his head. "Nothing here." Of course he'd seen Western supermarkets with their bounty in his travels to England and Italy and Canada. I glanced around at the wall-length produce bin that held nothing but dented, dirty cabbages.

"*Kapusta* and *kapusta*," I admitted. Cabbage and cabbage. Everything looked flimsy, primitive. The metal shopping carts, the sloppy jars of preserved fruits and vegetables with their torn labels and goopy glass. We moved through the aisles. At a meager selection of housewares, I raised a plumber's helper. "Look, Kolya, a gift for you," I said making a joke of his outhouse that needed no plungers.

Kolya and Alyosha grinned. One aisle offered toys, crudely painted dolls, machine guns. I exclaimed over a large pink plastic tank. "This must be one of those Soviet tanks for peace. I'll buy it for my nephew." I turned to see if they'd appreciated my joke but Kolya and Alyosha had vanished. I knew instantly that I'd made a mistake. One didn't make jokes about Soviet tanks in public, especially not a foreigner with an American accent. Their vanishing act was instinctive, ingrained.

I found them at the wine counter, choosing a bottle. Neither of them chided me for my error. Better to pretend it had never happened. We went out and sat in the parked car. Alyosha drank from the bottle of wine and passed it to me. Next, Kolya took a swig, surprising me, since he was still driving. They spoke to each other in a fast, slangy Russian I couldn't keep up with while rain spattered the windshield.

"What are you saying?" I asked Alyosha in English.

"We were talking about my mistress. Did you know I have a mistress at the school?"

"No. Do I know her?"

"You don't know her but she knows you. The art teacher, Alla. She doesn't speak English."

I racked my brain for an art teacher, tried to picture her in the lunchroom. "What does she look like? Is she beautiful?"

"No, but when you know her she is."

"Speak Russian," Kolya commanded.

It was strange to be privy to Alyosha's secret about his mistress: I was colluding, oddly in the position of being one of the boys, while Vyetta and her girlfriend fussed with chemicals and curlers. Was it my Americanness that cut through the male/female barrier, putting me in some category of my own?

The bottle passed forward and back again. Outside the car's steamed windows, shoppers sloshed through the rain. There should've been a saxophone doing the soundtrack. A blurry, soulful moment to obscure the reality of *kapusta* and *kapusta,* the pinched faces at my "party," the fear that made them disappear at my joke about the tank, which I clutched now in my lap.

A final party had been planned for the next night, at Kolya's house. Vyetta was already in the midst of preparations when we arrived. Kolya opened caviar cans while Vyetta cut sausage and bread into attractive oblongs. As usual, I sat bewildered in the face of their expertise. When I offered to help, Vyetta waved me away, licking the sausage grease from her fingers. "You are our guest," she said.

We began with vodka and *zakuski.* Kolya's sister Masha arrived. I'd never met her before, although she lived upstairs. She was a wiry toughie with a warm smile, wearing corduroy jeans. She'd been trained as a refrigeration technician but worked now in a beer hall because the money was better. Her dark-haired husband, Sasha, a former chemical engineer, drove a taxi for the same reason. I studied Masha closely, searching out some clue to Kolya in her features and gestures.

Kolya's father made his first and only appearance in my life: a small, thin man stooped by labor who backed out of the room quickly. He'd come into the kitchen to retrieve a pair of rubber boots drying by the stove. And still Kolya didn't introduce me.

Kolya had brought shoes for Masha, blue leather pumps procured through some mysterious under-the-table trade. She tried them on eagerly. I was pleased with Kolya for providing for his relatives, taking care of everyone. They told me that Masha's husband, Sasha, wanted only to fish. That was all he cared about. That and the billiards table he kept upstairs in their room. Sasha raised his hands in front of his face, interlocking his fingers to make prison bars, and said to me intently, "We live like this here."

I glanced quickly at Kolya. He'd never admitted as much.

They all agreed that Sasha's father, a composer, was one of the few happy men in Russia, because he cared only for writing music, and that's what he did all day. "You must find the thing you love to do and then ignore all else," Sasha said.

Kolya got drunk and began to sing my praises to the group. He put his arm around my neck and kissed my hair, while I slid lower and lower from exhaustion and vodka. Then everyone was gone, the room a shambles, and we were drunk, crawling into bed.

"I can't now," Kolya said, meaning make love. "I am too drunk. Tomorrow, in the morning." His words annoyed me, as though he were explaining away some inability to complete a duty. Perhaps because I needed the reassurance of his touch, I was seized with a need to clarify our situation.

"Kolya, don't go to sleep yet. I've got to talk to you about something. Remember when you were talking about Jews?"

Kolya groaned and pulled a pillow over his head. "Sleep, Lora," he begged.

I yanked the pillow away. "It's important."

Kolya sat up. He spoke in the voice of a patient first grade teacher. "Listen, the Jews are no good. I will explain. The Jew always helps his family to get a job, even if his family is stupid. It is bad. It is like this. The gypsy, he has something bad and I have something good. He talks and talks and talks and talks and in the end, I have the bad thing and he has the good thing. But the Jew, I have something good and he has something bad and he complains and complains and in the end I give him the good thing. See? The Jew always says black when I say white. The Jew loves to argue. And I am a little like gypsy, a little like Jew."

"I love to argue," I said stonily. It wasn't a bad description of Jews, I thought. Jews *were* always complaining. Look at Grisha. . . . Look at me.

"Lora, I am tired of this theme. Listen, you are very intelligent but you do not understand everything I say. It is a matter of language. Do you understand everything I say in Russian?"

"No. . . ."

"So."

"But my grandmother . . ."

"Your grandmother means nothing. Finish." Feeneesh, he said, in English.

"No. We must talk about this. It is very important that I know who you are, what you think, before I leave."

"It is NOT important." Kolya was angry now. "All that is important is that I love you. And you love me. Do you love me?"

"Yes." The word slipped out. I wanted to call it back. It hung, homeless, in the air.

"And this is your home," Kolya said, reaching for me.

"I could live here for a year, maybe."

Kolya's reply was little more than a mumble. "And I want to live there a year or two, and then home." He grabbed his notebook. "Look." He wrote out for me the false equation I'd given him to account for my four grandparents.

Lora: 1/4 Jew
1/4 Lithuanian
1/4 Czechoslovakian
1/4 Austrian

"And I," Kolya continued:

3/8 Russian
1/8 Gypsy
1/8 Ukrainian
1/8 Polish
1/8 Swedish
1/8 Jew

"How can I be against if I am also part Jew? You saw the pictures from my wedding. My closest friend Dima. He is half Jew. Anyway, you are not a Jew! Do you hear me? A Jew wouldn't work on a fishing boat. You are not a Jew."

Kolya held the empty vodka bottle aloft. "Your grandmother's blood is like the drops in this bottle." He pointed to the last bit of moisture at the bottom. "That is all. You are not a Jew. You don't even know who you are. I know who you are better than you do. I know you, Lora."

I was defeated and absolved. He knew me better than I knew myself. In Kolya's world, I wasn't a Jew because he didn't want me to be one, and I didn't want to be one either. I was absolved through dishonesty. Like a Soviet, I could rewrite my own past. I wasn't a Jew; I was Kolya's, who loved me. But lying in the bed, I mumbled in English, "I hate you" and started to cry.

"Why are you crying?" he asked.

"I don't know," I whimpered, unable to explain the anguish of our argument. "Because I'm leaving, because I have a fever." I switched to English. "Stress."

"Stress," Kolya repeated the word thoughtfully. "Stress I understand." He put his arms around me, held me close. But when we were both nearly drifting into sleep, I heard him mutter, "Lora, why do you think they're better?"

In the morning we were polite with each other, as though the argument of the night before hadn't happened. But some fear had entered me now, and I couldn't stop watching Kolya to see if he was acting differently than he had before. "Why are you so quiet?" I asked him as we drove to town. "Usually you are always talking."

"I am sad," is all he would say.

Kolya parked at the Central Park of Rest and Culture, across from a gold-encrusted Buddhist temple that was closed. Once there'd been a time in Leningrad, before the revolution, when Buddhist temples and synagogues opened their doors along with the Russian Orthodox churches and received the obedient. Now there was a big red placard exhorting something about the Twenty-fifth Congress. We walked the icy paths of the park.

"This is our *Centralnii* Park," Kolya joked. "Only here you don't have to worry about muggers."

Ducks swam in the half-frozen ponds.

"*Ootki*," Kolya said, teaching me a new word.

I shivered and coughed. We reached a small café; surprisingly it was open. Kolya took my hand and led me in. The radio was playing cheerful pop music and the windows were clouded with steam. Kolya ordered coffees.

"I feel like I'm in a film," I said.

"Why?"

"I don't know. Like I've seen this all in a film. The café, the music. Maybe because it's our last day," I ended lamely.

"We have time. Lots of time."

"A few hours."

A woman wrapped in a white apron brought us coffee and *piroshki*.

"Look, Kolya." I pointed to a small boy at the table behind us wearing a cap with a long bill, like a duck's.

"*Ootka*," Kolya said, catching my joke.

The waitress set a plate of *piroshki* on the floor for a bored fat dog. It sniffed disinterestedly at the meat-filled pies and then slowly ambled outside.

"I've never seen a dog that wouldn't eat meat before," I remarked.

"A businessman dog," Kolya said. "He has had enough of meat."

"A capitalist dog."

"Going out to do business with the ducks."

We smiled across the table at each other.

Outside again, we walked along the empty, icy paths. We approached a curving lagoon; in its center was an island connected to the shore by a footbridge. I wanted to walk to it, but when we got closer we saw that it was blocked by a sign, "Closed."

Kolya waved his hand with that familiar, dismissive gesture. "A famous American artist came to Russia once as a guest of the government," Kolya said. "He was asked his impressions of our country before he left. He answered, 'So many closed doors.'"

I was surprised. Kolya rarely criticized his country in front of me. Encouraged, I said, "I heard a joke at the consulate on Thanksgiving. Do you want to hear?"

Kolya nodded.

"It's a Finnish joke. There's an American and a Soviet. The Soviet says, 'See, there's my car. Maybe, it's not the best car, and I had to wait

for it ten years, but I can't complain. And see, I have a very nice apartment. Maybe it's not the best apartment, but it has two rooms and I
can't complain.' And the American says, 'Well, I own my own house, and
I have two cars, and I *can* complain.'"

Kolya laughed. "The Finns are smart."

Some strange compulsion drove me on. "I know another one," I said.
"It's a Jewish joke. Brezhnev decides to make contact with the people.
His limousine stops, and he goes to the door of the apartment of an ordinary Soviet family. A little boy answers but doesn't recognize the great
leader. 'Little boy,' says Brezhnev, 'don't you know who I am?' The little
boy shakes his head. 'It is because of *me* you have this fine apartment,'
Brezhnev says. The little boy still doesn't know him. 'It is because of *me*
you have those clothes to wear, because of *me* that you have food on
your table. Don't you know me, little boy?' The little boy lights up with
recognition. 'Mama, Papa,' he calls. 'Come quickly! It's Uncle Isaac from
New York!'"

Kolya threw back his curly head and laughed and laughed.

"An English teacher at the Moscow school told me that one," I said.

"Oh? Your teacher is clever."

"He's very intelligent, but I have no respect for him," I said, echoing
Tanya. "He wanted to emigrate but he had no courage and now it's too
late and he just complains all the time. He's weak."

I knew it was wrong to do this. I'd been warned not to discuss one
Soviet friend with another since it was impossible to know exactly how
such information could be used. Spite prompted me, or perhaps some
desire to detach myself from Grisha, from a joke told to me by another
Jew.

Kolya shook his head. "That's not good. One must make a decision
and then stick to it."

Back at his house, Kolya wrote his phone number and address several
times. One for my suitcase, he said, one for my pocket, in case I lost it,
so I could be sure to call when I got back. He took my favorite gypsy
record and wrote in careful block letters: *pomni*—remember. He removed a carved wooden picture of a sailboat from his wall, a gift for my
father, and handed me a photograph album from which to take the pictures I liked. We sat together on his bed while I opened the old, cloth-
covered cardboard and flipped pages. The first held ancient, discolored

portraits of *babushki* in headscarves, old men in workers' caps, relatives long dead. I flipped past snapshots of Kolya at a low table playing chess with a child, snuggled in bed with a baby beside him, holding a stuffed rabbit toy above the baby's face, Kolya as a young gymnast, drunk at a wedding, skiing with his son in some faraway mountains.

"Are you sure you want me to take them?" I asked. "Won't your son want them someday?"

"Better with you," Kolya said.

Why better with me? Did he mean he'd have to leave it all behind if he came with me?

These are the pictures I chose: Kolya as a child of four, wearing an outsized Soviet seaman's cap and baggy shorts, his arm around another smaller child; Kolya at age six, staring intently into the camera with knit brows, behind him a boggy landscape of forest pools and in his hands a bouquet of wildflowers.

"You were so serious," I said.

Kolya waved a hand. "Always thinking, thinking."

I took one of Kolya, a teenage seaman, dreaming over the rail of a ship. He wears a cowboy hat, its strap bent over the sharp jut of his cheekbone, and the coast of Cuba tilts on the horizon. In another, a sexy, hardened Kolya with a bandaged hand lined up with a group of men on the deck of a small working boat. A headshot of Kolya in uniform, and Kolya in swim trunks on his own small sailboat, raising the sail on what looks like a homemade mast.

"There's so much water in these pictures," I said.

"The only place I feel free is on the water. No one to tell me what to do."

When I closed the crumbling album I said, "I do not know why, but now I am sad."

"Of course," Kolya said. "It is my whole life."

Without me.

We made love silently. Uneasily, I watched Kolya's face for clues for his true feelings, but I'd never been able to read it. Was this separation sadness, or a realization that I, even a partial Jew in his mind, one who liked to argue, was too tainted for him? I didn't think of rejecting him for what I'd called stupidity in Tanya. I only wanted to keep what we had.

✦ ✦ ✦

Alyosha, Vyetta, Kolya, and I sat around the corner from my hotel in Kolya's car. Streetlights lit the rainy sidewalk. I memorized Kolya's hand resting on the wheel, that neatly hidden missing finger. The plastic American dollar key chain dangling from the ignition. From the back seat, Vyetta tried to show me Russian fashion magazines. I held them blindly. Why did I have to say good-bye to Kolya without privacy when I didn't even know if I would be coming back? But Alyosha and Vyetta wanted to say good-bye too. Vyetta chattered on about fashion until Alyosha hushed her. "Not now," he said.

Kolya said, "Lora, it's time." He walked me to the corner. "You will come back in summer."

I shrugged. "By summer you will be married, probably."

"No," Kolya said. "It's better alone. Sleep in the day, eat at night."

"And with me?" I asked, meaning, better alone than with me?

"With you it's good." Kolya said something about having plans to go on a cruise abroad, to Italy, but I couldn't catch it all. This was news to me. Was he referring to a chance to defect? How stupid I was not to know the language better, not to know who he was or half of what he said.

Kolya pressed his lips to mine gently. I wanted something more, a brilliant, passionate kiss that would make a statement, that would tell me he loved me and everything would be all right. That we would be together. A kiss that would tell me I loved him.

"You must come back in summer," he said.

I took his hand and kissed it.

"No, no," Kolya said in English, shaking his head.

Perhaps only men kissed hands in Russia and I was making a final gaffe. What did I know, I was only a stupid *Amerikanka*. I dropped his hand, walked away and didn't, couldn't, look back.

On the Midnight Red Arrow to Moscow, I was sick with fever and exhaustion and paranoia. Snow blew against the train window, making a crinkling sound like shards of glass being ground underfoot. When I dozed off I was woken by a nightmare in which someone—Kolya?—accused me of being a Jew; in the dream I protested, "No, I'm not!" The snowy fields rolled out beyond the frosted glass, stretching the miles between us.

I was lodged in the gleaming twenty-two-story Hotel Intourist—so I'd have a last impression of up-to-date Russia, as in Leningrad, I supposed—and was bustled about the city for final "exploitation" at every International Peace Club and House of Friendship they could fit me into. Elena Glebovna, the bulldog-faced Education Ministry official with the Madonna ring, was very pleased that I'd learned some Russian. "All you need now, Laurie, is a Russian boy," she crowed. In my moments of privacy, I sat on my narrow hotel bed and fingered Kolya's pictures, imagined his touch. At night I went out into the cold street to find an automatic intercity pay phone, as Kolya had instructed me not to call from the hotel.

He was drunk with his friend Vova. "My love," he said in Beachspeak, then switched back to Russian. "I waited for your call. Vova says I'm very sad, Vova says I have to wait for summer. Summer, Lora, everything will be fine. We'll be together, I know. I'll wait for you."

"I don't know how to wait," I said. As though, because I'd never had to, I shouldn't have to, as though I were entitled to whatever I wanted when I wanted it, my American birthright.

I called again the second night and cried on the phone. "I don't want to leave. I don't want to go home."

"*Lyagushka,*" Kolya said tenderly, "*vsyo budet khorosho.*" Everything will be fine. But all I could think of was his telling me: you have to say it is good even when it isn't.

At my final visit to School 45 I pleased Alexander Zakharich when I bestowed on him the remainder of the American texts I'd saved from Leningrad. He rubbed his hands together greedily, and tucked them away in his private closet. The English teachers gathered for a last goodbye, lined up like children for a photograph in Zakharich's room. Tanya winked, Natasha beamed, Emma scowled as usual, Grisha stood composed though I felt his dark eyes searching for mine. As they were filing back to their classrooms, Grisha caught me in a doorway and whispered in my ear. "Laurie, I must see you alone before you leave. "

"I'm free for a few hours today," I offered. "How about three-thirty?"

"I have a private lesson, but I'll cancel it."

"They've got me staying at the Hotel Intourist now. We can meet at the Prospekt Marxa metro station. It's nearby."

Grisha said, "I know." His smile looked so familiar, I felt a sweep of nostalgia for the way we'd cruised the city's metros, arguing, expounding.

"You know, I've missed you," I blurted, cheap with words now that I was leaving and none of it would matter.

Grisha breathed in sharply. "Three-thirty," he said.

"Good thing you're here," I said when Grisha came striding toward me at the metro entrance. How tall he looked in his black fur cap. "Now I can smoke without everyone thinking I'm a whore. That's one thing I won't miss at home."

"What will you miss?" Grisha asked, fishing.

I leaned over my cigarette and matches to protect them from the wind and to avoid his eyes. What had I done, arranging to meet him when he knew nothing of Kolya?

Grisha grasped my elbow. "Well, I shall miss you dreadfully."

"*Dreadfully?* You make it sound like a nineteenth-century romance novel."

Grisha grinned. "In my own language, I'm quite up-to-date. Okay. I will miss you *terribly* and think of you every day that you're gone."

I shivered, coughed, stepping from foot to foot. "Where shall we go?"

"Let's go to your hotel. You're too ill to walk about the streets."

I looked at him incredulously. "But they won't let you in."

"Perhaps I can pass, if we both speak English and you show your hotel card. It's easier at a big hotel where they don't notice everyone. The *fartsovchiki* manage their transactions that way."

I appraised his jeans and leather coat, frowned at his peeling artificial leather shoulder bag that marked him as a Soviet.

"Let me carry that when we get there," I said.

Outside the hotel, long red Intourist buses were discharging loads of foreign tourists, returning from their afternoon excursions to the Kremlin and Red Square. We chattered our way through the door, blathering in our perfect English, while I thrust the hotel *kartochka* in the guard's face. Grisha walked forcefully past him.

He glanced around at the sleek fluorescent surfaces. "This is my first time in an Intourist hotel. When I was leading groups of foreign students, I was permitted to pick them up at the Sputnik Hotel, but that's more like a dormitory for students. This is quite all right."

"Let's go to one of the buffets," I suggested, leading him to the elevators. "I need to drink something hot."

A gaggle of enormously tall blond West Germans crushed into the elevator with us. Their shiny parrot-colored parkas puffed against us, their ruddy good health sucked up all the oxygen. They smelled foreign even to me, some meld of spearmint and fresh air that they'd managed to squeeze out of the wintry Moscow vapors. Could they smell Grisha's Sovietness? We battled our way between the Germans to get out on the sixth floor.

"I think this one takes rubles," I said, thrusting open the glass doors to a buffet that looked the same as any other: the same cup of napkins cut economically into skimpy quarters on each table, the usual display of boiled eggs, bread with caviar, sausage, cheese behind the glass counter, the candies and cigarettes and cognac on a mirrored shelf that you'd see in any train station buffet. Except for the Pepsi and Fanta.

"Do the currency ones look different?" Grisha asked.

"They're the same. Only they sell Marlboros and Cinzano."

There were few other coffee drinkers scattered about at the low tables with stools. Grisha ordered in English, meeting the squinting eye of the busty counter woman. She turned up her nose as though mortally offended—but it was no different than she would have treated me. We stirred our tiny cups of foamy coffee and stared out the window at the darkening city, which was beginning to sparkle as streetlights lit up the enormous thoroughfares. I'd forgotten how vast the streets were in Moscow, as though all built for monumental parades, so that you had to use the pedestrian underpasses to cross. How much more human scaled was Leningrad, Kolya's city.

Grisha took a bite of a cream-filled pastry and put it down. I gave up trying to break a massive lump of sugar in half and dunked one end into my cup, crumbling it where the coffee softened the crystals.

"I will miss you terribly and think of you every day that you're gone," Grisha started up again.

"I might be coming back," I said, making a stab at bringing up Kolya.

"Really?"

"Yes, in summer. I'm not sure yet. . . ."

"But if you come back, you will let me know?"

"If you want."

"Will you truly come back?" Grisha put his hand over mine. I slid mine out, glancing around at the counter woman who was engrossed in a crossword puzzle.

"Don't worry. She thinks I'm one of you, remember? Listen, in summer I go with my family to my parents' in Odessa. But if I know that you are coming I will make some excuse to return." Grisha pulled out a scrap of paper and wrote down his parents' phone number in Odessa.

I couldn't help asking, "Does Tanya know that you are meeting me here? Perhaps you told her just to make her jealous."

"Tanya? But I can't even think of Tanya anymore. You still wish to punish me for that? Won't I have punishment enough? You are leaving and I must stay here forever."

I dipped my head at the weight of his words.

Grisha leaned forward, lowering his voice in case the counter woman spoke English. "Let's go to your room," he urged.

I panicked. "We can't."

"We'll pass the floor lady just as we did the guard. Let's try."

"Grisha . . ."

"What?"

"I met someone in Leningrad."

Grisha stiffened. "A man?"

"Yes." A woman passed, carrying a plate of *sosiski,* rubbery pink hotdogs, to a table. She returned immediately for another plate heaped high with cookies. This constant eating—I felt feverish and repulsed, repulsed by myself for bringing Grisha here before telling him about Kolya.

"And you're lovers?"

I nodded.

Grisha slammed his fist on the table. "So this is all quite a farce now. Why did you let me think . . . you said you missed me, you brought me here. Damn you! I thought we would go to your room. How stupid of me. So, you found someone else, but I primed you for him! Don't you know that all Russian men are dying to sleep with a foreigner?"

"You don't know anything about him! Anyway, you're the one who is married. You're the one with the mistress. You don't have any right to judge me. And if you wanted so much to be with me, why didn't you make it happen? You act like I betrayed you but you offered me nothing."

We sat in silence. "No, I suppose I have nothing to offer you," Grisha finally said. "Well then. Do you love him?"

"I don't know," I said miserably. Why couldn't I say yes? "He doesn't speak English," I added.

"So you found a way to learn Russian. A very commendable method. And what is his profession?"

"Something in a store. Car parts."

"Car parts. Of course. Is he a Jew?"

I shook my head.

"Does he know that you are?"

"Kind of. Not completely." I looked up at Grisha fearfully. "He doesn't like them very much."

Grisha leaned forward again and gripped my forearm. "Someone who doesn't like Jews. So now you understand. You've become a real Soviet, a good little Soviet Jew with a lover who is an anti-Semite. It's quite funny, actually. I thought you were so different but you really are just like us."

I began to cry. "I couldn't help it. I was so lonely and I've been here so long and it's dark all the time, and I think I love him." The counter woman glanced over at us with disapproval: a foreigners' love quarrel. I wiped my eyes and blew my nose in one of the meager napkin fragments that sat in a cup on the table. "I'm sorry. I should've told you before I invited you here. I couldn't talk about this at the school and I *did* want to see you. But I've made a mess of everything."

"Laurie, are you going to try to marry him?"

"I don't know. Let's get out of here. People are looking at us." I stood up.

"They don't understand what we're saying."

We took the elevator downstairs. Grisha leaned against the stop button and grabbed me as the elevator lurched and halted. He ground his hips into mine, pressed his lips against my throat. "See what you'll miss? Take me to your room. Now."

I pushed him off. "Stop it, please stop it. I can't. Don't you understand? Something has happened to me."

Grisha released me. The elevator gears ground again and we descended. I stared at my stained suede shoes, wet at the toes. When the elevator stopped I glanced up. Grisha's rage had given way. His dark eyes flickered with the old yearning, disappointment, and something else, an emotion I could barely recognize since I felt it so rarely myself. Compassion?

"In any case," Grisha said, "I shall not forget you. I shall think of you for a very long time."

I went downstairs to the hotel lobby, after another feverish night without sleep, to call Kolya. It was six-thirty a.m. At seven the woman from the ministry would come to drive me to the airport. I'd used up almost all of my rubles on gifts for family and friends and I had to beg coins in exchange for my last rubles from the stone-faced hotel guards sitting beside the reception desk. An elderly man and woman, they wore dark blue jackets with red armbands and watched me impassively. I had no choice but to call Kolya from the automatic intercity phone booth in the lobby; I didn't have time to go out on the street. I wondered if these two with the armbands could listen in. It scared me that I'd somehow misplaced Kolya's official Komsomol photo, a wallet-sized identification picture he'd given me, in my hotel room. Or someone had been in and taken it while I was out.

I deciphered the posted code and called Leningrad.

Kolya answered, knowing it had to be me. "Lora, good morning."

"Wait," I said, "I have to put more money in. *This damn machine,*" I added in English.

Kolya laughed. "You don't like that machine?"

"Kolya."

"Listen, Lora, I am waiting for you. I'm already making plans for when you come back in summer. We'll do everything. I love you."

"Kolya, today I'll be in England. An island."

"I know. I've been everywhere."

"Not everywhere. There's one place you haven't been." I looked over my shoulder at the stony guards. I couldn't bring myself to say *America* aloud.

"I will," Kolya said. "Lora, I love you."

"You'll have another woman, that's natural."

"No, no, I'll be waiting, remembering. I miss you very much. I love you, Lora. I love you."

"There's no more money. No more time left," I said, beginning to cry. The phone clicked off, dead, before I had a chance to say good-bye. When I came out of the booth I felt fractured. No sleep, my persistent fever, Kolya's voice so close, so familiar, so certain, Grisha's desperation. I couldn't stop sobbing.

"*Devushka*," girl, "don't cry," the old guard woman said, her stern Soviet demeanor cracking. She rushed over to put her arm around me. "Don't cry." The old man hurried over too, begging, "Please don't cry."

"I don't want to leave," I said. "I don't want to go home." I cried harder because they comforted me with a warmth no stranger would show at home. But this was Russia. The same people who consoled me so sincerely could just as sincerely report me.

New York: Sailing—June 1983

I was scheduled to return to Russia in less than a week, my ticket was purchased, and my visa still hadn't arrived from the Soviet embassy. If it didn't come, I couldn't go. This was only a little more unbearable then the uncertainty of what I would find when I got there. If they didn't allow me to return, Kolya would never know what happened. I could hardly write to him and say, Sorry, your government decided it didn't like me. He probably wouldn't receive such a letter, and if he did it would compromise him. If they didn't want me, I had compromised him already.

In the two letters I had sent him in the past six months—more than two might seem too personal to any snooping official—I referred only to something we'd done or seen, depending on his memory to supply the associated emotions. But I'd received no letters from him.

"If he hasn't written he doesn't want to burn his bridges, he doesn't want to take the risk," an émigré friend advised. "Forget him. Nothing can come of this anyway. They're not letting them out."

I knew the odds were against us, but I believed that we would be the exceptions, the special ones for whom doors would open and bureaucracies mesh. So what if he hadn't written? I'd never promised to return; he had a child to protect. Why should he take chances until he was sure I was coming back? Anyway, he might have written but the letters hadn't gotten through. Nothing was simple in this situation and every action had ramifications I could only guess at.

But as the weeks passed and my visa didn't arrive, I'd grown paranoid. Was it the wallet-sized ID portrait from his Komsomol days that had disappeared from my last hotel room? Or was it Galya who reported on me? Could I have said or done something construed as anti-Soviet at the school in Leningrad? Something on the phone when I first got back?

"You are a fool," the defector Vasily said when I asked his opinion. "You are nobody and you think they care about you and your little nobody boyfriend? You think they have not more important people to listen to?"

Vasily believed they listened to him. He said the KGB had beaten him up in Greece for handing out anti-Soviet propaganda to Russian tourists last winter. Although he worked as a shoe salesman in Queens, Vasily devoted his life to an anti-Soviet organization, a collection of disgruntled defectors and Ukrainian nationalists who dreamed of restoring their pre-revolutionary homeland. The group had collaborated with Hitler in World War II. Vasily swore that their appeal was broad now; they had Jews in their ranks too. I didn't believe him.

Here, in New York, I'd become obsessed with the idea of Russian anti-Semitism, and it was only at home that I was brave enough to argue about it. In my first weeks at home I'd continued to have the nightmare I'd had on the train—someone was calling me a Jew and in the dream I kept saying, "No, I'm not." I'd even visited a hip synagogue on the Upper West Side a few times in an attempt to confirm my Jewish identity. Much as the chanted Hebrew prayers remembered from my Sabbath school days moved me in some eerie, inchoate way, I couldn't force myself to feel I belonged, and I stopped going.

Vasily had invited me out to dinner a few weeks ago and offered to pay my way back to Russia if I'd do a "favor" for his organization while I was there. He wanted me to smuggle in money for them.

"Are you out of your mind?" I asked in the middle of a Greek diner on Broadway and Eighty-fifth. "You're crazy. You think I want to get involved with something like that and mess things up with Kolya?"

"You are selfish," Vasily said, looking at his watch. "You do not care about others, only yourself."

"A lot you care about what happens to me. I could end up in Siberia, and I don't even believe in your cause."

Vasily studied me. His eyes looked unpleasantly close together and his Slavic nose was too geometric, as though pinched from clay. "You realize, of course, that your Russian boyfriend only uses you, to get out?"

"Not everyone is a sleaze like you," I said, pushing back my chair. Kolya didn't want to get out. He wanted *me*.

Despite the exchange of insults, Vasily insisted on paying for our meal, the ingrained role of a Russian male, and we hurried away on opposite sides of the sidewalk. It wasn't just Vasily's dangerous "favor," or his slur on Kolya that infuriated me, but I'd been flattered when he called. I thought he wanted my company. We'd met at a party in February, six weeks after I'd come home, and slept together shortly after. I'd thought how much simpler it would be to fall in love with a Russian in New York instead of one in Russia. Vasily seemed possible. He was engagingly literate, if morose, and nearly handsome. Then he disappeared, saying Russian women were more passionate. How could I have been passionate, when I was thinking of Kolya, and Vasily was a terrible lover from the beating-a-drum school of sex? Vaseline, my girlfriend called him, when he slipped out of my life.

Kolya, forgive me. I lost faith.

What would happen to me if my visa didn't come and I was left to this life, here?

Walking up Columbus Avenue this hot June evening, past the glittering shops, the smug, overdressed couples, I consoled myself with the thought that it didn't matter that I was alone now. None of them knew or could understand my particular drama, not even my closest friends. I was special now by virtue of my vigil, my hopes. I'd been raised above the ordinary and made unique. I didn't have to be talented or ambitious. My life was shaped by a necessity it had always lacked. Kolya had given it shape.

Something disturbing happened earlier today. I received a call from an émigré, the teacher of a Russian language class I took this spring at Hunter College. Sophia Kuzminskaya was a small, graying, harried woman in her forties with a teenage son. She'd been embarrassed the first week of class, covering her mouth with her hand, because her teeth were being repaired and she wore some kind of temporary, ill-fitting caps. A week later she had gleaming new American teeth. She told us about her husband, who hadn't received an exit visa from the Soviet Union and was now living in the limbo of the *refusenik* who no longer had the right to work. I'd mentioned that I was hoping to return to the Soviet Union this summer.

Sophia had asked me to meet her in the cafeteria at Hunter. She was waiting when I arrived. I picked up an ice tea, tasting of artificial lemon, and she sat behind a styrofoam cup of coffee, which she didn't touch. She leaned anxiously over the table. I wrapped my straw around my index finger and waited. She looked at me with her sad, brown, beseeching eyes and I knew I didn't want to hear what she would say.

"I must to ask you favor," Sophia said. She'd only learned English recently; she'd been a teacher of history in Russia. "You go soon to Soviet Union?"

"I'm not sure," I hedged. "My visa hasn't come." I was sorry now that I'd mentioned it to her months ago, trying to ingratiate myself, perhaps, because she came from Kolya's city. It had made me feel closer to him.

"It will come, don't worry," she said, brushing away my words with that Russian gesture, the downward wave of the palm. "Why should you not receive visa? You are not dissident, you are American, you have dollars, *valyuta.*"

Sophia opened a plastic bag and drew out a pair of jeans with the tag still attached. She pulled out a calculator, a Walkman cassette player. Was she asking me to sell these things on the Russian black market for her?

"For my husband," she said quickly. "He is good man, very good man. They say he has state secrets. What state secrets? He was in army, everyone was in army. . . . Now they do not let him work. I must to help him. He has no money. It is very simple. You call from street, of course, not hotel. He will meet you. . . ." She looked up at my dismayed face and grew more urgent. "If jeans too heavy, at least this?" She pushed the Walkman toward me, biting her lower lip.

"Sophia," I said, "I'm really sorry. I'd love to help you but I can't. Your husband is a refusenik and it would be dangerous for me."

"What danger? You are American? For you is no danger."

"It isn't that, it's just that I might be getting married to a man there and if I saw your husband it might make things . . . more difficult. I know the KGB frowns on Americans who talk to refuseniks. I'm sorry. I can't take the risk."

"I understand," Sophia said. She stuffed the jeans back into her bag. "Everyone must to think of self, of course. I understand very, very well." She gathered up the Walkman, the calculator, and stood. "I understand you, but you do not understand me. When they do not allow your Russian boy to leave, then you will understand me."

I sat a long time at the table, across from her untouched coffee. Although I believe she was speaking without malice, her words resounded like a curse. I would have liked to help her. Perhaps I was as bad as Vasily said, someone who thought only of herself. But things had grown complicated in a way I'd never known before. Every action had a price.

I couldn't sleep. In my stuffy maid's room cum studio apartment, I held a T-shirt under the faucet and then put it on, pointing the fan toward my bed to chill my hot skin. I lay on my back, staring up at the ceiling, trying to drown out thoughts of Sophia by playing back the memories of my time with Kolya from beginning to end like Alexander Zakharich's movie, struggling to salvage one more gesture, one more conversation. It was my nightly ritual. I'd made a religion out of waiting. The longer we were apart the more I remembered, the larger Kolya loomed.

I studied his photographs, willing them to life. I spoke to him in my head all the time. Walking through Central Park I explained everything to him in Russian: see the roller skaters and the yachtsmen with their toy sailboats on the Seventy-second Street pond? Every time the elevator opened down the hall I imagined, for one impossible second, that it would be Kolya, come for me as he'd promised.

A friend had taped my gypsy record. I popped it into my cheap cassette player. The strains of the violins leading into the melody filled me with a sweet poignancy, a sob-in-the-throat longing more real than any emotion engendered by the day—I was teaching high school English again. My favorite song on the record was still "*Prosti menya za vsyo*"— "Forgive Me for Everything." Kolya had tried to translate it for me from Russian into simpler Russian. The only line he'd made me understand was "and only now I know that no one can replace you." At home I had transcribed and translated the words with the dictionary. One line in the song disturbed me: "I did not mean to deceive you," but it was overridden by the last line: "Surely everything can be understood and forgiven with love."

I rarely played my gypsy record lately because the walls were thin and it drove my neighbor in the next maid's room crazy. She said she was worried about me. Even I was worried about me. There was something suspect in all this. How, another friend asked, could I love an anti-Semite? But it wasn't clear to me that Kolya really was one, just an offhand comment, a knee-jerk Russian reaction. If he was, I believed, he could be healed of this Russian disease by the fresh New World air. He would be as changed by my country as I had been by his.

"I don't want you to go back," my friend Kate insisted. "I'm afraid you won't come home."

When I'd used up every memory, lying there in bed, I imagined our reunion: it would be summer. The evening sun would shine high overhead, Nevsky Prospekt filled with couples strolling arm in arm. I'd wear a white dress. I wouldn't be myself, but someone much prettier, like in a perfume ad—there where they had no perfume ads. On a street corner, Kolya would lean against a wall, as casual as any local boy waiting for his girl. Head tilted back, he'd watch me with that familiar expression of amusement. I'd come toward him in a crowd of shoppers, dodging their string bags filled with mackerel cans, whole dead fish, cabbage. He'd reach out. . . .

But I couldn't make the fantasy go further. The picture refused to take shape. I was too uncertain; it had been too long. There were so many forces against us. Finally, I fell asleep to the creaking fan and dreamt of a sailboat on the Baltic coast. In my dream, the water glittered before a line of coast black with firs. We moved lightly over the water, the sail filled with wind. When Kolya released the main sheet, we drifted slowly through a warm, sweet-scented dusk. Kolya laid out pieces of newspaper, sliced sausage and bread with his pocketknife. I watched the swift, sure movements of his hands. The oily sausage ripped between my teeth. We drifted for hours, until the water grew shallow and ahead of us lay an unfamiliar coast. The keel bumped on the sandy bottom. We stood thigh deep on an unknown shore. It wasn't my home or Kolya's, but a place where we could live.

Return

What I'd feared was intentional was only a bureaucratic snafu, a wrong address. My visa came and I departed for London, where I joined a British language-study program—the cheapest return ticket to Russia I could find. We would fly into Moscow, then take a night train to Leningrad, the *Krasnaya Strelka,* the Red Arrow. I was the only American. The rest of the group was made up of English, Irish, and Scottish twenty-year-olds, an elderly female professor of Russian from Birmingham who served as their escort, and one British man in his late fifties who, it became clear soon enough, traveled to Russia in order to meet a ready supply of young women who found his foreign passport sexy.

By the time we were through customs, bused to our hotel, and checked in, it would be far too late to find an intercity phone to call Kolya. He wouldn't want me to call from the hotel. I hadn't slept in forty-eight hours, and I'd begun to feel crazed, the culmination of six months of waiting, not knowing. Everything that had frightened me the first time here, like the Sheremetyevo Airport security, seemed insignificant now. All I could think of was a telephone. What if Kolya had gone on holiday? What if he wasn't home?

We were brought to a dormlike hotel run by Sputnik, the Soviet youth travel organization. It was illegal to stay in Russian houses; you had to register in a hotel. They wanted that *valyuta.* Two Russian men in their thirties sat on the steps of the Sputnik Hotel joking and commenting on the students as we carried our baggage in. "This one is good," a chunky man in a warm-up suit remarked in Russian as I passed. I'd forgotten how instantly I was transformed in Russia into someone noticeable, my New York ordinariness, my invisibility left behind.

"You, yourselves, are not so beautiful," I said in Russian.

"Oh-ho. She speaks the language. Where are you from?" his buddy called.

"The United States," I said.

"No! But you look just like an *Odessitka*." A girl from Odessa. A Jewess, he meant.

"My *babushka* was from Odessa," I answered, brave now where no one knew me.

"Ahhhh." They nudged each other and laughed.

The Sputnik was a sixties modern structure with few amenities, located far from the city center. We were given a smarmy Sputnik guide, Valery, who was thrilled with me because I'd been to Leningrad before. His was the sort of job both Grisha and Alyosha had had while students at language institutes. I wondered about Grisha. Now I was in his city but I wouldn't call him. He'd said he'd come from Odessa but I'd only be in Moscow a day, and anyway, our last meeting had been too ugly.

In the morning, while the students took a bus tour of Moscow, I insisted to Eleanor, the British professor, and to disappointed Valery, that I knew the city and didn't want a tour. I slipped off to the nearest metro and rode to the center where I found the cavernous Central Telephone and Telegraph Office. I couldn't make sense of the directions for the automatic intercity phones, the city codes and the blips and bleeps that told when to drop in kopecks. I had to ask for help from a dark Central Asian soldier trying to call Tashkent in the booth beside mine. His accent nearly defeated me.

When I finally connected, Kolya's mother answered. I didn't put in my coins fast enough and lost her. The second time I asked for Kolya but lost her as soon as she said, "Wait." The third time Kolya answered.

"It's Lora," I said.

"Lora!" I felt him bolt upright across the hundreds of miles. A sleepy Sunday-morning Kolya trying to clear his head.

"I'm in Moscow."

"Lora."

"I will be in Leningrad tomorrow. In the morning, by train." But I didn't put the needed coins in fast enough and lost him again. He answered this time and I cursed the phone. Last winter he'd laughed at my struggles with the automatic phones but now he only asked, "When?"

"I don't know. Maybe seven, eight. I'm not sure."

"I will meet you."

"No, you don't have to." I thought of the group, the guides, the way I'd be hurried to some bus to whisk me away to the Leningrad Sputnik hotel.

"I'll be there. I'll find the train number. I'll meet you, but then I must go to work. Understand? I'll greet you and then I'll go to work. Call me not tomorrow, but the day after, in the morning."

Why not tomorrow? "How are you, Kolya. How's your son?"

"The day after tomorrow. Understand? In the morning."

"Kolya, you didn't write to me." I wanted to stop my words, my incriminating tone, but the nights of no sleep, the weeks of waiting for the visa, everything piled up to keep me from thinking. "Why didn't you write me?"

One day last winter we were sitting in Kolya's car waiting for Alyosha and Vyetta, and I started chiding Kolya about something. He turned to me, raised a finger, and said carefully, "You often scold me, and that isn't good." I'd apologized immediately. He was right, it wasn't good. Why hadn't anyone else ever stopped me? Why couldn't I stop myself now?

"I wrote, two letters," Kolya said.

"They never came. Perhaps it won't be good for you to meet me?"

"Nonsense. Tomorrow Lora, *poka*."

It was that simple. Forty kopecks after six months. Another soldier waited for my phone. I walked out onto the streets of Moscow where summer sun beat down and the Soviet tourists were lining up to view Lenin in his mausoleum. Red Square looked like a Hollywood set to me. In front of the building housing Lenin's waxed remains, long-coated, jack-booted soldiers goose-stepped like Nazis. Who said you could tell the level of freedom in a country by the manner in which their soldiers marched?

I felt sick. What could he have, should he have said to reassure me? I wanted professions of love. Russians had learned to be reticent on the phone. Yet, last winter when I was leaving, Kolya had offered them. Forget it, I told myself, the guy was just waking up. Now I had an afternoon to live through, an eight-hour train ride, the drinking, smoking,

laughing British students sharing my berth, their gaiety and complaints, while I nursed my hopes like an illness.

In the afternoon I walked with a couple of the English kids into a
deep woods full of paths not far from the Sputnik Hotel. We passed tables of men playing chess, picnicking families, women gathering berries
or mushrooms. Their heads spun around at the sound of our English
with its mix of accents. People exclaimed delightedly at the reddish
Russian squirrels that leaped on branches or ran to steal crumbs. Far
down the path the forest opened to a pond rimmed with sunbathers
and swimmers, teenagers and fat old *babushki* in their underwear. Across
distant fields our hotel rose, stark and unnatural.

I lay down on that hot, sun-baked grass and closed my eyes, hoping
to be healed of all worries by this well-worn Russian soil, by something
radiating off the solid oiled flesh of the sunbathers.

On the way back we stopped to drink water from a spring with a
family that offered its glass jar to drink from. I leaned over the rocks
and cold water ran down my throat. I was here but not here, wandering through a Russian summer dream.

On the train I couldn't sleep, as usual. My hair was greasy from the
bunk, my eyes had dark circles. I wasn't ready for Kolya, I was supposed
to be beautiful, as in my fantasy reunion. Beyond the windows the same
fields I'd seen frozen were green and grassy like in the landscape paintings I'd visited with Anna Iosefevna in the Russian Museum. Shishkin's
and Levitan's landscapes. We were riding into the White Nights of
Leningrad, where dusk didn't fall until midnight and dawn came two
hours later. The train was an hour late arriving. We sat on the tracks
outside of the city while I thought of Kolya waiting for me. I didn't want
him to meet me there, in the midst of sixty students and the chummy
guide, it might be dangerous for him. But when he wasn't there on the
platform, I was bereft.

Russian couples met and embraced, men held bouquets for their
women. One of our students got lost so we waited a long time in the
parking lot. I stood in the bus aisle, glancing anxiously through the
windows, studying every white Zhiguli. Nearly all the cars were white.
Why had I never learned Kolya's license plate number? But of course it
was too late already; nine, then nine-thirty, and he had to be at work.
He might have come earlier and waited until he had to leave.

We drove through brilliant sunshine to the Leningrad Sputnik, as lacking in charm as the one in Moscow. Lots of plate glass, visible metal beams, faded posters celebrating international goodwill, and space-age abstract decoration—plastic quasar beams shooting from the ceiling of the dining room. I was assigned a roommate, a plump, bespectacled girl named Fiona who lived in Birmingham with her auntie. She'd never been away from home before and lay curled up on her bed hugging her pillow with her face to the wall.

I sat at a table of students from Birmingham, all of whom wore the same style metal-rimmed glasses, paid for by the National Health, they said.

"This is right garbage," a boy named Ian with bleached, punked-out hair declared, pushing away a plate of *kasha* and gristly beef. I shrugged. The food was about the same quality as what I'd gotten in the school cafeterias. We were traveling on the cheap; there'd be no caviar and chicken Kiev like the proper Western tourists got in their slick hotels.

"Did you hear about our *skan-dal?*" asked a girl named Pamela.

"One day in the Soviet Union and already they're in trouble," Ian said, grinning his bad British teeth over a slice of buttered bread.

"Maybe we'll get lucky and they'll send us home," a third girl, Nora, offered.

"Don't you want to be here?" I asked.

"No, we have to come. It's part of our course of study. The government pays for it," Pamela explained.

"So what happened, what was the *skandal?*" I asked.

"The knickers," Ian said, pointing his bread at several of the British girls walking by in huge elastic-waisted, garishly patterned boxers. A few of them had discovered the colorful men's underwear at a Russian shop and thought they'd make great shorts, causing an uproar with the *babushki*. I remembered Grisha's words about it not being permitted to wear shorts on the streets of the city—I could just imagine what the *babushki* thought of girls flaunting men's underwear. The students thought it "brilliant" and didn't care a whit. Though I couldn't imagine not wanting to be here, I would have liked to have been as blithe as they were, as uninvested in this trip.

That evening I called Alyosha. He seemed confused and surprised by my voice. He had trouble shaping his English. It was summer and he was out of practice.

"Kolya said he'd meet me at the station and he didn't," I reported.

"It was a misunderstanding," he said.

"No, he said he'd come. Does he want to see me? Tell me if he doesn't want to."

"He wants to see you very much. It must have been a misunderstanding. He had to go to work. He has a new job now."

"Doing what?"

"I'm not sure. Something at the port."

"How is Vyetta?" I asked.

"Both of them are fine. Do you know why I say both of them?"

"No." I thought, in a bizarre burst of paranoia, that he meant Kolya and Vyetta. Were they having an affair?

"Because we are going to have another child! Vyetta is pregnant."

"Congratulations!" I said with too much relief.

"When will we see you?" Alyosha asked. "Are you bored in your hotel?"

"No. It's okay. I've heard that there is a pond not far from the hotel; I will go swimming this afternoon. Tomorrow I start Russian classes at the Polytechnic Institute."

Alyosha said, "I will call Kolya at work. He already called me. He couldn't say on the phone, but he said he needed a translator. He meant you'd arrived. He gets off work tomorrow morning. He works a twenty-four-hour shift. We will meet when your class is over. He will come here and you will call us after class. Okay, Laurie?"

I put my bathing suit on under a pair of lightweight slacks, donned a T-shirt, and started walking in the general direction of the pond. The neighborhood was undistinguished—five-story apartment buildings, low, gray institutes, a furniture factory, a grassy vacant lot. Soon I noticed a *gaii*, a car policeman, cruising very slowly behind me. Why car police when I was on foot? He pulled to the curb and stopped beside me. I decided to settle the matter by asking where the pond was.

"Get in," he said, smiling, "I'll give you a ride." He had a blandly handsome Russian face and looked amused. "Where are you from?" he asked. He'd, of course, noticed my accent.

"America."

"Where?"

"*S.Sh.A*," I said, the Russian initials for the U.S.A.

He couldn't believe it. We drove a short distance. The apartment buildings surrounded grassy lots and a series of crisscrossing paths.

"Through there," the cop motioned.

"Is it dangerous?" I asked. "I mean, if there are no people?"

"Why dangerous?" he asked, puzzled.

"In New York, whenever there are few people, it is dangerous." I was trying to please him, though telling the truth.

"You are safe here," he said.

I could feel him watching as I walked away. Here I was a princess, a pinup girl, here I was stylish. In New York I'd met a seriously obese American grad student who spoke beautiful Russian. She'd studied in Moscow and often traveled as an American tour guide to the Soviet Union. She had Russian boyfriends in every city. How seductive this place could be to Westerners with deficient egos; here every American was a star.

At the pond, I stretched out my towel on the industrial-grade gravel that served as sand and removed my outer clothes in the midst of Russian sunbathers. I was the most tan of all the swimmers and sunbathers. I'd spent hours sunning myself on the tarry roof of my building in New York to look good for Kolya. Of course, as an olive-skinned *Yevraika*, I had an advantage. I hoped I hadn't made myself too tan, in this land where darkness was suspect. Last winter a man had spit at me and called me *Tsiganka*—Gypsy—on the Leningrad metro. I'd been riding with Sasha Ivanov. I would call him soon, but not until I knew my plans with Kolya.

Volleyball players shouted and thunked their ball. *Babushki* scolded children for swimming too soon after eating. Everyone at the pond was in twos, threes, or more. I overheard two teenage boys discussing me. "Why is such a person alone?" one asked. It wasn't normal here to do anything alone, especially lie around in a bikini.

At breakfast I learned that the students segregated themselves by homeland—the Irish and Scottish kids refused to sit with the English, though I, as the only Yank, was neutral and could sit with anyone. We walked several blocks to the Polytechnic Institute, where we were tested for language ability. It was a quintessential Soviet building—pale green paint running halfway up the walls, faded yellow covering the rest, a large entrance hall with standing displays of political propaganda, a gritty, echoing stone floor, walls hung with photos of Lenin, Andropov, and scenes of factories and mighty dams, the eventual creations of the real

Polytechnic Institute graduates, I supposed. After brief tests we were released.

Although I'd imagined myself in flowing white, I dressed to meet Kolya in baggy black cotton slacks and a short-sleeved jersey of tiny red, white, and blue stripes. When it came down to it, I couldn't play the role I'd set forth in my fantasy. I only realized the irony of my unintended patriotic costume later. It was as though Kolya had met me, after so long, wearing a red shirt emblazoned with a hammer and sickle. When I saw him standing beside the metro entrance, I couldn't meet his eyes. How tired he looked, how small. He had come from his all-night job and hadn't slept. He hugged me and I noted deep lines about his eyes. How wizened he'd grown in half a year. Though I knew it was petty, I didn't like the hideous Soviet synthetic knits he was wearing— clothes for his job. He wasn't the Kolya I remembered but a new Kolya, exhausted, anxious, resigned. He put an arm around my shoulders and led me quickly to his car, parked around the corner. Why hadn't he brought flowers? Russians always brought flowers.

The familiar dollar key chain dangled from the ignition. "Alyosha wanted to come with me but I told him not this time. Just you and me." He started the car and wove through Leningrad traffic, white or black Moskviches and Zhigulis, the occasional Volga, drab green army trucks and delivery vans. I'd forgotten how unlike our vehicles theirs were: monochrome cars and flimsy-looking trucks with their obviously bolted seams. Except for the Volgas carrying important personages, the vehicles had no shine.

"Your Russian has improved, you speak much more freely," Kolya said, turning to smile.

"I took classes in New York all spring," I said. "You've learned no English?"

"No time," Kolya said. Leningrad gave way in a series of bridges, then marshes with long waving grasses, the industrial edge of a harbor, firs. When the *gaii* stopped us at their checkpoint, Kolya showed his papers and we drove on. I no longer felt alarmed. It was all part of my Leningrad movie. But the gloomy darkness of fall and early winter had dominated my movie. Now light filled the stretches of fields and glittered on the gulf to the west.

Kolya asked, "How is your family?"

In my nervousness, for reasons I didn't understand, I couldn't stop speaking of problems. "My sister has lost her job. And my father has lost his business." I presented Kolya with the most unflattering portrait of America, better than *Pravda,* and it wasn't one he'd be able to interpret correctly. My sister would quickly find a new job and receive unemployment until she did; my father was a lawyer as well as a businessman and had been living on investments for years. I was performing an act of sabotage.

"You have your problems and we have ours," Kolya said softly. "I am accustomed to ours."

I didn't mention his not meeting me at the station.

As always, we had to make stops once we left the highway and entered Kolya's region. I sat in the car while he talked to an aunt about a cousin in the hospital. Nearing Kolya's house, bulldozers blocked the road. We waited for the roaring monsters. The earth was torn up in sandy swatches. Many of the hand-built, charming little houses with their carved decorative trim had already been flattened.

"Your house still stands," I observed.

"Yes, but not for long."

Kolya's room was a mess. His bed wasn't folded back into a couch, clothes lay strewn about, vodka bottles littered a table. Why hadn't he cleaned up for my arrival?

"I was very drunk," Kolya said, putting a hand to his head. "Vova and I."

Sunday, after he'd received my call, he'd gotten drunk. And hadn't been back from work since the following morning. His room had changed. The bed stood near the back window to catch the summer air, and through it I could hear children playing. Kolya drew the curtain shut quickly. Perhaps his son, visiting his *babushka*? The rumble of a bulldozer and the steady pounding of a pile driver served as background to the kids' voices. Kolya switched on a tape deck, American pop, to drown out the noises and perhaps to cover our voices.

"Do you understand the words, Kolya?"

"No."

The song playing was "Breaking Up Is Hard to Do." I didn't translate. Kolya led me to his opened bed and began to undress me. I wanted to say, No, wait, let's talk first, but I felt as lacking in will as I had the first time here.

"You are very tan," Kolya said.

"I'm white, too," I said, gesturing toward the pale lobes of my breasts, the triangle of white at my groin.

"But very little!" Kolya laughed, and for a moment I recognized him.

We hugged and clung to one another but it wasn't making love for me; it was more like swimming when tired, trying to keep my head above water.

Kolya smiled. "I haven't become worse?"

"Maybe you've had a lot of practice while I was gone," I said, then quickly added, "it's just a joke, don't tell me. Do you think I've changed?"

"No, I saw immediately that you were exactly the same."

Now we would lie here and talk, straighten everything out. But Kolya sat up abruptly. "I want water," he said, "to swim, to wake up."

We dressed. I opened the plastic bag I'd carried and drew out the gifts—a calculator that would be useless to him when the battery wore out, sunglasses, T-shirts.

"Ti molodetz," he said, kissing me. You're wonderful.

We drove to a river and I sat in the car while Kolya disappeared behind a screen of green fiberglass, reappeared in trunks. I hadn't brought a suit. In a car next to me, two men and a girl sat smoking. They wore Western clothes and looked terribly bored. *You have your problems, we have ours. I am accustomed to ours.* Did that mean he'd decided not to leave? I couldn't ask outright, didn't have the courage yet. Across a stretch of beach Kolya dove under water. He surfaced and swam toward shore. I felt no closer to him than if I were back in New York. Kolya appeared, dripping but dressed, beside me.

"These people, are they foreigners?" I asked, gesturing toward the next car.

"Russians," Kolya said, toweling his curls.

I didn't understand anything about how things worked here.

"Now we will go wherever you want to," Kolya said.

I requested a park. Driving there, Kolya related for me the plot of an American novel he'd read in translation about a man who'd lost his sons. I began to fall under the sway of his voice again. Perhaps it would be like last winter again, how I didn't think much of him at first, and then he'd grown on me until he'd become as necessary as breath. His tired eyes didn't matter. But was this story meant as subtext? His son lay between us. What fairy tale had he created for me last winter, a place of easy exit visas he'd invented for the world within his room, that small island we'd shared.

When I asked for a park I was thinking of the one he'd taken me to our last day together, with the *ootki,* and the dog that wouldn't eat *piroshki.* I would have liked to see it with leaves, in summer, but Kolya drove us to a much wilder park, with paths that cut between the birch and fir trees. Again I chattered nervously as we carried a blanket into the woods, past the crumbling relic of a wooden peasant shack.

"I wanted to write something about Russia this spring, perhaps an article, but I was afraid that I wouldn't receive a visa if I did. Not that I am against the Soviet Union, of course, but I would have to tell the truth."

Kolya said wearily, "Lora, you must do what you want to do. If you want to write an article, you must write it."

Did that mean he didn't care if I couldn't come back? Or that I shouldn't let the fear of losing a Soviet visa keep me from writing? I didn't stop to wonder what such an article might mean for him.

He spread the blanket and we stretched out. Kolya lay hunched and distant, seeking sleep. He seemed unreachable, the things we needed to discuss far out of reach as well. A pack of heavyset women in nylon warm-up suits jogged past.

"Why if they run are they so fat?" I asked petulantly.

"For that reason they run," Kolya said, as though explaining the obvious to a bad-tempered child. "Look," Kolya said, pointing upward, "a circle."

Above us the birches parted to reveal a perfect ring of impossible blue. When I looked up I saw not the sky but the replay of my Kolya movie, the string of images I'd savored all spring. The movie played with a terrible insistence, more real than this moment, than Kolya lying pained beside me. The movie played on: the park, the ducks, the icon to Saint Nikolai, while Kolya stared silently up at the circle of sky. I thought: I hate my life.

Kolya said, "Now I will drive you back to your hotel and I will go home and sleep. And you will sleep."

I nodded. Why didn't he want me to stay with him, as before?

He pulled up to the corner beyond the hotel. "Tomorrow I have to go to Vyborg," he said. "Business. Something for work. I will be back Thursday. Call me Thursday."

Two days? After six months, I would have to wait two more days.

Kolya kissed my cheek. "Lora, *vsyo budet khorosho.*" Everything will be fine.

Back in the hotel my British roommate was crying into her pillow with homesickness. She hadn't wanted to come. She'd only come because it was a college requirement. The food was awful and she didn't see how she'd live through a month away from her auntie. I listened unsympathetically to her sobs and thought: I have only twenty-six more days.

For five rubles I purchased a massage from the masseuse whose office was on the same floor as my hotel room. He doubled as a physical therapist. I'd seen a small crippled boy, helped by his mother and *babushka,* entering the masseuse's office this morning. I almost never saw disabled people, save for a few one-legged war veterans, in Russia—where did they hide them?

The masseuse, whose name was Boris, was built like an Olympic wrestler. He had a broad, square face and flashing gold teeth. He spent an inordinate amount of time on my chest. "*Mokraya, tyoplaya,*" he crooned—warm, wet—and tried to kiss me, though I turned my face. After the session he plied me with hard candy and asked me to meet him after work. I refused, but I'd found comfort in his eager touch. Maybe it was only my foreignness that drew him, but I didn't care. I needed badly to be wanted and I didn't know if Kolya wanted me anymore. I lay in my narrow bed while Fiona sniffled, remembering the feel of Boris's sweating palms.

A Ring That Fit Neither of Us

Sasha Ivanov and I walked through summer drizzle, looking for a place to sit with a little privacy so I could give him the gifts I'd brought for him—cigarettes, sunglasses, acrylic paints. We didn't want it to look like he was a *fartsovchik* making a deal. Sasha's face was drawn, his large mustache droopy; he smoked nervously and spoke in an insistent monotone. His American girlfriend, Annie, had come for a week's visit recently. Things had not gone well.

Sasha had spent months preparing for her arrival. He'd sold off three-quarters of his impressive record collection to get money for the marriage and his plane ticket to the States. He'd bought her a beautiful jade necklace as an engagement gift. For months she'd been writing him love letters with questions such as, "What do you think, should we live in New York or Washington? Would you mind Washington very much?" He met her at Pulkhovo, the Leningrad airport. Annie insisted she wanted to take the metro to his place, alone, for old time's sake. He hadn't understood but had indulged her, carrying her bags to his apartment, where he'd waited hours for her to show up. Officially, she had to register at a hotel, so he thought, perhaps, she'd gone there first.

When she got to his place they'd made love, then she'd fallen asleep immediately. She'd slept through the night and through the next day until four o'clock in the afternoon. When she woke up she'd said that she'd decided not to marry him. She'd come back to make sure.

Sasha then had to accompany her to the welcome party he'd planned with all his friends and relatives. People brought gifts, which Annie cheerfully accepted. She offered Sasha, as a gift, a story she'd written that had been published in her college literary magazine. It was all about a girl who resembled Annie very closely and her relationship with a selfish college boy whom she loved wildly. Annie had written an inscription to Sasha on the title page. He wanted to kill her. What, he wanted to know, did all this mean? When Annie hit Helsinki on the way home, she'd called, crying. Would he hate her forever? Maybe, she said, she'd change her mind with time.

"Shit," Sasha said, shaking his head. "I think American girls all crazy. She was living with that asshole all year and sending to me love letters."

"She's a spoiled brat," I said. "I can't believe she did that."

"She is a fool," he said. "She lost everything. She'll never find a man who loves her as I did." He was trying to bolster himself. He'd lost immeasurably more than she had—a love and a chance at an exit visa.

We finally sat on a bench in the drizzle. Sasha held my umbrella overhead. He said his umbrella had fallen apart and he couldn't find one anywhere. I promised to leave mine with him when I went home. Sasha was wearing the other gift Annie had brought him, an argyle sweater vest.

"What happened with your friend?" Sasha asked. He threw the butt of a Marlboro into a puddle and lit another.

"I don't know. I've only seen him once. He's got a new job and . . . I'm supposed to call him in half an hour."

"Can you believe what she did?" Sasha asked, unable to think of anything but the Annie story for long.

Sasha wandered the sidewalk while I phoned Kolya. His mother answered and said Kolya was outside. I waited while she called him.

"I was working on my car," he said. "It was a long, hard trip to Vyborg. Call Alyosha and Vyetta," he said. "We are making plans for Saturday, to go together to their dacha."

"Saturday?" I said, incredulous. "Don't you want to meet me tonight?"

"Tonight I must work on my car. Tomorrow morning I must go to work and work twenty-four hours again. So tonight I must sleep."

"If you don't want to see me you don't have to," I said. I began to cry, half in hurt and half in shame. I couldn't believe this any more than Sasha could believe his Annie.

"Lora," Kolya said, "You are making me feel very bad. Of course I want to see you. But do you want me to throw my job away?"

"I don't want you to do anything you don't want to do."

"Lora, I'm looking forward to Saturday. There we will be together. Saturday. Call Vyetta, she will explain."

I hung up the phone. Sasha looked at me questioningly. I said, "Everything's fine. We're going to a dacha Saturday."

Sasha and I continued our aimless walk through the evening shopping crowds. I thought, later I'll call and hang up, just to see if Kolya's really home sleeping. Maybe he has a girlfriend now and hasn't told me. Maybe he . . .

"What is he doing in Vyborg?" Sasha asked suspiciously. "It's on the Finnish border. Is he involved in smuggling?"

"I don't know what he does," I said.

A block from the Sputnik, Alyosha crossed the street to meet me and then Kolya ran up from his car, grabbed me and kissed me on the sidewalk. He wore jeans and a red crewneck jersey that made his shoulders look wide. The kiss he planted on my lips felt real.

Driving to Alyosha's dacha, I told Kolya about the masseuse who had tried to kiss me. "He wasn't very professional," I said.

Kolya laughed. "Oh, he was very professional." He seemed cheerful, the old Kolya, despite the fact that once again he'd worked all night without sleep. It was a sunny Saturday and we were going to be away overnight, even though it was illegal for me to travel more than thirty kilometers beyond Leningrad. Alyosha shrugged it off. "Who will know?" he said.

I'd brought presents, which Vyetta exclaimed over—cosmetics and earrings for her, clothing and tapes for Alyosha. I should have brought jeans for them all, the most valuable commodity, but I was afraid that they'd be taken from me at customs, that I'd be accused of preparing to sell them on the black market. And, I didn't have enough money to buy them, after I'd paid for my ticket and the language program.

Kolya and I sat in front and Vyetta and Alyosha sat in the back seat. A fluffy little rat of a dog nestled on Vyetta's lap. Their little boy, Danya, was already at the dacha with his *babushka*. The tape deck blared American pop from its usual position of honor between Alyosha's feet. Fields spread forth between deep forests. This wasn't the same wintery black and white but a wholly Russian world of green fields and meandering streams, grazing cows, and rubber-booted peasants.

After more than an hour of driving we left the "highway," a two-lane blacktop, and pulled onto a series of sandy lanes that wound through a village of dachas—hand-built wooden houses much like those in Kolya's neighborhood. In contrast to the puritanical rules for city dress, the dacha people walked barelegged, bare-bellied, in bathing suits or even underwear. The houses lay close together but every fenced yard was rich with vines, fruit trees, gardens of sprouting vegetables and berries. Roses hedged most of the yards and purple lupines grew everywhere.

Alyosha's dacha was a ramshackle three-story building on the edge of a perfectly round pond. It had a crazy, unplanned elegance with its large, sun-filled windows and unpainted shiplap boards. Every inch of ground around the house was thick with growth: fat strawberries, green tomatoes, cucumber vines, onions. A wealth of food compared to what you could find in the city. "The land was all swamp when we got it," Alyosha said, "but my mother filled it in bucket by bucket; the neighbors call her the Lady Horse." She owned the house but not the land, Alyosha explained. All land belonged to the State.

On the lake side of the main house stood a small green shed, the summer kitchen. Alyosha's father, a hunched silent man, sat within.

Galina Ivanovna, or The Motor, as Kolya referred to Alyosha's mother, because she talked incessantly and made everyone work at her own fever pitch, wore a bathing suit over her large belly and grinned gold teeth at me. She shrieked her gym teacher's voice in a Russian so fast I understood nothing beyond the fact that I was very welcome.

She immediately put Kolya to work digging a hole so she could replace a rotted post that held up one end of her hammock. I watched the sledge rise and fall, the tense and release of Kolya's well-muscled calves as he pounded in the post. When he finished I helped to tamp the fresh earth with my bare feet. The hammock was strung on its new post. Gingerly, Galina Ivanovna sat to test it. The new post held but, as if in slow motion, the other post toppled. Galina Ivanovna looked up at us from a tangle of hammock strings. She was the first to laugh.

"Let's swim," Kolya said, before she could put him back to work.

There was no beach on this side of the lake. The birches and grass ran right to the water. We walked to a small opening beyond Alyosha's lot. Vyetta stood shivering with her pregnant belly jutting through the nylon of her bathing suit. She couldn't decide if it would be bad for the baby to swim. It was early summer and the water was still very cold. Alyosha's belly jutted a little bit too, but his shoulders and arms were powerful. He'd built this house without the benefit of power tools, which no one seemed to own. Across the pond on the public beach swimmers screamed as cheerfully as swimmers anywhere. Kolya, Alyosha and I dove in.

"She swims well," Kolya said as I propelled myself with a practiced pool crawl. I swam harder, trying to impress. Why did he speak of me to Alyosha in the third person, as if I weren't even there? Kolya and Alyosha headed back to shore but I kept swimming. I was safer here where my stroke carried me, where I knew what to do. It was back on shore that I was afraid, where I watched Kolya for clues.

"Enough," Alyosha called to me, "it's very cold." But I swam further. "Laurie, now we must go to the forest to cook *shashlik*!"

I'd once seen a Russian movie called *Moscow Does Not Believe in Tears*. I thought it strange when the man took his new girlfriend and her teenage daughter to meet his friends on a hillside beyond the city. They cooked meat on skewers and sat around drinking. I hadn't known then that it was a normal Russian entertainment. It had seemed exotic to me.

Kolya, I, Alyosha, Vyetta, their solemn little son, Danya, and their terrier dog crowded into the car. To Kolya's relief, Galina Ivanovna would stay behind and bundle birch leaves for the *banya*. First we had to find the exact spot in which to make our fire. Kolya drove through a pine forest on a pitted dirt track, while berry pickers and mushroom gatherers ran from our path. An old man skittered away on a bicycle. The road was filled with puddles and mud.

"Do you have such bad roads in America?" Kolya asked.

"In Vermont where my mother lives the roads are just as bad."

Kolya hit the steering wheel. "*Nashi khuzhe, nashi khuzhe,*" ours our worse, Kolya joked, reversing the usual Soviet maxim—ours are better.

When we found the right spot, with a view of a little pond in a glen and a pit for a fire, we stopped. Vyetta set to picking berries. They were greedy for any food that could be gathered, storing up vitamins and flavor against a long cold winter. No, I could not help cut the onions, that was men's work because it made the women cry. Alyosha cut meat for the *shashlik* skewers, mixed in onions and herbs. Kolya gathered downed wood and hacked it into kindling. "Rest," they said, "you are our guest." When I begged to help they gave me the cucumbers to wash.

We sat on a blanket, drinking vodka with chasers of weak pink juice, eating our *shashlik* and salad. "Give her the best one," Kolya said, "she is our guest." It sounded too formal; I was their guest, not his intended. But in the car driving back to the dacha, Kolya was as jovial as he'd been last year. Vyetta passed me berries from a pail in the back seat. I offered berries to Kolya, who insisted that I place them directly against his lips, since he couldn't take his hands from the wheel on such a bad road. He looked happy, kissing my fingers, smiling sideways at me.

Alyosha's tape deck blasted American tunes: "been lonely sooooo long." They found it funny when I insisted I could identify if a singer was white or black from his voice. They didn't believe me. I translated for them, since even Alyosha couldn't catch the English words.

Piles of leafy birch branches lay bundled in front of the small log building that housed Alyosha's *banya*. It had a narrow curtained ante-room with a table bearing a pitcher of juice and a vase of lupines, a dressing chamber hung with thin towels and strips of sheet. While we waited for the wood stove to heat, I sat on Kolya's lap beside a table set up in the yard and we all downed vodka shots. I ran my fingers through his thick curls and he gripped my waist. When it was ready, Kolya and I went into the *banya* first. The stove hissed, making a wall of choking heat. We clung sweatily to each other on a bench, kissing. I'd drunk enough to stop worrying; everything was as it should be. The *banya* heat was our heat, a pressure that took my breath away. Then the door flung open and Galina Ivanovna came in wearing overstretched, raggedy underwear, her great breasts flopping. We broke apart.

"*Tebye nravitsa*, Lora?" Galina Ivanovna asked. Do you like it?

"*Ochen zharko*," I said. Very warm.

"Cover your hair," she counseled, handing me a strip of sheet.

Alyosha came in and threw a dipper of *kvass*, a drink made from fermented rye bread, against the brick stove, and the *banya* filled with hot, bread-scented steam. Sweat ran. "Bend over," Alyosha ordered, and he beat my back, my legs, and chest with birch leaves in a practiced rhythm. Kolya beat the branches against his own body, then we ran out into the night, steam rising ghostly from us, and jumped into the lake. A few nighttime swimmers watched us. My accented Russian to Kolya, my English to Alyosha, boomed across the still water. Would it compromise them somehow? No one seemed worried. Kolya looked white and slender, an apparition in the steaming night.

"Ready for another time in the *banya*?" asked Alyosha. "If you are very brave you must take five turns."

Vyetta appeared, crying. We'd left her little dog in the forest and we had to go and search for it. No, we couldn't wait for the dog to find its way home; we had to go now. Kolya didn't like to drive when he'd been drinking but there weren't likely to be *gaii* cruising the forests. We bumped over the dark pitted roads while Kolya grumbled. When we came back without the dog, after an hour of searching, Vyetta was still crying and Kolya was annoyed.

"Don't you want another turn in the *banya*, Laurie?" Alyosha asked. But I wasn't brave. The mood had broken. I was tired from drinking and Kolya hadn't slept in forty hours. Kolya led me up to the room that Vyetta had prepared for us. It was a beautiful room. A vase of fresh flowers stood on a bureau with a carved wooden mirror stand. Lacy curtains. Like a bridal suite, except for the lumpy single bed. Once again I felt distant, and afraid. I couldn't lose myself in him as I'd done last winter. I couldn't let him lose himself in me. I didn't know who was responsible for the distance between us.

"*Yesho?*" he asked. More, do you want more? As though he were serving tea and cakes instead of making love to me. He'd never had to ask before. Still, when the crooked little bed let out a wooden shriek and collapsed beneath us, we both laughed.

I woke to find Kolya sleeping. I wanted to touch him, to turn to him and wake him so that we would make love as we'd done last winter, in those mornings before he had to sneak me back to my hotel. But I couldn't do it. He was so exhausted. And, I was afraid that he might not want me. I watched him sleep while the sun moved across the pale walls and turned his brown hair gold. Outside I heard Galina Ivanovna giving orders, Vyetta's high, querulous voice, Alyosha's bark as the women prepared breakfast in the summer kitchen. Alyosha's little boy peered through the gap in our curtains, a small serious face peeking in. I crept out and went swimming. In the break between birches, a woman threw sticks into the lake for her shaggy, dripping black dog. A tiny lone figure strode across the distant sandy shore.

We were drinking tea around a folding table in the yard when Kolya appeared several hours later. "You didn't wake me," Kolya complained. "You let me sleep too long."

"You needed it," I said. I'd let him sleep too long, or had he been sad to find me gone?

"Now we'll swim," he said. "My head hurts."

Kolya pulled an inflatable rubber boat with attached oars from a storage area under the house and carried it to the shore for me to lie on. He brought a blanket for himself, the same blanket we'd lain on in the forest. It wasn't a blanket, he told me, but a Finnish flag. How he'd gotten it, I didn't ask.

"Too many people here," he said, leading us away from the place where swimmers and fishermen and sunbathers had already gathered, to a grassy clearing behind trees and marsh grass. Did he just want to get away from crowds, or was he afraid of my accent identifying me as a foreigner? We lay in the sun without speaking. In the face of so much silence, I put the inflatable boat into the water, lay down and paddled away. Across ten yards of water I watched Kolya huddle into a fetal curve. He looked vulnerable, naked in a way I'd never seen him, like a small wild animal cringing in open light. I wanted to go back to him, to put an arm around him and say, "It doesn't matter, Kolya, none of it matters," but I couldn't see beyond my own need for reassurance. It was his role to tell me everything will be fine, *vsyo budet khorosho*. I paddled through weeds, over water that sparkled like broken glass. My legs looked impossibly blobby and white to me in the overexposure of sun reflected off water. Everything had grown distorted. Kolya was watching me now.

"*Do svidanya*," I called softly. Good-bye.

Kolya lifted his hand in a small wave.

In the afternoon, Kolya and I sat in his car, waiting for Vyetta and Alyosha so that we could drive around the village hanging signs about the lost dog. "Vyetta is always late," he grumbled. He didn't like her much. I'd known that last year. She was a dissatisfied woman who complained and argued with Galina Ivanovna constantly.

Across the lake the swimmers screamed and splashed. A fly buzzed against the windshield, blind to the open window beside Kolya's head. Kolya took a cheap tin ring in the shape of a horseshoe from his pocket. "Look," he said, "Anatoly found this and gave it to me." His son. I turned the cheap metal in my hands, a five-and-dime ring, a gumball machine ring, if there were such things in Russia.

"It's strange," he continued, "although my hands are not so large, the ring is too small for them."

I slid the ring on my own hand, on my left hand, the American wedding finger. In Russia they wore their wedding rings on the right. The ring was too big for me; it tilted, swung upside down. I slid it off and handed it to Kolya, the ring from his son that fit neither of us.

"In America," I said, "this shape means good luck."

I picked up a book off his dashboard, a novel in Russian that I had no hope of reading. From out of its pages drifted a picture of Kolya's son.

Vyetta and Alyosha decided to spend one more night at the dacha in case the dog was found. Kolya would drive me back to Leningrad. He said he had to be back by six to pick up his son and drive him to the train station. His son was going to Kiev to visit his *babushka*. The narrow road was congested with Sunday traffic. Kolya drove fiercely, speeding up to pass on corners. I gripped the dashboard with whitened knuckles. Kolya drummed the wheel nervously. His son would be waiting. He'd miss his train. We hit a traffic jam at a train crossing. Kolya was crazy with nerves. I no longer believed it was his son who was waiting. A girlfriend? A business deal with a shady character? I remembered Sasha Ivanov's words about Vyborg and smuggling.

"The heat is awful," Kolya complained. Last night's embraces seemed as long ago as last winter's. Kolya wanted to get away from me, I was convinced of it.

"Drop me at the next station," I said. "I'll take the train back to my hotel."

"No, no. I'll take you to your hotel," he insisted.

Around the corner from the Sputnik he stopped but didn't turn off the engine. "We'll make more plans for the week. Call Vyetta tomorrow. I have to go to Vyborg again tomorrow. Call Vyetta."

In the Sputnik, Fiona still lay with knees drawn up, facing the wall, crumpled tissues surrounding her. I flopped onto my bed and stared at the ceiling.

A Conversation That Will Not Be

The hydrofoil, a speedy, low-slung ferry, whizzed across the sparkling Baltic to Petrodvoretz, the czar's summer palace. Kolya didn't sit by me but drifted from window to door, lost in his own calculations. Perhaps this would be my only boat ride. I'd asked Kolya about his sailboat but he said it needed work and he had no time to fix it. This trip had been planned without consulting me; I was as passive now as any Soviet, moved along by forces I couldn't understand.

Alyosha bought beer at the ferry snack bar and happily guzzled. Vyetta chattered. Her dog had been found and all was well with the world. I watched them in silence. At the hydrofoil landing, a platform connected to the mainland by a long cement dock due to the shallow gulf, policemen hurried the crowd. A Japanese delegation was being led through and they wanted us out of the way.

"*Buistreye!*" the policemen shouted. Faster!

Kolya shouted something back.

The cop turned and waved a menacing arm. "Less conversation," he hissed. We hurried along.

"Japanese are better than Russians," Alyosha said. "Do your police act like that?"

I thought of mounted police warning crowds to get back at parades or accidents in the city. But to make way for foreigners? No. I felt embarrassed for my humiliated friends. The palace rose like a dream beyond a long colonnade of golden fountains. A red flag waved in the breeze from the palace roof.

"*Sovietskii vlast vesdye,*" Kolya said quietly. Soviet power is everywhere. "What?" I asked, though I'd heard him.

"The riches of the people," he said bitterly.

Vyetta said, "It's eleven; now the fountains will turn on."

Great golden Samson rent the jaws of the lion at the head of the Grand Canal that led down to the gulf in a golden shimmer. Spectators patiently waited for the daily show: old pensioners with their canes, pimpled young soldiers with shaved scalps, gaggles of schoolchildren, peasants from villages and collective farms in their shabby padded jackets and their cheap rubber boots. Scattered among the drabness were the brightly dressed Western tourists, their pedantic Intourist guides stuffing their ears with English, German, French.

The first fountains came on. Water shot in jets from the mouths of golden fish. Slowly, more and more of the fountains spurted their water into the sky. Though beautiful, it was an odd anticlimax. Water, an element, rose through air to fall again. The foreigners grew bored and wandered away, but the Soviet spectators, except for Kolya who stared off into a middle distance, silently stood in their clumps, watching and waiting, as though there'd be more. They'd been promised a show and they stood gazing stubbornly at the gilded statuary, the narrow water jets, the yellow fantasy palace spread against the sky, the red Soviet flag hanging limp now, as water shot and fell, shot and fell. The spectacle was already over and yet went on and on, a sleight of hand as breathtaking and unyielding as the revolution. Their patience in the face of thwarted expectation pained me: We were promised. We're still waiting.

"Would Lora like ice cream?" Vyetta asked, breaking from her trance. "Our Russian ice cream is very good."

"Not right now," I said.

Alyosha bought beer and we strolled through the enormous park, past ponds and gardens, a checkerboard fountain, Peter the Great's playground—a magical stone paved square that squirted water if you stepped on the wrong spot, his sumptuous bathhouse. Kolya put an arm around me as we walked. Ahead of us, Alyosha and Vyetta walked arm in arm. Two couples. I stroked Kolya's hand. But on the hydrofoil going back he stood again to look at the view, his back to me. Through the scratched Plexiglas windows, Leningrad sped toward us, ships, piers, stone embankments, the Hermitage's blue stone topped by titans.

Driving back through Leningrad, Kolya and Alyosha made plans.

Vyetta and I would take the train to join Alyosha at the dacha Saturday morning. Kolya would drive out to join us on Sunday when he got off work and stay Sunday night. Everything was agreed. "Do you understand?" Kolya kept asking me. "Alyosha will explain it again in English."

I understood. Today was only Wednesday. I wouldn't see Kolya until Sunday. "Drop Alyosha and Vyetta off first," I said. "I want to talk a minute."

Kolya couldn't refuse in front of them but as we neared the Sputnik he said, "Talk. We can talk while I drive."

"No," I said, "stop."

Kolya parked not far from the hotel, the engine running. "Lora," he said, "this conversation will not be."

"Yes, it will be." I turned the keys and pulled them out of the ignition.

Kolya sighed. He leaned back against the driver's door, studying me from the greatest possible distance. The late sunshine struck his eyes and turned them a greeny blue, the color of the Mediterranean. Like the sea in Italy where he'd hoped to go last year but had somehow lost the chance.

Outside the car, everyone looked cheerful. Men waited for their girls at the door to a furniture factory, swimmers returning from a nearby pond carried towels. There was a great air of normalcy from which I felt excluded. Kolya lay his forehead on the steering wheel. I thought, this is a moment I will remember forever: the sun filtering through the open car window in Kolya's curls, the weight of the keys in my own hand with their plastic dollars. A conversation that would not be.

"Kolya," I said, "you've changed. Last year you did not drive me back to my hotel, you asked me to stay."

"Last year was last year. This year is different."

"Explain!"

"Ah, you are an American. You want everything in a little box. Listen, Lora, I don't want you to think I've done badly to you when you go home so I take you back to your hotel."

"You have already done badly to me. This was your idea, Kolya. You asked me to come back. You insisted. You said you loved me."

Kolya looked up. Softly he said, "I loved you at the dacha."

I stared out the car window at a policeman across the street. He loved me at the dacha a few days before, but not now. "You said you wanted us to have a child."

Kolya smiled. "Let's."

I hit the dashboard angrily. "Thank you. You here and I alone with the child in New York. A nice plan."

"Lora, do you want me to leave my country? Do you want me to leave my son? I have to build a life for him here."

"I don't want you to do anything you do not want to do. But last year you said everything would work out, we'd live here and there and he could come with us when he wanted."

Kolya let out breath. "That would have been better."

"You said it was possible."

"Now it is not. Lora, listen. Nothing is possible now. Things are not the same. Our relationship is very difficult, very complicated. You live there and I live here. Do you want to live here?"

My eyes swept the street—factory, hotel, trolley, police. I tried to will myself into this picture but it wouldn't take shape. I couldn't see myself carrying a string bag, waiting in line, fearing police. "For a year, maybe," I said. "After that, no."

"And I? If I left I couldn't come back."

"But last year you said it was possible!" Last year, last year, I kept insisting, as though the fact that he'd said it had made it true, and now he was only being contrary. I knew it was hopeless, maybe it had all been fabrication, what he wanted to believe, or maybe it was that his job had changed and he no longer had the means. Maybe Andropov's crackdowns had forced him to leave his old job and had made his contact with me more dangerous. He was right, the risks were all his; I could come and go as I liked. And yes, he'd said, last winter, he wanted to live in America a year or two, and then return. But my worst side took over. If I couldn't have Kolya, or my Kolya movie, I wanted an admission, an apology, some satisfaction. I wanted some truth.

"It was your idea, Kolya, not mine. I worked six months to earn the money to return. I had two jobs, I waited for you." Now I was lying. I hadn't had two jobs, I'd just tutored students on top of my two-thirds teaching job, and I'd slept with Vasily. I'd wanted to fall in love with someone else but it hadn't happened, and in that space Kolya had grown too large, grown to be everything, while I must have shriveled in comparison to the enormity of the problems my return meant for him, and now I couldn't be compassionate but had to wring something from him.

"You said you loved me, Kolya, I never said I loved you."

"Do you, Lora? Do you love me?"

I wanted to say yes, I wanted to believe it because if I hadn't, what was I doing sitting in this car now, what had the past seven months meant? Or I wanted to wield such love as a weapon, as further proof of the magnitude of his crime. If I had loved him, then he had betrayed me. But I felt too doubtful about both of us, humiliated to be sitting here whining accusations. Maybe I had only loved Kolya loving me, loved what loving Kolya would have meant: waiting to return, to file for marriage, waiting again to see if permission would be granted for him to leave. It would have become a crusade. . . .

"I can not love anyone who does not love me," I said stonily.

"I can't either," Kolya said. "Lora, you too have changed a little. Last year you were so afraid, and now you are not afraid but you invent problems. You make complications. You worry about losing your visa. I have to be careful with you with your articles, your writing."

Was that it? Why had I been such a fool to mention it to him that first day? Worrying about my visa and too self-involved to imagine he might worry about himself. I'd become a threat in so many ways.

"You aren't satisfied ever," he continued. "You search and search and are not satisfied with yourself. You are always thinking. You mustn't think so much. It's better just to live."

"I was always like that," I said. "I haven't changed." Hadn't he praised what he now criticized?

"I understand you," Kolya said softly, "because I am the same. Always thinking, thinking. Listen, Lora, now you will go to your hotel and we will be together soon at Alyosha's dacha. Saturday you will go on the train with Vyetta, and I will come Sunday when I get off work."

"I won't be waiting for you," I said. "I've waited long enough." I handed him the car keys. "Do you want me to send you the photographs? Your boy will want them when he's grown."

"Keep them," he said.

We Don't Ask Questions Anymore

Vyetta met me at the station for trains headed north. She carried a basket and a suitcase, both of which looked heavy. Her pregnant belly pushed out one of Alyosha's plaid flannel shirts but she'd tied a ribbon around her throat to feminize the outfit. She was a beautiful woman, with bow lips, a pale heart-shaped face, and blue eyes. Why did Alyosha need a mistress? Was it her character or did Russians just have to have affairs?

When I offered to carry her bag she refused. "But you're pregnant," I persisted.

"I'm stronger," she said. "I'm used to it."

We had to shop first. Alyosha expected us to arrive on the ten a.m. train, but Vyetta had found a place where they were selling a certain kind of flat squash that her grandfather liked very much, and which she wanted to cook for me in a special dish. The squash stall wasn't open yet. We secured a place in line (Russians customarily respected line placement even if the person left) then wandered through a nearby shopping "center"—a few stalls selling bread, juice, eggs.

"See, those are ours," Vyetta instructed me, pointing to a stack of egg crates, leaking squashed yolks. "And those are from Finland," she said, pointing to clean, uncrushed crates. "You see the difference," she concluded.

It was noon before we got on the train. It was an old-fashioned train, unlike the shiny *electrichkas,* painted olive drab inside and trimmed in wood. We sat on wooden benches, squeezed between peasant women with big sacks of food, children with fishing poles, men carrying plastic satchels. Vyetta had brought a Soviet fashion magazine for me to examine. I feigned interest.

"How is it with Kolya?" she asked.

"Not so good. We had a fight."

"It doesn't matter," Vyetta advised. "If a man loves a woman he forgives everything. Talk to Alyosha. Maybe he will know what is with Kolya. I myself don't know Kolya very well."

The train rocked along. Forests, swimmers, fields slid past the windows. After what seemed like thirty stops we finally reached our station. Across a swatch of grass, Alyosha stood under a tree to get out of a sudden rain. He leaned against a bicycle and smoked a *papirosi*. He grinned at us with amused acceptance. He'd probably been waiting for an hour and a half, allowing a half hour for his own habitual lateness. He strapped all of our packages onto the bicycle and we trudged along a sandy path while the vacationers streamed about us. Alyosha and I spoke English; Alyosha stopped the bike from time to time to translate for Vyetta.

There was a placidity about Alyosha that I liked; though it wasn't sexy like Kolya's constant motion, his restless energy, it was comforting. It went with his large, just slightly overpadded body, his sturdiness and slow cigarette puffs.

After we'd stowed our packages, Alyosha retreated to the attic of the house to work on an unfinished room, and Vyetta sent me after him to discuss my Kolya problem. The third floor was a shambles of lumber, nails, unfinished walls. Alyosha held a hammer and looked around the room at all the work left to do: every board to be cut by handsaw, every nail to be retrieved from a bucket rather than a tool belt.

"I don't understand," Alyosha said. "I thought you two were together. I thought everything was fine."

"No. I only see him with you." I sat down on a block of wood.

"I don't understand," Alyosha repeated. "Before he got this new job, just weeks ago, all Kolya talked about was when you would come back. He was always singing your praises. He didn't forget you when you were gone."

"Now he's changed."

"And he's made no plans? It is already too late. You will leave soon." Alyosha shook his head. "Laurie, even I don't know him anymore. Since he began to work at this new job he is like a different man. Always busy, always nervous. After you left, he went from his old job. He had no work, no money for a long time. He had to leave. It had become dangerous for him. You see, after Brezhnev died, Andropov made changes. Kolya still has no money now. The day we went to Petrodvoretz, I paid for everything. Kolya had not enough money to pay for your coffee. Now he has this job he must keep it."

"Why did he leave the old job?"

Alyosha waved away the questions. "Problems."

"Because of me?"

"No. I don't know. Something. Laurie, listen, he is crazy! If it were not for all this now, the dacha, Vyetta, my child, I would change places with him gladly. I would go with you."

I looked at the gapped floorboards. What to say to such a comment? Go with me because I was an exit visa? Was it a compliment, a secret admission? I didn't want Alyosha, I wanted Kolya.

"Kolya doesn't want to leave his country," I said.

"I always thought he was a man who didn't care where he lived."

"That's what he said last year, this year he cares."

"He is a fool! He is out of his mind." Alyosha shook his head, looked around the chaotic room, sighed. "There is so much work to do here," he said. He sat down on the block of wood beside me and put a heavy arm around my shoulder. "Laurie," he said, "let's have a cigarette."

In the evening we played Monopoly on a board sent by an American friend back in the days when Alyosha had been a Sputnik Youth Organization group leader. He'd gotten too friendly though, and the work dried up. That's how he ended up as an English teacher, much like Grisha. The Monopoly game was intact but for the playing pieces—the car, the dog, the iron, the top hat had been pocketed by a custom agent. Alyosha had carved and painted little wooden cars to replace them, so we wheeled around the board on handmade matchbox cars.

Vyetta was the most talented player and wiped the rest of us off the board. She was mollified by her victory. She'd been angry all evening because her mother-in-law had cooked the squash her style, and Vyetta hadn't gotten a chance to impress me. The two women kept up a running quarrel in the kitchen. Alyosha ignored them. After all, it was his mother's house.

While we were playing Monopoly on the sunporch, a middle-aged friend of Galina Ivanovna's dropped by, a friend of my last year's school director Tatiana Nikolaevna, it turned out. She said she knew who I was. I was gripped by fear—now everyone would know I was beyond the thirty-kilometer restricted area, but Alyosha waved my fear away. "She won't tell," he assured me. Dacha life had its own set of rules, its own freedoms.

I slept alone in the bridal chamber, and despite my protestations, woke eager for Kolya's arrival. We swam and ate breakfast at the outdoor table. Alyosha stuffed the fire compartment of a big samovar with pine cones and twigs. I carried plates down to the pond to wash. I swung in the hammock, which had been rehung. Kolya didn't come. Hours passed. In the afternoon, Vyetta, Alyosha, and I took pails and walked into the forest to hunt for berries. Perhaps Kolya would arrive while we were gone.

Russian forests are different than ours. There is little undergrowth, as though everything had been settled a long time back and new trees didn't bother to grow in. The forest floor was spongy and mossy and pooled, rich with berries and mushrooms after the rain. It was easy to walk through, unlike our brambly blackberry tangles and thorn patches, our poison ivy and sumac clusters. Alyosha and I walked ahead. Vyetta bent assiduously to the task of berry gathering. Our English echoed through the woods. Other gatherers could be spotted or heard from time to time.

I wanted to talk about Kolya; like Sasha with his Annie, it was my only theme now. But Alyosha wanted to talk about life in Russia. Once he'd wanted very much to leave. There had been a time when he'd been slated to study in England, but at the last minute they told him to forget it; there would be no trip for him. He was given no explanations and would never receive them. He was very angry then and would have done anything to leave. But time passed and he reconciled himself.

"Aren't you afraid then to have me here, to keep up contact with me?" I asked.

"Afraid of what?" Alyosha asked.

"That you might be harmed, like you were for being friendly to Westerners when you worked for Sputnik. Kolya is afraid," I said, sliding the topic back.

"Kolya is very strange," Alyosha said. "You know, Laurie, last winter we had a falling-out and it has never been the same between us. We were at a party, at his house maybe, I don't remember, and I was very, very drunk. Kolya was drunk too. I came outside and Kolya was standing talking to someone, doing some business, and he got very angry at me and accused me of spying on him. For what would I be spying? I was very insulted. After that Kolya apologized to me a million times, but it was never the same. He didn't trust me and there must be trust between friends. He trusts no one, I think. And he was involved in dangerous business, so he had to worry."

"What do you mean dangerous? Selling things?"

"He was no *fartsovchik*, no black marketeer, like the ones who want to buy your clothes at the hotel or on the street, but he did business on the side. Listen, Laurie, everyone who can does such business. My father, you know, now he is a drunkard and sick and does not work, but for many years he was a butcher and he did very, very well. There are two cuts of meat in the Soviet Union, a different price for each. He simply sold the worse meat for the price of the better meat, and believe me, people were happy to buy it at any price. He made hundreds of rubles a day that way. And for a salary, officially, he made only 150 rubles a month. Who can live on that with children? You tell me. How much do you earn at home?"

"Seventeen thousand dollars a year and that is considered very low."

"And I am a teacher, you know how we live. We teachers have no chance to make money on the side."

I thought of Grisha and his private lessons, but they probably hadn't amounted to much. Goods, not services, were at a premium here. "What did Kolya do?"

"He didn't do anything, he couldn't, it was too dangerous. But somehow he managed. But he couldn't do it for too long. If they caught him, they would have sent him straight to prison."

I remembered those late-night phone calls, his rough, barking voice.

"But he never told me about any of it, so why should he be afraid that I know?"

Alyosha shrugged. Here they were used to no answers.

"I think it is something else," I said. "I think Kolya is against Jews."

"I don't think so," Alyosha said.

"Yes. And . . ." I couldn't say it without checking first. What if Alyosha learned of my heritage and was sorry he'd invited me here? What if it put something between us? But there already was something between us if I couldn't tell. "Are you against?" I asked.

"Of course not," Alyosha said. "I believe what my father told me. The Jew is the person who hurts no one. Many of my friends are Jews. Would you like to meet them?"

"I'm one," I said.

"Yes?"

"Part," I said, still incapable of admitting it. "My mother. . . ."

"Then you can tell me," Alyosha said, "there is something I've never understood and even my Jewish friends don't have the answer. What was the dinner before Christ's death? They say it is Easter, but the Jews do not celebrate Easter, and anyway, Easter is, I think, a holiday after Jesus' death."

"It was Passover," I said. "The Last Supper was Passover, an ancient holiday commemorating the Jews' escape from slavery in Egypt."

"Ah," Alyosha said with satisfaction. I'd cleared up a mystery for him. "If you want, I could take you to see a synagogue."

"No," I said quickly.

"You know, Vyetta's grandfather is Jewish," Alyosha said.

Last weekend, Vyetta had taken me to visit her grandfather while Kolya slept. I'd reported to Kolya that the old man had shown me his fruit trees, his garden, his house, and proudly declared how well they lived in the Soviet Union. He was an ardent Soviet, a real patriot, and wanted me to admit how much better they lived than we did. He was an old man, and to please him I agreed and agreed. "Ah, you are a diplomat," Kolya had said. I hadn't liked the ring to his words, as though he suspected me of always speaking according to convenience. I hadn't known the old man was Jewish then.

Vyetta caught up to us. We were halfway around a deep sunless pool when it began to thunder and lightning. We stood under a tree but were soon drenched. The rain wasn't cold, though, and after half an hour the sun returned.

"Now you've experienced a real Russian storm," Alyosha said.

My clothes clung to my body, water ran from my hair. Kolya would laugh when he saw me. We came out of the forest and onto the dirt road. When we went around that next turn I'd see if his car was there, and if it wasn't . . . I knew it wouldn't be with a sudden certainty. Hadn't I told him I wouldn't wait for him any longer? But I'd been lying. There was the dacha, Kolya's empty parking spot by the wooden gate, the cool shimmering lake.

"Maybe he had trouble with his car," Vyetta said, coming to ply me with fat red strawberries while I lay, desolate, in the hammock.

"If he had car trouble he'd fix it," I said.

Alyosha walked back and forth carrying wood to heat the banya. He stopped to study my face and pat my head.

"Lora's sad because Kolya didn't come," Galina Ivanovna shrieked.

Alyosha, Vyetta, and I sat on the bench outside the *banya*, steam rising from our overheated flesh, drinking *kvass*. I could see specks of mold on the dark fermented drink. The evening darkened and the stars came out for their brief sojourn. I had never been anywhere more beautiful.

Alyosha and I walked through the center of Leningrad, over my favorite bridge, the Anichkov Most. The wild stallions were still in various stages of being tamed on the bridge's four corners. Vyetta wanted Alyosha to entertain me so I wouldn't be sad and lonely while she was at work. Alyosha had already phoned Kolya's ex-wife and his sister but no one had seen him. His sister said that Kolya's son was still in town, he hadn't gone to Kiev. A lie or a change of plans?

We were headed to visit the school where I'd worked, but then Alyosha said no one would be there. Why hadn't he said it before? It did no good to ask Alyosha such questions. I never got straight answers, just as he was never on time. He decided we should see a movie. There was an Italian film playing a double feature with a Soviet film at a theater near an amusement park. Of course, the tickets were sold out.

"This is what we do," Alyosha instructed. "We separate and go along the line asking for *lishnii bilyet*—extra tickets."

I walked along the line asking timidly. People ignored me or shook their heads coldly. Finally, defeated, I sat down on the stone theater steps. Alyosha appeared smiling. From behind his back he drew out two tickets and reached out a hand to pull me up.

We ate melting ice cream in the theater café because you can't do anything in Russia without eating, and then took our seats. The film was in Italian, without subtitles. A Russian male voice provided a monotone voice-over for all the parts. Throughout the entire film, Alyosha insisted on translating the Russian into loud English, word by word, even the parts I understood. Not one person in the theater complained.

It was an idiotic slapstick sex farce but Alyosha and the audience gasped and howled. The Italian interiors looked impossibly lush. It took place on a farm but the farmer lived with a maid and butler; he had a paneled library, four-poster beds. Throughout the film Alyosha held my hand. I sat quietly, embarrassed by his touch and his translation, thinking *Kolya, Kolya.* I lied and said I'd enjoyed the film when the credits came up. The second feature, a Soviet detective story, began. Alyosha stood and said, "Shit, let's go." Half of the audience got up to leave with us. We walked out into the bright afternoon light.

Alyosha said, "I can't stand that police shit after seeing the Italian film. It's such an insult."

Back at their apartment, Vyetta said, "Kolya hurt his arm. I talked to him at work. That's why he couldn't come. He says that you two should come visit him tomorrow night at work. He'll show Lora around. We'll plan a trip for when he gets off in three days."

Alyosha called Kolya. He reported, "I asked him what was going on but he wouldn't tell me anything. He didn't want to discuss his life with me."

"I am ashamed for you to see my apartment," Vyetta fussed. "It is old. We must do renovations."

I waved her words away. What did I care about renovations?

I wanted to see the place that had changed Kolya so much. I wondered why I couldn't call him at his new job but I could visit—perhaps he'd present me to his coworkers as Alyosha's friend. I had plans already to meet Sasha for dinner at his parents' apartment, and afterward, Alyosha and I would visit Kolya.

Yelizarovskaya was a region of old five-story buildings with crumbling balconies and dented cigarette urns tilting by doorways—Khrushchev's slums, they called them; it rhymed in Russian. "Don't speak English in the hall," Sasha reminded me as we approached his parents' building. "Better not to speak at all. Excuse me, but your accent." Since Sasha's sister had immigrated to England and his father had been demoted, his father had grown sickly and been in and out of hospitals. They didn't need any more problems.

I was surprised to see Sasha, always so gentle with his friends, short-tempered with his mild and frail parents. "You don't understand," he insisted, when his father commented that American writers would also be silenced if they were to speak out against their government.

After we ate cabbage soup and fresh *piroshki,* Sasha's mother shyly showed me photos of her trip to London; she'd been allowed to visit her daughter last year. The sister stood beside her bald English husband. She was as beautiful as a model, her ticket out of the Soviet Union. "London was lovely," Sasha's mother said wistfully. Of Annie's behavior, all she would say was, "She is very young."

I called Alyosha from the street, from the Yelizarovskaya metro station, and from my own station but he didn't answer. I tried one last time from a phone a block from the Sputnik. It was nearly eleven and too late to start a journey to the Pribaltiskaya region where Kolya worked. Already the White Nights were giving way to shorter days, darkening at eleven instead of midnight. But plenty of Russians were still out on the streets. They stayed up all night on the Neva embankments, singing, drinking, playing guitars. It was like that in Alaska—no one wanted to sleep in summer when winter was so long and dark.

"Where were you?" I asked, annoyed, when Alyosha answered.

"I have a problem," Alyosha said. "Vyetta is in the hospital. She has been bleeding since you left our house the other night."

"Oh, no," I said. "How's the baby? Is it very serious?"

"Well, it is not serious," Alyosha said. "Yes, well, it is but, no. Everything is all right."

"Tell me the truth."

"Don't worry, Laurie."

"What can I do?"

"You want to do something? Would you do something for me?"

"Yes."

His voice altered, became wheedling. "Come here. Come stay here with me. I am very lonely."

"Alyosha, I can't. Are you drunk?"

"No. Yes, well just a little."

"Alyosha, I can't come now. It's so late. I'll come tomorrow. I'll call you tomorrow. Did you call Kolya to say we won't be coming?"

"Maybe. It doesn't matter, Lora. Call me tomorrow in the afternoon after your class. We will go visit Vyetta. You won't come now?"

"Alyosha, it's not a good idea."

"Later, then."

Vyetta was in the hospital, bleeding, maybe losing their child and Alyosha wanted me to come spend the night. Kolya was sitting at work, waiting for us. Sasha was back at his apartment, rereading his letters from Annie. In the Sputnik, my roommate held a British version of a Harlequin romance before her face.

"Did you have a nice time?" Fiona asked, lowering the book when I came in.

I shrugged.

"I had quite a horrible experience today," she said. "I rang up the brother of a friend of a friend back in Britain to deliver some goods, jeans and such. The brother was very charming at first. He took me to an ice cream shop, walked with me in a park. Then he asked me to marry him so that he could leave the Soviet Union. When I refused, he became abusive and told me that I was a stupid, spoiled little Westerner who didn't care about anyone but myself."

"What a creep," I said dully, pulling on my nightgown.

"I'll say," she replied. "I've had quite enough of Russians!"

Alyosha had locked himself out of his apartment and left the extra key at the dacha, he told me cheerfully. He didn't seem perturbed by his predicament or worried about his wife. We were going to visit Vyetta at the hospital, but we needed to get into the apartment to gather items she wanted: sausage and pastries because the hospital swill was inedible, a watch, a book to read. Alyosha sent me to stand below his apartment at the back of the building, a four-story, pale cement structure with narrow tiled balconies on which people hung clothes and raised houseplants.

Ayosha planned to climb down to his balcony from the apartment above, break in, and throw me the key. The apartment, strangely, couldn't be unlocked from inside. I stood in the bushes, smoking cigarettes, waiting. Alyosha appeared on the balcony above his own with two heavyset men in undershirts and warm-up pants. A woman in a housedress came out on the balcony to join them. They were all laughing. The men had a rope. They tied a loop around Alyosha then wrapped a loop around their flimsy balcony railing. Gingerly, Alyosha lowered himself while the men held onto the rope. I could see a long rip on the inside of Alyosha's well-worn corduroy jeans. I wished again that I'd brought him a new pair.

The wife grinned, showing gold teeth. The men strained and whooped. Alyosha slid down the wall, jerky inch by inch, until his toes reached the railing of his own balcony. The middle-aged trio above him cheered. Alyosha scrambled over the railing and broke a window. He disappeared, reappeared smiling, tossed me the key, which landed in the dirt at my feet. I ran around to the front of the building and up the stairs to release him.

Alyosha reached up to sweep his hair back over his bald pate. "Laurie, let's have a little drink," he said.

Visitors were not allowed inside the hospital maternity ward. We stood outside the building, under the windows, joined by a collection of new fathers or fathers-to-be, and shouted Vyetta's name. Vyetta appeared at the window, waved, reappeared with a rope that she lowered over the side. The rope, with a plastic bag attached, crept down the four stories in imitation of Alyosha's recent descent. We filled the bag with goodies and Vyetta hauled it up. She was thrilled with the little two-dollar digital watch I had put in the bag, thrilled that I'd anticipated her need since Alyosha had forgotten to bring the one she'd asked for. She didn't know my suitcase held a pile of such small gifts bought on the New York streets.

"Did you go to see Kolya at work?" she called down. "How are things going with him?"

I shook my head. Still no word.

"I feel terrible," she said. "I wanted you to see more, to travel and visit Pushkin and Pavlovsk. Tell Kolya he must take you there. I would have brought you."

"Don't worry," I yelled back up. "You must get healthy."

"Masha, Mash, Mashinka," a skinny boy with a big adam's apple called to his pregnant teenage bride.

Alyosha glanced at his watch. "We'll be back tomorrow," he yelled up.

As we left we passed a friend of Vyetta's coming to visit, a nurse at the hospital. She and Alyosha conferred in rapid Russian, then she turned to study me closely. She was an attractive short-haired blonde with a worried expression.

"She understands," Alyosha said. "You know why? Because she and I spent a night or two together. She is worried now when she sees you."

"There's no reason to worry," I said.

"No?"

Back at the apartment Alyosha and I made a dinner of eggs and a mayonnaise-laden salad. He brought out a vodka bottle. Danya, he said, was with his *babushka* at the dacha. Like many Russian kids, he spent more time with his grandmother than his parents. Alyosha's father, who had left Galina Ivanovna this week because he couldn't stand her noise, drank silently with us in the living room while we watched a TV movie about World War II. When it was over, Alyosha's father retreated to a tiny back bedroom. I wondered what the old man thought of me sitting there with his son while his son's wife was in the hospital.

"I've got to go," I said.

"Stay," Aloysha said.

"What will your father think?"

"He is very discreet. He has seen a great deal and he keeps his mouth shut."

"Tell me what Kolya said when you called him."

"Kolya, Kolya, always Kolya. Listen, Lora, he is planning a trip for us but I don't think he is very enthusiastic. He was angry that we didn't visit him at work but he will not speak to me of his feelings about you. It doesn't look very good. You understand?"

"I just want an explanation. I can't go home without knowing what really happened. I don't even like him anymore," I bluffed.

"So forget him. Think about me."

The phone rang. It was Alyosha's mistress, Alla, the art teacher at the school, whom I'd never met. They spoke briefly.

"She understands everything," he said. "She wanted to know about Vyetta, but she also wanted to come here to be with me. I told her no, so she understood that you are here."

"Oh, god. I'm going to go home now."

"Stay," Alyosha pleaded. He put his arms around me and kissed me. In the next room his father coughed. I leaned my head into Alyosha's striped nylon pullover and started crying. Alyosha stroked my hair. Oh, to be touched. Everything I was doing was wrong now, everything had gotten so mixed up, but my humiliation, Kolya's defection, were overruled by vodka and Alyosha's desire. To be simply wanted, even in so meaningless a way by a friend whom I didn't desire, was irresistible. I let Alyosha lead me into the bedroom.

"I know you are only doing this because Kolya hurt you," Alyosha said, "not because of me."

I couldn't deny it. I appreciated Alyosha's bulk, his rough, ungraceful, force. "You're such a bear," I said, using the Russian word, *medved*. I would be covered in bruises in the morning. But all I could think of was Kolya, Kolya. I wanted to forget everything but we were a failure as lovers. "It is only Alla who can make me feel a man when I am this drunk," Alyosha said. We fell asleep, curled close. We were friends, not lovers, after all.

In the morning I hid from his father's blank gaze, crept out of the apartment building like a criminal, snuck back into my hotel in shame. I had betrayed Vyetta after giving her a cheap gift. And Kolya would meet us Saturday for another outing. We would continue this farce right up until it was time for me to go home. My mouth tasted of cigarettes, my head spun with vodka. I sat in the classroom in the midst of British students, and, when asked by the Russian conversation teacher, a sweet woman with the body of a hippopotamus, how I spent my free time, I said, "Badly. I think I'm sick from the water. May I leave and go back to the hotel?"

Saturday I waited for Alyosha at Finland Station, in front of the glass box enclosing the engine from the train Lenin had ridden into Russia after the revolution. It was one of those monumental meeting places; lots of Russians lounged, backs to the sepulchered locomotive with its requisite wreath of fresh flowers. Young men in pointy- collared shirts irreverently crushed hollow-stemmed *papirosi* under their platform heels. Grandmothers gripped children by the hands and lugged enormous shopping bags of produce. And sexy Russian girls wore sundresses, too much eye make-up, and habitually bored, belligerent pouts

Alyosha was late, as usual. I feared that if we missed our train, Kolya, who was supposed to pick us up at the train station in Zelyonigorsk, would be angry again. Maybe he wouldn't even show. I spotted Alyosha standing by a platform, engaged in an intense conversation with a buxom blonde woman wearing a blue knit dress, high heels, and matching blue disc earrings: Alla. Her face was strong-boned, older than Alyosha's, dignified but worried. She kept fiddling with one of her earrings. It pained me to see how she'd made herself up for such a brief rendezvous with her lover. Alyosha had invited her along but she hadn't been able to arrange for her mother to stay with her daughter, so she couldn't come.

Alyosha waved me over. Alla looked at me, direct, knowing, but not harsh. She was a lovely woman and I could barely meet her eyes. Here was someone else I'd betrayed, not just Vyetta, as Kolya had betrayed me. *If* he had betrayed me. . . . Alla stared long at Alyosha before we turned to walk to our platform.

The train to Zelyonigorsk was filled with Saturday vacationers, travelers to dachas and to the public beaches at Solnichny, everyone carrying bundles and crowding each other on the hard wooden benches. Alyosha led me to the space between two cars to smoke. A young woman stood in the passage, restraining an enormous brindled Great Dane. Alyosha used to have two such dogs; he'd shown me a picture in his album. It surprised me that here, where food was so hard to come by, Russians were as eager for pets as we were.

Outside the window, lush July leaves slid past. Tracks, gravel, factories, then fields and little villages, each with its depot and myriad footpaths winding near the tracks.

"I won't spend the night," Alyosha said. "I will visit, and then come back on the train."

"Why?"

"It will be strange for the three of us. If Alla had come, that would be different, but with you and Kolya and me?"

"You *have* to come. I don't want to go without you. I don't even want to see him."

"You do."

"Let's just keep going, or turn back and go somewhere else. What's the point? He doesn't want to see me. Let's just go to the beach."

"You don't mean that Laurie. You love him."

"So I'm a jerk."

"What means jerk?"

"*Idiotka.*" I crushed my foul Bulgarian cigarette out on the wooden floorboards. Alyosha began to hum. I lit another.

Kolya was waiting for us in his car, one arm in a sling, his excuse for not coming to the dacha, an accident. I thought he groaned too pointedly and hated him for faking, hated my mistrust. He looked glum.

We spent the next two hours traveling from store to store and region to region, over dusty unpaved roads with glimpses of the Baltic through pines and spruce, past sunbathers en route to the beach, in search of a chicken to skewer over our campfire. The first store, a grubby cement bunker with glass doors, was closed for its daily sanitation break. A barrel-shaped woman in a white coat and paper headdress waved us away through the glass. Nor were there chickens to be found at the roadside food kiosks, just the usual cabbage, onions, and an occasional squash. At each stop Alyosha bought a beer, growing more cheerful as his face grew more flushed. Several long strands of hair had fallen over one ear, giving him a cockeyed, unbalanced look.

Since he was driving, Kolya could only drink *kvass*. There were many *gaii* checkpoints on the road north. I wouldn't drink the *kvass* because the glass, swished around on a little water sprayer between customers, was *communalnii*, and many of the drinkers lined up behind the mustard-colored *kvass* tank had cold sores on their lips. I was shamed by my squeamishness but unwilling to take the risk. Now I was thirsty as well as bored.

"Why don't we just eat bread and cheese?" I asked. "Why do we need a chicken?" What I really wanted to know was why Alyosha hadn't picked up a chicken in Leningrad before we left, where there was at least some chance of finding one.

Kolya turned to me, taking my measure with cool blue-green eyes. "You don't care about your stomach. That's not good."

"We don't have to at home," I said crossly. "It's easy." He'd decided I wasn't a real woman, a Russian woman, who knew the sacred importance of food, but a spoiled American who figured if you didn't have a chicken for the campfire, you could always get one tomorrow. I'd ignored the point that this was a daily struggle; if one was to ever eat chicken, one had to search relentlessly. I didn't care enough about my stomach and so could never properly care for him.

After a few more futile stops we parked behind a tourist restaurant. Alyosha disappeared inside the back door with a couple of packs of American cigarettes and a bottle of Cinzano I'd bought at the hard-currency store. He returned triumphant, dangling a stringy fowl with its head still on, clawed feet stiff as talons.

"Do you have such excellent chickens in America?" Kolya joked, eyeing the skinny bird.

"Of course not," Alyosha answered with the intonation of a properly trained Young Pioneer. "Everyone knows Soviet chickens are best chickens in the world!"

They broke up laughing. Alyosha popped a tape—Marvin Gaye—into the player between his legs and we continued north. The blacktop gave way to a bumpy dirt road and Kolya opened his first beer, gripped clumsily in his injured hand while he drove with his left. I sat beside him in the front and shifted the gear stick for him. "Now," he'd say, and I'd push.

"What does that sign say?" I asked Alyosha in English, nodding toward a large orange placard covered in black Cyrillic too dense for me to read as we rushed past.

"Restricted area. No foreigners allowed."

"Are you kidding?" If caught, I could be called a spy.

"Don't worry about it," Alyosha said. "You always worry."

We turned onto a track that ran through a forest. Kolya stopped on a small bluff overlooking a lagoon and beyond it, the wide Baltic Sea. Kolya had brought along a tiny TV. He plugged it into the cigarette lighter on his Zhiguli and set it on the hood.

"Why do you want to watch TV when you're camping?" I asked Alyosha in English.

"We might get a station from Sweden," he said. The TV wavered with static and then a Soviet movie appeared. "They block the Western stations," Alyosha said disgustedly.

Kolya spread a few pages of *Pravda* on the trunk of his car and laid out cups, vodka, green onions, dill, and a chunk of bread. It was, of course, time for a drink or two or three or four. We got drunk quickly and stumbled down to the water. Kolya lay on his belly on the pebbled beach and I sat down beside him. He rolled over.

"You want me to do what I can't do," he said.

"I don't want you to do anything," I hissed and scrambled up.

"Where are you going?"

"I'm going to search. That's what you said Americans do, isn't it? Search and search." I set off down the pebbled beach, cutting my bare feet on the rocks. Finally I lay down and took off my shirt to absorb the sunshine. Back in the trees a family of volleyball players in warm-up suits had set up a tent and a net and were doggedly tossing a ball around. Let them see my lacy bra, I didn't care. Russians wore their underwear at beaches. When I came back to the car Kolya and Alyosha were drinking again. I still had my shirt off. Alyosha looked at me, said nothing. I wanted Kolya to know about him. I wanted him jealous, as I was jealous, though I wasn't sure of what. Kolya reached out and stroked my arm, kissed me.

"You're such a fool," I said, echoing Sasha Ivanov. "You'll never have another chance like you had with me." Kolya looked at me hard, pushed me away. I turned to Alyosha. "Come on," I said in English, "let's swim."

"Speak our language!" Kolya commanded.

"What for?"

The lagoon was shallow and brackish. Kolya and Alyosha were in the water by the time I put on my bikini. Dusk was falling, and the sky streaked pink, a strange soft dusk over the slate of the Gulf. How had it gotten late enough for dusk to fall? I stood up to my thighs in warmish water, looking out at the cloud banks or land mass that might have been Finland, remembering my sailboat dream.

Kolya looked me over appraisingly. "That's good," he said to Alyosha, nodding at me. He drew it out, *khoroshooooooo.*" That. I wasn't even "she" anymore.

"Lora," Alyosha called in English, "you have to decide." Grinning, he combed the wet strands back over his baldness, caressed his belly. "Which of us do you want?"

"Neither of you," I said.

"Speak ours!" Kolya yelled.

They leaped and knocked me down. I came up sputtering with a mouthful of gulf. My thigh was bruised and my knee bleeding. Kolya pulled me down again. Alyosha wandered down the beach and returned paddling a little rubber raft that a fisherman had left on shore. I screamed a banshee cry and tipped him over. The volleyball players looked over at us. Alyosha clobbered me with the rubber raft. On the beach I hunched in sudden pain. Water, night air and vodka had combined to give me a swift, violent headache. I crouched with my hands on my head. When I began to cry, I couldn't stop.

"Lora," Kolya said, kneeling beside me. "What is it? What's the matter? Don't cry, please." His tender voice made me cry all the harder. What was the matter? Why should anything be the matter? I'd only come five thousand miles for him and here I was drunk and shivering on the Gulf of Finland, and he was going to let me go.

"Go away," I said. "Leave me alone."

"No," he said. "No."

I stumbled up the beach wrapped in a towel and climbed into the car. I woke in the dark. Alyosha was sitting on a log in front of the fire. The chicken was cooking on skewers. Kolya lay beside me, sleeping. When he woke he turned to me and said, "You are always drunk."

"I'm rarely drunk," I said. Almost never, at home. And not as often as any Russian.

We sat around the fire eating chicken, potatoes. Kolya didn't speak to me at all, but straight to Alyosha, in a Russian so rapid I couldn't hope to understand. I spoke English to Alyosha, touched his knee, his arm for emphasis. "Speak our language," Kolya snapped. Alyosha brooded. When Alyosha said how useful the newspaper *Pravda* was, very good for lighting a fire, Kolya warned, "Careful. She'll put that in her book too."

How much he feared me now. He was giving lie to all the things that had made me think he was untamed. No one was untamed here.

"She understands more Russian than she lets on," Kolya said. "The more complicated the subject, the better she understands."

Alyosha said, "That's because some of our most abstract words are Latin-based, the same as in English."

A bandy-legged *babushka* came over and scolded us. It was her rubber raft we'd taken, and when we overturned it, we'd lost her husband's fishing net. She wanted the men to find it. Alyosha and Kolya apologized. They went back to the water and retrieved it after a lot of splashing.

"I'm glad I'm not a *babushka*," I said, watching the old woman lurch away with her net.

"Yes, like this is better," Kolya said, rubbing my tanned arm. Then he turned a gimlet eye on me and said, "Here we are not afraid to grow old."

He was turning everything I said against me, selling himself a bill of goods. I had to be someone he couldn't love now so he could live with his decision. "Where will you sleep?" I whispered to Alyosha.

"In the car. You will go with Kolya in the tent."

"Better if I go with you."

"Better if Alla had come," he replied.

I followed Kolya down to the tent like a sleepwalker. He opened the flaps to a view of the perfect rising moon. Now we would go through our farce, lovemaking that wasn't love, then roll away to our corners. I would have done better to sleep with Alyosha in the car, or let the two of them have the tent and take the car myself, but Kolya's touch, empty as it was, still controlled me. It was as though his touch possessed the secret of what had happened between us and through his touch I would discover the answer and be at peace.

"We live well here," he said as we lay under the covers. "The beach, friends, simple." He sounded like Galya to me. What was he doing, excusing his decision? Or was he so afraid of me now he had to speak like some official Soviet rep?

"We live well at home too," I said.

"We have our problems and you have yours. I don't want to trade ours for yours. Do you understand?"

"Yes. Yes. Yes. Yes. Yes. I understand."

"We aren't afraid to grow old here," he repeated.

Oh, but I was afraid. I was afraid I would go home to nothing and grow old. Kolya lay beside me, the moon shone through the tent flap, the voices of the volleyball players who'd brought out their own bottle echoed through the trees and over the water. Up in the car, Alyosha slept.

We were sitting around the smoky campfire reheating the potatoes for breakfast when a uniformed border guard appeared, carrying a rifle. "Don't open your mouth," Alyosha whispered to me. I looked about wildly. The clues—the Cinzano bottle, the Marlboro packs—were already exchanged for the chicken. We were all Soviets here.

The guard stopped before us. Every aspect of him stood out sharply, surreal in its detail: a belt buckle with the five-pointed Soviet star. The creased leather of his belt. His bland, square, childish face with its eerie pale eyes. If he addressed me, my life would be over.

"*Spichki?*" he said. Matches. He wanted matches. Alyosha offered a light. The guard fumbled for a cigarette, resting his rifle against his hip, lit up, smiled. One of his front teeth was stainless steel; it caught the morning sun. He drew on his cigarette, pleased with himself. Noting the empty vodka bottles, he tapped his throat with two fingers, the sign for drinking. "A good party, eh?" He was just a simple soldier boy on lonely forest duty.

"Very good," Alyosha said. "Too bad you couldn't join us." When the guard was out of sight, Alyosha said, "That reminds me of the anecdote about the border guard."

I couldn't listen. My heart was still beating too fast, I was sick with the ebb of adrenaline. Across the fire, Kolya gouged at embers with a stick.

Alyosha turned to me. "You can talk now. The guard is gone."

I didn't know what to say.

"You didn't understand the joke," Alyosha said. "I will tell you in English."

Kolya said quietly, "She understands everything perfectly."

I understood that I would never understand.

Alyosha and I stood knee-deep in water washing the dishes with sand and grass while Kolya dismantled the tent.

"Laurie," Alyosha said. "A deaf *babushka* was riding the train. Two other old ladies are talking about the size of cucumbers. One says, 'How small they are this year.' She holds her hands apart, like this, to show how little they've grown. The deaf lady says, 'Never mind, dear. The most important thing is that a man be good.'"

Alyosha laughed and laughed.

"So many anecdotes," I said, glancing around at Kolya who was eager to get on the road, to dump us at the Zelyonigorsk station and be on his way to Vyborg.

"I'm very fond of anecdotes," Alyosha said. "Laurie, you have to laugh."

Russia Is a Fish

Alla, Alyosha and I sat at a table in a disco bar, trying to hear one another over the earsplitting music. Vyetta was still in the hospital. She'd lost the baby several days ago but the doctors wouldn't let her go home. The bar had a twenties Chicago gangster theme with flashing disco lights added. A mock-up of a twenties roadster took up half the stage. The DJ rapped in Russian and spun American discs. Every so often a deafening taped Tommy-gun shoot-out and the cry "Mafia!" interrupted the music.

I hadn't wanted to join them but Alyosha had insisted that Alla wasn't angry with me, she understood everything. In the blare of American rock music she said, in Russian, of Kolya, "He is secretive. Like a shellfish."

"What?" I didn't know the last word.

"*Molusk.* You understand the word? He pokes his head out, looks around, jumps back inside."

"Yes."

A dark man with a mustache, a Georgian, came to our table and asked me to dance. Alyosha winked at me, urged me on.

My Georgian spoke incomprehensible Russian. Perhaps it was his accent. He tried to hold me close and croon into my ear.

"Excuse me, I speak very bad Russian," I said, leaning back.

"Where are you from?"

"America. S.Sh.A."

He stopped in the middle of the dance floor and stared at me. "*Nyet.*"

"*Da.*"

"*Nyet.* And who is that one, the man at your table?" He nodded toward Alyosha.

"*Znakomi,*" I said. An acquaintance.

"You should have said KGB," Alyosha said with a laugh when I returned to the table. Across the room, the Georgian sent me moist glances and whispered to his friends. Alla and I went downstairs to use the toilet. The women's room was occupied, so Alla went into the men's room with me to stand guard. While I balanced over the seatless commode, Alla leaned against the door and told me about her life.

"I thought I would die when my husband left me, I loved him so much."

How could he have left her? Standing there, rosy from dancing, she looked to me exactly what any man would want. It was a stupid question. The answer was: because. Now she loved Alyosha, who could not leave his wife and child.

"I wouldn't ask that," she said. "It's enough for me when we can be together. Like a holiday." She turned to bang on the door in answer to some desperate drinker's complaint. "It's not so bad for me," she added quietly. "I'm not alone. I have my little daughter."

Back upstairs Alyosha and I watched Alla dance. The music had switched to a silly Finnish chicken dance. La dee da dee da, then everyone clapped. Da da da da. Clap clap clap. The floor full of dancers flapped their arms like chickens, shook their chicken tails, spun. Alla, in her pretty blue dress and her flying blonde hair, twirled and laughed, laughed and twirled.

"I couldn't keep it from her," Alyosha said. "She knew before I said a word."

We three decided to abandon the bar and go to Alyosha's house to make something to eat. In Vyetta's kitchen, Alla sliced tomatoes with assurance, whipped up a beet salad with cilantro, placed the bread in pretty circles around the plate while I watched.

Someone knocked on the door. Alla and I hid in the corner of the kitchen while Alyosha talked. It was Vyetta's grandfather, come to ask how she was. We stood in silent collusion, listening to the old man's questions. "What did the doctors say? Must they operate? The child could not be saved? Perhaps she needs better doctors? The clinic isn't good enough. We must transfer her." Alyosha answered in reassuring tones.

When the grandfather finally left, Alla pointed toward our reflections in the kitchen window. "He saw us," she said. "Look." Thoughtfully, she put a piece of bread to her lips.

Driving out of the city, Alla, Alyosha, Kolya, and I passed the park where he and I had walked last winter, on my last day in Leningrad. Kolya looked out the window and said, "Do you remember, Lora? That is where we saw the dog who wouldn't eat meat."

"He went outside to converse with the ducks," I said. I couldn't believe he remembered. I turned to look at him from narrowed eyes. Kolya laughed.

Kolya pulled into the dirt road that led to the river not far from where we'd danced on my first trip up the Baltic coast. I recognized the boatyard, although now barefoot kids in trunks wandered through the dust. Alla and I hid behind a tree to change into our swimsuits. A brown horse popped its head over a slatted board fence to watch us. Kolya parked the car, returned carrying oars. We clambered down an embankment and into a wooden rowboat.

This send-off, this final party, was Kolya's idea. "You should have told me you wanted a boat ride," Kolya scolded. "I would have taken you sooner."

Why he was bothering with all this now I couldn't say. We would camp on Kolya's Island, the one he'd drawn a map of a million years ago. In the morning they would bring me back to the Sputnik before Kolya had to be at work.

Rowing to the island, I put on Alla's yellow visored cap to shield my eyes. I leaned back against the thwarts and raised my black cotton gypsy skirt high over my bikini bottom to sun my legs.

"The hat suits her," Kolya said. "The color."

I pulled the visor lower and looked out at him warily. Now that I was leaving he could compliment me.

"She looks like the Mona Lisa," Kolya added.

We rowed past fishing boats with racks of nets, kids on a dock who shouted when we passed. A speedboat zipped through the channel. Alyosha rowed, sweating and squinting in the brightness. He winked at me, his familiar face placid, kind.

"It's so beautiful here," I said, dragging my fingers through warm water alongside the boat. "This is just where I want to be."

Kolya smiled. "I try," he said.

The hollow echo of last winter's words, what he'd said each time I'd praised him for the caviar, the meals he'd cooked for me, his knowing touch, outraged me. I reached out a foot to tip him backward into the water, but he laughed and leaped overboard, to come up shimmering twenty feet behind us, shaking the drops from his curly hair.

I wanted to say to Alyosha, row faster, let's leave him behind. I wanted to jump in too, to immerse myself, but I knew I wouldn't be able to pull myself aboard and didn't want them to haul me in like some lumbering sea creature, at home neither in water nor air. Kolya swam easily up to the boat, lifted himself up. The water ran over his smooth, tensed muscles. He hovered over the thwarts like a gymnast, then he was in. Again, there was more than simply air between us. The water sparkled mercilessly. Alyosha rowed.

So this was Kolya's Island. Just like in his drawing, a sandy clearing surrounded by marsh weeds and forest, a perfect place to hide. Kolya set up the tent. Alla and I cleaned the chicken in the gulf, then sat in the boat to peel potatoes. Kolya came over to give orders. "Who made him a general?" I asked and Alla laughed. Her knife moved expertly, the skins piled up in the bow, flew over the thwarts to float on the warm sea.

A fire had been built. Blankets and logs set out. The chicken went into a pot with the potatoes. The vodka bottle was stuck in the sand beside another Cinzano bottle I'd brought along from the dollar store. While we were downing vodka around the fire, two small boys appeared in our clearing, carrying their shoes. They looked startled and shy. Alla picked up two of our precious oranges and tossed one to each boy. "Opa!" she said. They both fumbled their catches. Russian kids were great with their feet, soccer players, but unable to catch. The boys had probably been walking home for dinner through the shallow water and taken a shortcut across our island.

"That one," Kolya said, nodding toward a boy with curly hair and rolled-up pants, "he reminds me of my Anatoly."

Clutching their oranges, the boys hurried off without a word.

"I used to play here too," Kolya said. "Always, as a child."

I thought of the photographs I still possessed: Kolya at four, wearing a seaman's cap; at six, holding a bouquet of wildflowers. When Kolya began a story in Russian too fast and slangy for me to follow, I got up and wandered through trees until I came to a rock looking out over the gulf. The sun was lowering, the days getting shorter. I committed this scene to memory—the lovely lights on the freighter anchored to the west, the gray-green darkening water. What would I do with all these pictures, this burdensome album?

Soon it would be fall. I knew what autumn meant in Leningrad. Foggy canals and wet, cold pavement. But Kolya's golden-lit house no longer existed. His phone had already been disconnected, according to Alyosha. Our room had been torn apart. Where were all the things I remembered? The lamp, the table, the shelves of books, the driftwood and curios, the crumbling photograph album? Where did he live now, in his car, as he said he would?

Kolya walked up behind me. "When I was little I came here often," he said, using the overly slow voice he reserved for me now, enunciating too well. I wanted to say, "I understand, my Russian isn't *that* bad, but then I decided there was another reason for his emphasis. "For me, this is home," Kolya said.

"It is very beautiful here."

Kolya sat down on the rock beside me, stared out over the gulf. "Soon this place won't exist anymore. They plan to make a new harbor here and they will fill this coast in with sand."

"Kolya," I exclaimed. "How can you live here? First they took your house, and now your island."

"Lora, it doesn't matter. There are many more beautiful places, many you haven't seen. See that island across the water? Someday it will be possible to live there. I'd like to live there, away from all the people. There is so much here you haven't seen. Come back and I will show you."

I kept my eyes on the water.

"When will you come back?" Kolya asked. "It is good with you, interesting." And then, so that I wouldn't misunderstand, he said, "We are all friends, you, me, Alla, Alyosha. When you come back we'll be good company."

When I didn't speak, Kolya got up and went back toward the fire.

"Come join us, Lora," Alla called out. "Dinner is almost ready." She parted the willow trees and appeared, blonde hair tangled with leaves, large breasts jutting in her overbuilt one-piece bathing suit: a beautiful figurehead riding the prow of a ship. Alla sat down beside me. Her bare toes on the rocks looked strong and square.

"Only I understand you," she said, touching my hair.

"At least you still have Alyosha," I responded stupidly, selfish with my loss.

"Phew." Alla laughed. "Who knows? They say I love you, I love you, but you must never believe. It is how they are. When they say it, they mean it, but they mean it only for one day. So you must enjoy that one day."

"For you that's enough?"

Alla's smile was edged with weariness, the lines about her mouth suddenly deep. "What choice is there?" she asked.

Alla and I snuck around the island and pushed the heavy rowboat into the warm water. At first Alyosha and Kolya chased us, splashing and making indignant noises, but we were faster and easily left them behind. I turned to look back at them: Kolya, small, wiry, a flush of sunburn where his open shirt left his pale skin exposed this afternoon; Alyosha, bulky and bearish, large hands hanging at his sides. Alyosha was probably thinking of the vodka bottles waiting by the campfire.

As we rowed, Alla sang in Russian, I in English. I had forgotten the words to my American song but it didn't matter. To Alla, who spoke no English, it was just melodic noise.

"*Smotri*," I said, pointing. Look. A few hundred yards away a sailboat glided gracefully in from the gulf, headed toward the river from which we had come earlier in the day. "*Idi syuda!*" Come here! We called but the sailboat took no notice.

"They are afraid of us," I ventured.

"Like all men," said Alla, and we both laughed. Alla's spine, exposed by her bathing suit, made a line of bumps between the strong muscles of her back. Her sinewy calves flexed impressively with each pull on the oars. Why were the oars so heavy? Russian oars, long squared-off blocks of wood, they were much bulkier than they needed to be. When I offered to take a turn, Alla refused and I relented; I knew she was stronger than I.

"I still love him," I said, surprising myself. Now I could say it, when I was leaving.

"I know," said Alla, "I see it. That dirty dog."

What had Kolya done? What made him any more culpable than I?

This morning, Alyosha, Kolya and I had stood in the sun beneath the window of the cement-block hospital, waving and calling to Vyetta, while Alla hid around the corner in Kolya's parked car. I felt guilty, looking up at Vyetta's wan face. We were tricking and deserting her: Alyosha, I, Kolya, Alyosha's mistress. Vyetta smiled down at us from the fifth floor. She shouted that she was glad we were going on a farewell trip, that I would have a chance to see more of their country before I went home. She was sorry that she couldn't come with us and be my guide.

Alla and I turned the heavy rowboat back toward the island. The water was so warm, so shallow, it seemed I could just get out of the boat and walk away. We were delighted to be here, delighted by our theft of the boat, our mock escape. On the island, Kolya and Alyosha were waiting. We had only run away in order to come back.

We sat by the fire, poking the logs, gnawing chicken on skewers, drinking Cinzano, drinking vodka. Kolya was attentive, the gracious host, filling my glass, offering morsels. The clearing darkened and fell into shadow. When the sun disappeared, the air turned chill. All the vodka was gone. Alyosha complained that he was wet and cold. Alla said, "You need exercise to warm up," and pulled him up from the fire. "Opa," she shouted, running at him across the sandy clearing. She leaped onto his back and they fell. Laughing, they rose, and Alla backed off for another go.

Lurching a bit from the vodka, I got up and trotted across the darkened sand to join Alyosha and Alla. I'd leave Kolya to his empty solicitations, I thought. Alla and I struggled to hold Alyosha down. Without realizing quite how I got there, I found myself lying with my legs around Alyosha's waist, being dragged through the sand. I giggled hysterically as the sand slid into my clothing, my hair. Only inches away, Alla was whispering to Kolya, who had her pinned. "Stop," she said, "you're hurting me. Please stop."

"Enough?" Kolya whispered. "Enough?"

I couldn't stop laughing and my arms were still around Alyosha's broad back, but the wave of jealousy was enough to take my breath away. When Alyosha and I rose, the two of them were gone.

Now the game was really over. Alyosha and I sat uneasily by the fire. How silent it was. It wouldn't take much time, the two of them grappling in the bushes. We'd all drunk too much. "Where have they gone?" I asked in English.

"I don't know," Alyosha said. "Why don't you go look for them?"

"I don't want to."

"Lora," he said. His voice sounded pained. "Does it really matter?"

"Alla wouldn't do that to me," I said plaintively.

"Why not? To get back at me. She is not stupid."

The silence vibrated with betrayal. I had betrayed; I had been betrayed. There was Alla and there was Vyetta. What did my knowing them both mean? We had all conspired.

"I must go find them now," Alyosha said. "Or I will lose my good friend." I didn't know which one he meant—Alla or Kolya. If he were speaking Russian instead of English, I would have known by the built-in acknowledgment of gender. It seemed ironic that Russian should be more precise.

But then Kolya appeared out of the forest and Alla from the other side of the clearing, where the boat was tied. She was dripping wet, wringing her long hair. I wondered if she had time to circle around the tip of the island, to fake coming from another direction. Did it *really* matter? Alyosha leapt up joking, too obviously relieved. He didn't want to know. It was the same as in the forest with our blueberry pails: We don't ask why anymore. "You've been swimming?" Alyosha asked joyously. "Now I want to swim too. Alla, will you join me?"

"But of course," she said.

Kolya went into the tent and I followed. He slid his fingers under the blankets tentatively, under the sweatshirt I'd borrowed from him. We could hear Alyosha's and Alla's muffled laughter from the direction of the boat. I turned to Kolya. "With you I cannot."

"What with me?" He hadn't heard. He sounded amused, as though expecting a compliment.

"I cannot."

We lay silently, side-by-side in the tent.

"When will you come back?" Kolya asked gently.

"You want me to come back but not for you."

Kolya sighed. "Lora, even if you lived here I don't think we would have been married very long. We are too much alike."

Odinakovui. Yes, we were alike. Neither of us could bend. "I won't come back," I said.

"You will come back many times," he said, "but you will never live far from your country. Here we live well. We are good company, you, me, Alyosha, Alla. You will come back."

"With a husband," I said.

"No problem. Leave him in Moscow and come here to me." Kolya kissed me with such passion it brought tears to my eyes. "Lora," he said, "I remember *everything*."

Alla and Alyosha shook the tent violently. "Can we come in?"

The four of us lay crushed together in Kolya's two-man tent, Alyosha against one wall, then Alla and me, then Kolya, who was turned away now, touching as little as possible. I was sure that in the darkness Alyosha and Alla were wrapped in each other's arms. In the breathing silence of the tent, Alla began to speak, amazingly, in English.

"My friend," she said to Alyosha. It was a tiny child's voice, her voice in a foreign language. Words that came from classrooms so long ago they were distorted by the distance from memory to mouth. "My friend," Alla repeated, "I so happy when I with you."

"Am," Alyosha corrected. "I *am* so happy when I *am* with you."

"Leave her alone," I protested. "She speaks well."

Kolya lay silently beside me. I sensed him listening attentively to the sound of the words.

"My friend," Alla said. "My dear, dear friend." This island was another country, and whatever language we spoke here was not spoken anywhere else. It was the language of one day only and there were few hours left to this night.

Yes, they lived well here, but every moment had to be surrounded by a border guard to make it precious. We were alike and not alike. They lived under water and I in air. When I looked into the water I envied the richness of their world, its density and peculiar pressures, yet if I were to stay down there I would drown. And they would suffocate above the water, in all that intoxicating air. Our meeting point was only at the surface and we all had to hold our breaths.

The four of us sat in the rowboat, piled with dirty pans, empty bottles and blankets. Now it was Kolya who rowed. Again the sun was shining and the sky a perfect brittle blue. The thwarts of the wooden rowboat were plastered with tiny, glassine husks of winged insects. They covered the seats, the oars. I touched one gingerly. It was as delicate as crystallized air.

"Why so many?" I asked. "Why have they all died?"

Alyosha shrugged away my question. The answer was too trite: the Russian equivalent of mayflies, they spent their one day in some wild carouse.

We rowed around the island, across the stretch of gulf, to the mouth of the river. It was early still and inside the channels the fishermen were arranging and mending their nets. A few of the small wooden boats were heading out. The droplets from the oars sparkled in morning light. Against my skin my skirt was damp and cold. Kolya's familiar back bent with each stroke, so close I could reach out and touch it. Beside me, Alla arranged her pretty blue party dress; it was spotted with wine, covered with twigs. She reached up to clip a barrette around her tangled blonde hair. Her gesture lingered, as though everything imprinted itself on my retina.

The docks and shacks slid past, then rowboats tied to pilings, and the same brown horse staring over the fence. We were almost there. For me there would be packing, then an all-night train to Moscow, a plane to catch. Kolya would go to work without having slept, Alyosha return to his wife, Alla to her little daughter—each of us consigned to our lives. The fishermen would head in this evening, tomorrow set out again. Russia was a fish, slipping through my fingers.

Before I left last winter, I asked Kolya what I should say if I returned and called him. He answered, "You must say, *priyekhala*." I have arrived.

Saint Petersburg—June 2002

Kolya was right. I would visit the Soviet Union many times, though I would never live far from my country. I would cross-country ski on the frozen Gulf of Finland, watch women in head scarves and long black dresses jog on a track in Tblisi, search for Chekhov's "Lady with the Pet Dog" in Yalta, touch the blue mosaic tiles of minarets in Samarkand, converse with soldiers just back from Afghanistan in the open market of Tashkent. I would visit Alyosha and Alla at their apartment, at their dacha—yes, Alla, for Alyosha left Vyetta and married Alla within a year—whenever I was in Leningrad, and they would visit me in Vermont.

In 1990 they'd arrived with goods to sell for cash because they weren't allowed to take much money out of the Soviet Union: a dozen jars of caviar, a box full of *znatchki*—little pins with pictures of Leningrad's bridges and Lenin's portrait—and a roll of gauze because they'd heard that gauze was *defisitni* in America. They found Vermont a bit dull ("absolutely the same as in Russia," Alyosha kept saying) and so we headed to New York. They were obsessed with seeing or acquiring everything that they'd been denied all their lives—Stallone movies, pornography, VCR's. A year later Alyosha returned with a school group and apologized—such hunger was a mania, he said, a madness.

My last trip to Russia was in 1988. Gorbachev was talking *perestroika* and Sasha Ivanov had begun to sell his paintings legally in the West. Russian television spouted corruption exposés. No one cared about what was happening in America; their own country had become too interesting.

Now, fourteen years later, wealthy "New Russians" in expensive business suits brandish their cell phones while my nine-year-old daughter and I await our flight from Frankfurt to Saint Petersburg. I have to keep reminding myself not to say Leningrad. At Pulkhovo Airport I walk under a sign reading "Nothing to Declare" and find, to my bewilderment, that I've passed through customs. There isn't a soldier to be seen.

Alyosha picks us up at the airport in a friend's shiny purple Toyota Rav 4. Ads for Marlboros and Calvin Klein loom over us on billboards that once heralded the Politburo. Pornography is rampant. A hunting shop on Nevsky Prospekt sells rifles and shotguns over the counter. In front of the Hermitage, a cop pulls over a driver who leaps from his vehicle, rubles waving in his fist. No one bothers to hide the bribes. Money, Money, Money. The Soviets used to say, "We pretend to work and they pretend to pay us." Now everyone must hustle.

The stores are full of the goods that have made the "New Russians" rich, everything you could buy at home—Revlon cosmetics, CD players. Food is plentiful and fresh. By our reckoning, the prices are cheap. A can of red caviar costs four dollars, but a teacher's salary is only the equivalent of three hundred dollars a month. Alyosha still spends an inordinate amount of time shopping, going from store to store to compare prices. He must work two jobs to feed his family.

Tatiana Nikolaevna, the director of my old school, speaks of the terrible cost of medical care these days. No one knows where it will stop. Her Cheshire cat smile is gone. "Of course there is much more freedom now," she says, "but there is so much uncertainty. . . ."

Alyosha hasn't lost his love of anecdotes. "Two old men sit on a park bench. One tells the other he was a Bolshevik. Before the revolution he sold pencils on the street. Lenin made him a commissar. Stalin sent him to the camps for twenty years. Khrushchev released him. During Brezhnev's reign he had to sell goods out of the back of a store to survive. He was arrested by Andropov's men and sent again to prison. Yeltsin released him."

"And how do you live now?" asks the other old man.

"I sell pencils on the street," says the old Bolshevik.

"An interesting story," says the listener, "but wouldn't it have been simpler just to skip your revolution?"

Alyosha's face is puffier, florid, his remaining hair short rather than combed over. He no longer has a complex, he says, about being bald. He wears a Russian Orthodox cross around his neck, though I doubt he is religious. Everyone wears them now. He makes several stops a day at what he calls "filling stations." My daughter and I follow him down the stairs into a dim basement. A door opens into a small cement walled room with a lone barmaid standing behind a high glass counter. She smiles warmly; Alyosha is a regular.

"*Kakaya krasavitsa*," what a beauty, she says of my little daughter, who is straining to see over the top of the high counter. The barmaid fills a glass with one hundred grams of vodka for Alyosha's quick and necessary chug.

"These are our friends from America," Alyosha tells her.

"So far? Then you must take a gift," she says, climbing on a chair to reach an old Soviet flag hanging on the wall that is stuck with medals her patrons have left for decoration. She clambers down and hands my daughter a flat disk hung from a faded ribbon. Inscribed on the back are the words, "Hero of Soviet Labor." I don't believe the wall display expresses Communist nostalgia; rather it is an ironic statement. Medals for what? What use were the sacrifices they made in the name of building communism?

Such enormous changes are unimaginable: it is as if ten years ago the United States became a Communist country and we were expected to adapt overnight. No one here wants to talk about the old days; they're too busy just getting along. And to Alyosha and Alla's sixteen-year-old daughter, communism is ancient history, as distant as McCarthyism would have been to me. Still, Alyosha says, "We don't know how long this will last."

The barmaid, an attractive fiftyish woman in a gray knit dress, insists we take more gifts: juice, candy, a small baked fish laden with butter and sour cream that she has probably brought for her own lunch. Such generosity—this aspect of Russia hasn't changed.

Nor this: At Alyosha's fiftieth birthday party, his friends toast and sing. Valerii, a teacher in the school I worked at, and now Alyosha's boss at a private school, pours me vodka and asks, disapprovingly, "Why did you give your daughter a Jewish name?"

Though I could say that Rebecca isn't a particularly Jewish name in English, I prefer to answer, "Because I am a Jew."

Alyosha, Rebecca, and I ride the metro. The whir of the trains rushing into the stations—*davai, davai, davai*—and the smell of stale underground air pull me back. But no one relinquishes a seat for women, young or old. Grisha was right. The men only gave up their seats because they had to. Beside Alyosha, a small *babushka* mutters loudly.

"What is she saying?" I whisper to Alyosha.

"She is crazy."

The old woman opens her purse, takes out a marker, walks over to a poster beside the metro door announcing a rock festival and writes on it with angry black strokes the word *obscene*.

Alyosha explains, "The festival is on the anniversary of the siege of Leningrad."

How do these old folk who survived the siege, who believed in the sacredness of their suffering, cope with this strange new disorder? Yet it is only this perplexing and perilous freedom that allows her to express her outrage. Little more than a decade ago she would have been arrested for antisocial vandalism. Not that she would have dared.

On the train to the dacha, still olive green, still filled with wooden benches, entrepreneurs walk the aisles hawking toys and ice cream. I ask Alyosha about his son. I know that Vyetta wouldn't allow the boy to see his father or even his *babushka* after the divorce. He used to sneak away from Vyetta's family's dacha to visit them and report that Vyetta and his stepfather fought all the time.

Alyosha says, "He came to me at work not long ago and said, 'Father, you won't see me for a long time. Better to forget about me.' You see, Laurie, he must serve an eight-year prison sentence. He became a heroin addict and was caught selling drugs. I am certain it would not have happened if he had lived with me." Alyosha's eyes fill and he has to move to the gap between the cars to compose himself.

"I'm sorry," Alyosha says when he returns. He has paid a large price for loving Alla. Yes, they have a treasured daughter, but without leaving the country, he has lost his son.

At the dacha, roses grow riotously over the wooden fences that separate the houses. My daughter picks bouquets of lupines. Galina Ivanovna still shouts like a gym teacher and still bustles about without cease. Her face is rosy, her smile glints gold. She speaks in constant diminutives and endearments, "Lorichka, *khoroshinka maya*," caresses my hair, praises my daughter's behavior. "I was a teacher," she says. "I know." She bundles the birch leaves for our *banya* and sits naked beside me on the bench, breathing eucalyptus-scented steam in the choking heat, her pendulous breasts resting unselfconsciously against her belly. "*Kak khorosho*," she says. How good. But tomorrow, when we get ready to return to the city, she will weep. She has grown lonely since the death of her husband, with whom she couldn't live and couldn't live without.

My daughter and I get into the same little green rubber rowboat in which I rowed away from Kolya and take turns with the stubby oars, pulling our way through the lily pads that have begun to choke the edges of the round lake. Imposing summer homes stand out on the opposite shore. The "New Russians" have built brick mansions in the midst of simple dacha colonies, fortresses with few windows and huge gates, attack dogs patrolling their holdings.

In the sylvan pine forest where we picked berries and ate *shashlik* so many years ago, trash litters the ground and plastic bags cling to the branches of trees. "It was never like this," I say. "All this garbage. Don't people care?"

"It is our freedom," Alyosha says with a shrug.

They want us to see a local curiosity, an animal cemetery located in the forest not far from the public beach. Trash surrounds this island of lovingly raked dirt, this collection of elaborately decorated graves celebrating the lives and loyalties of cocker spaniels and Rottweilers, cats and pet rabbits. "Look," my daughter says, "here's the grave of a rat! And here's a hamster!" Ferns and flowers in jars of water lean against hand-painted inscriptions, portraits and photos, even a few professionally carved tombstones. I marvel at the owners' grief and devotion in the midst of a forest of trash.

Alla still wears pretty jewelry and dresses carefully but her beauty has solidified. She is more nervous now, understandably preoccupied with making arrangements for a three-year move to the Middle East, where they will teach in the embassy school—the only way for them to increase their pay. As though it were still the Soviet Union, this involves payoffs to doctors and dentists so they will sign official release forms for travel. Alla must bake *piroshki* for one, bring dollars to another. She is also concerned with Alyosha's drinking. She says, "At night I have no one to talk to, no one to give me advice."

She loves her art students and proudly shows me the remarkable

Chinese-style landscapes her young pupils have produced. When I give her a set of the latest water-soluble oil paints for her birthday, Alla says, "Thank you, Laurie. You are the only one who still thinks of me as an artist."

Her old playful nature surfaces when she and my daughter, who has just returned from the circus and is wound tight, perform an improvised operetta for us, a duet about a crystal of sugar and a cup of tea.

My daughter has trouble sleeping in Saint Petersburg. It is too light outside, even at midnight. She cries because she misses her daddy, who couldn't join us—he is a builder and summer is his busy season—but on the plane home she will cry because she misses her new Russian family. "People are different in Russia," she says. "Nicer than at home."

Kolya comes into her bedroom, at Alyosha's and Alla's apartment, to meet her. "*Kakaya sympatichnaya devushka*," he says. What an appealing little girl. Rebecca tells me later that she thinks he's the ugliest man in the world.

The years haven't been easy on Kolya. He has shriveled the way some very slender people do. His face is deeply lined, his profile sharper, his gypsy nose curves lower, his eyes seem smaller. One shoulder hunches in toward his body, a protective gesture or evidence of some new injury in a land where good medicine is difficult to procure and more difficult to afford. There is gray at his temples and his curls are shorn—for summer, he says, when I ask about them.

"*Ni izmenilas*," he says of me. She hasn't changed. Of course I have. I gave birth too late to be a *babushka* yet, but I'm almost fifty years old. It isn't just that I've aged, become a woman who turns no heads; I am no longer, as Tanya put it, "a woman who loves no one."

"May I sit next to Lora?" Kolya asks. Alyosha moves and Kolya squeezes in beside me on the couch that serves as Alla and Alyosha's foldaway bed. It is Alla's birthday and the low table in front of the couch is littered with vodka glasses and a bakery torte. Kolya will have neither; he never eats sweets and he can't drink since he's driving. It is a narrow room, the large television set looming not far behind the low table, books and student work stacked on every surface, the requisite breakfront taking up most of one side. A reproduction of Saint George slaying the dragon decorates a wall.

After a discussion of Cairo, where they will soon work, a city that Kolya visited as a young seaman, Alyosha and Alla discreetly slip out of the living room.

"Lora, I think of you often," Kolya says. "I still have your picture."

"I have yours," I say. "From when you were a little boy."

"Ooh," Kolya says, a sound I can't interpret—almost pained. "Lora, I often think of how good it was with us together. When my spirits are low, I remember how it was with us and it helps me."

"I don't believe you," I say. He doesn't have to play a role for me now.

"Why should I lie, Lora? What good would it do me? I am a man who must tell the truth."

I shrug at that one. Maybe he remembers me fondly; maybe he thinks he does now that we're sitting beside each other. Surely it's easier to remember how good things were than to make a life with someone. Easier to forget how bad things were, too.

Kolya already knew I was married and had a daughter; Alyosha didn't volunteer the information that Kolya had asked about me the last time they spoke, more than a year ago. Alyosha has never forgiven Kolya for changing his mind about me. But I have no reason for anger. Maybe Kolya didn't handle it well when I came back, but I didn't either. Who had practice in such things? And what does it matter now?

Alyosha insists, "Kolya is a strange person, Laurie. I don't understand him. He wants to live alone. Without my family, I would be nothing."

In a country where it is odd to be alone, Kolya is strange. He isn't so strange to me. Why expect everyone to follow the same path?

"Do you have a girlfriend?" I can't help asking.

"Sometimes, but no one lives at my place." Is this a rule, or an offering?

When I mention Vyetta, Alyosha's ex, Kolya says, "Oh, it's been so long I forgot he even had a first wife."

"I remember your life better than you do," I joke.

"Lora, do you remember when we broke the bed at Alyosha's dacha?"

"No, that's something I forgot. Something *you* would remember."

"Two times!" Kolya says.

We laugh.

Kolya leans forward to kiss me; his tongue darts between my teeth. I'm shocked. Is this why he came? Did he really expect to spend the night here with me? I pull back, say, "I can't. I have kissed no one but

my husband in fourteen years." Yet, some old chemical lurch hits me in
the chest. What is it about this small unhandsome, elusive man that still
moves me? I want, I want—I don't know what I want, or if what I want
has anything to do with the Kolya sitting before me. Perhaps even now
I want to be the young woman who—if only for a moment—crossed
the line between nations poised to destroy each other and, in a softly lit
room on the shore of the Baltic Sea, believed that everything was possible because Kolya did a handstand on a chair.

"Then I won't bother you," he says gently. "I won't make things bad
for you."

"Tell me about your life," I say.

Kolya's big problem is finding work that interests him. He has had
many jobs but none that make him feel worthy as a man. In all areas of
business now there are bandits, he tells me, criminals, and he can't work
with them. I assume they are a different order of criminal, guilty of
crimes beyond the low-grade wheeling and dealing Kolya used to do.

He tells me he lives in an apartment, but he has a cooperative dacha
on an island near Vyborg, and a sailboat. If only I'd called him sooner,
he would have taken us sailing. Why didn't I call him sooner? This is my
last night in Russia.

"I didn't have a current number for you," I say. "It took a while to
find you. Alla played detective to track you down." That's true, but it's
also true that half my trip passed before I decided to call him. I knew
Alyosha wouldn't approve and I wasn't sure if I wanted to see Kolya. I
wasn't sure if he'd want to see me.

I show him photographs that I have sent to Alyosha and Alla over the
years—our house, our Vermont land, my husband on a ladder with a
hammer. Kolya inspects each picture carefully. "Very beautiful," he says
of a photo of my daughter and me riding our horses in a green field
rimmed by apple trees.

"Vermont," I say. *You were going to build me a house there.*

Kolya runs a finger over the cover one of my novels in which Alyosha
has stored the photos.

"It's a pity I have no talent for languages," he says. "I'd like to read
your books. Will they be translated, do you think?"

"Probably not, not into Russian."

"Perhaps you will come back to take a job here again?"

"Not likely." I ask Kolya the question that has been on my mind since he walked in. "Do you ever regret your decision not to come with me?" Quickly, I add, "I know it was much harder for you than for me. If it didn't work out I could always say good-bye to you, but you could never go home."

"It was fate," Kolya says, still playing the gypsy, the seaman. But then he bows his head and says, "Lora, forgive me. I was afraid I would have nothing there."

The words *prosti menya*, forgive me, stop my breath. Wasn't that all I wanted to hear so long ago? "You'd have had me," I say, though I doubt it would have been true for long. He was wise not to stake his life on me. It was another five years before I was ready to settle with anyone. I can no more tell him the truth now than he could tell it to me twenty years ago.

"Yes, you," Kolya says. "But I would have lost my son, my friends, my family."

Who could have prophesied that in ten years' time no one from Russia would have to make such decisions, that all relations between Russians and Americans would become so much simpler? They would rise and fall on love's success or failure, the inevitable culture clashes. They wouldn't require national betrayal and dishonor, permanent dislocation and loss of a child as a price. Because we met in the last days of Brezhnev's regime, I'll never know if Kolya and I had a chance. It was the same with Grisha. The great dying ogre that scorched so many lives merely singed me with its breath, yet it showed me how easily we can all be consumed.

"I understand your decision so much better now that I have a child," I say. "Back then I could think only of myself." I wonder if Kolya would have managed any better in America. Maybe there, too, he would have jumped from job to job, woman to woman. At least in Russia he has his sailboat, his dacha, his friends and family. He still has the water on which to feel free.

"I know we will meet again," Kolya says. "I am certain."

"When we're eighty. Or a hundred."

"Every age is a good age," Kolya says with a smile.

Before he leaves, Kolya pulls out a gift he's left by the door. It is a pressed copper drawing of a square-rigged ship in full sail. I remember it hanging from a wall in his house. "My grandfather made it," Kolya says. "He was a seaman, like I was, and a bit of an artist."

"Then I can't take it. Your grandfather made it."

"A gift only has worth if it's something of value to the giver," Kolya says. So I take the heavy object and wonder what I will do with it at home.

Kolya goes into the kitchen to thank Alla, whom he tells, "You can't know how important this was to me." At the door Kolya hugs me. "I love you," he says softly. "Call me. From home."

At home I am playing around on the computer when I discover a web site for the school in Moscow where Grisha and I worked. I'd seen him there once more, in '84 for just a moment. I was working as a guide for an earnest peace group from Berkeley who'd brought a "peace quilt" they'd made to bestow on the Soviet people. (When they presented it to a museum in Leningrad, their last stop, a museum official took me aside and showed me, with a wink, a room full of American peace quilts they already possessed.) In Moscow I brought the group to tour School 45 and display their quilt.

"I've never told anyone your secret," Grisha whispered that day from his classroom.

"What secret?"

"About being Jewish."

"Oh, that. It doesn't matter anymore," I said, distracted by my duties, callously dismissing this last link between us, a secret I'd entrusted to him. Under Grisha's restraint—the mask that a Soviet had to wear when twenty foreigners were milling about, smiling with international good-will—he radiated not the old hunger and longing for what I'd once represented, but an affection I didn't deserve.

I call the number of School 45 and talk to a secretary who tells me, "Grisha is no longer at our school. He immigrated to the United States. Perhaps ten years ago."

Immigrated? I want to dance a jig in my living room. He did it! He did it! "Where does he live now?"

"I think Washington." She has no number or address.

When I find him, thanks to the computer, he is only home for a day before he's off again to Russia and Europe. He works for the U.S. government as an interpreter at high-level meetings abroad. Now he is using his skills to play a part in the world, just as he'd once hoped. His voice is unfamiliar. He has traded his perfect British accent for a perfect

American one. And he is a bit formal, perhaps puzzled at this visitation from such a distant past.

"I owe you an apology," I say.

Grisha brushes it off. "No. No. That's old history. You owe me no apology."

Perhaps my call is history too and he doesn't want to be reminded of his old life.

"You taught me a lot and I'm grateful," he adds.

"You taught *me* a lot. You were my source of truth in Moscow." What did he mean, I'd taught him a lot? That American girls weren't so different from Soviets? We could all be broken? Or that there existed a place where it was legal to wear shorts in a park?

"Are you still married?" I ask, figuring he's probably had two more wives by now.

"Sort of," he says.

Sort of? He was "sort of" married in Moscow. "Why did it take so long to emigrate?" I ask, expecting to hear about trouble with exit visas.

Grisha says, "A matter of temperament, I suppose."

We change and we don't change. But I am so happy for him. It seems too great an irony. Grisha, whom I condemned for inaction and complaints, is the one who took a risk. And Kolya, adapted to life in a nation that has disappeared, believes that Russia has grown worse since the end of the Soviet Union. No matter how valid his reasons, Kolya, the untamed one, was afraid to take a risk.

"What ever happened to Tanya?" I ask Grisha.

"Which Tanya? There were four Tanyas in our school."

"Your *girlfriend*," I say. "The one you were sleeping with."

"But I slept with all four," he jokes, and it is then that I recognize him. The formality has dropped away as it did in a long ago classroom, where friendship was a crime.

In the background his grown son announces it's time to leave for a birthday party for Grisha's father. Yes, his father and mother are here too. I wonder about his father, the old true believer who had to watch his dream of the worker's paradise die and now lives in America, perhaps supported by his son.

Grisha and I talk of getting together; we decide to keep in touch by email. I try to imagine his life in the Sheratons and Hiltons that he is lodged in most of the year. Does he walk the streets of London, Moscow,

Tblisi, Tashkent? Is he sick of hotel food? What of the prostitutes hanging around his hotels? Does he maintain lovers in the cities he returns to, or is that all behind him now that he has other freedoms? I try to picture him as a fifty-year-old man in a business suit, translating for generals and politicians, but it is the Grisha of twenty years ago I see, dark-eyed and yearning. Does he still yearn?

"And how have you been, Laurie?" he asks.

His family is calling; they're late for the party. How to sum up all those years in a few words?

Vsyo builo khorosho, vsyo khorosho, vsyo budet khorosho.

Everything was, everything is, everything will be good.

About the Author

Laurie Alberts teaches fiction and creative nonfiction in the Vermont College MFA in Writing Program. She is the author of three novels, a story collection, and another memoir, *Fault Line*.